The Making of the Chines

In this innovative and well-crafted study of the relationships between the state and its borderlands, Leo Shin traces the roots of China's modern ethnic configurations to the Ming dynasty (1368–1644). Challenging the traditional view that China's expansion was primarily an exercise of incorporation and assimilation, Shin argues that as the center extended its reach to the wild and inhospitable south, the political interests of the state, the economic needs of the settlers, and the imaginations of the cultural elites all facilitated the demarcation and categorization of the borderland "non-Chinese" populations. The story told here, however, extends beyond the imperial period. Just as Ming emperors considered it essential to reinforce a sense of universal order by demarcating the "non-Chinese," modern-day Chinese rulers also find it critical to maintain the myth of a unitary multi-national state by officially recognizing a total of fifty-six "nationalities."

LEO K. SHIN is Assistant Professor of History and Asian Studies at the University of British Columbia.

The Making of the Chinese State

Ethnicity and Expansion on the Ming Borderlands

Leo K. Shin

University of British Columbia

CAMBRIDGE
UNIVERSITY PRESS

CAMBRIDGE UNIVERSITY PRESS
Cambridge, New York, Melbourne, Madrid, Cape Town,
Singapore, São Paulo, Delhi, Tokyo, Mexico City

Cambridge University Press
32 Avenue of the Americas, New York, NY 10013-2473, USA

www.cambridge.org
Information on this title: www.cambridge.org/9780521189897

First published 2006
Reprinted 2007
First paperback edition 2011

A catalog record for this publication is available from the British Library

Library of Congress Cataloging in Publication data

Shin, Leo Kwok-yueh, 1967–
The making of the Chinese state: ethnicity and expansion on the Ming
borderlands / Leo. K. Shin.
    p.   cm.
Includes bibliographical references and index.
ISBN 0-521-85354-0 (hardcover)
1. Minorities – Government policy – China – Guangxi Zhuangzu Zizhiqu –
History.   2. Guangxi Zhuangzu Zizhiqu (China) – Ethnic relations – History.
1. Title: Ethnicity and expansion on the Ming borderlands.   11. Title.
DS793.K6S54   2006
323.151′2809 – DC22   2005036512

ISBN 978-0-521-85354-5 Hardback
ISBN 978-0-521-18989-7 Paperback

For my mother and father

Contents

Illustrations

Tables

Preface

Identities are made, not born. Although I claim no originality for this insight, it is striking how much our understanding of the world has continued to be anchored on the premise that identities – in particular racial, ethnic, and national – are self-evident. In the context of China, not only do we often learn from textbooks and popular media that the country has had a continuous history of over five thousand years (a "fact" that has been used to show that China is either steady or stodgy), we are also constantly reminded by official propaganda and well-intentioned observers alike that the Chinese nation (*Zhonghua min zu*), internally diverse as it might be, is ultimately united by blood as the descendant of the Yellow Emperor. Although the optimistic scholar might view such efforts to promote an essential Chinese identity as so transparent as to be unworthy of intervention, it remains the case that, despite all the harms that have been done in the name of racial, ethnic, or national unity, we who live in the new millennium are still very much, in the broadest sense of the term, prisoners of modernist identities.

To claim that identities are constructed is not to deny that they could be deeply meaningful. Rather, it is to insist that, in order to capture more fully the complexity of the human past, we must approach the formation of identities not as an aside but as an essential component in historical inquiries. For many, the history of China is, at its core, a history of the realization of the Chinese people as a nation. But while the conventional story of the emergence of China as a modern nation-state is in many ways seductive, it is also fundamentally flawed because it takes for granted that "Chinese people" are *inherently* a nation and that "China" is *inherently* a nation-state. I do not share the optimism that we can actually "rescue history from the nation" or that we can now write a history of China, however "China-centered" it is meant to be, that is completely outside the influence of the modern nationalist discourse. What I believe we can do is to imagine alternative narratives, to take not for granted the "Chineseness" of China, and to ask, as some have begun to, "how China became Chinese."

xiii

This book has been long in the making. It has taken more time than I anticipated because the sources I discovered along the way have led me to tell a story that is fundamentally different from the one I had in mind. It is with great pleasure then that I am finally able to formally acknowledge with much gratitude teachers, colleagues, friends, and family members who have sustained me through the years.

At Princeton, where this book first took shape as a dissertation, Professors Yü Ying-shih, Willard Peterson, and Susan Naquin set for me not only a high standard for scholarship but also in their own ways examples of how to be an engaged scholar. The late Professor Frederick Mote first opened up for me the world of Chinese history when I was still a wide-eyed undergraduate student. For helping me find my way, I am forever grateful. Professor Denis Twitchett has been a constant source of inspiration and support since my first day as a graduate student. For his sage guidance, I am most thankful. Others at Princeton were supportive in different ways: Yuan Nai-ying and Tang Hai-tao *lao shi* taught me more than they perhaps realize; Martin Heijdra, fellow Ming historian and Chinese bibliographer of the East Asian (formerly Gest) Library, is a walking encyclopedia; Hue Su, the graduate secretary, offered much-needed encouragement; and fellow students helped make graduate school an intellectually exciting experience.

Beyond Princeton, I have also benefited from the kindness and generosity of friends and colleagues. I cannot hope to repay them all, but let me at least acknowledge the following: Lin Fu-shih, of Academia Sinica in Taiwan, helped arrange my visit to the Fu Ssu-nien Library; Fan Honggui and Wu Guofu, both of Guangxi University for Nationalities, welcomed me to Nanning and arranged for me to visit Tianyang (where the native domain of Tianzhou was); Tonami Mamoru and Sugiyama Masaaki facilitated my visits to the justly famous library collection at the Institute for Research in Humanities at Kyoto University; Dorothy Ko introduced me to useful materials early in the project; Robert Marks kindly shared with me his data on Guangxi and his enthusiasm for maps; Daniel Bryant sacrificed his research time in Taipei to photocopy for me sections of a hard-to-find local gazetteer; Tsukada Shigeyuki of the National Museum of Ethnology at Osaka and Taniguchi Fusao of Toyo University, from both of whose scholarship I have drawn much inspiration, kindly sent me copies of their important publications; Pamela Crossley, Helen Siu, and Donald Sutton not only invited me to a conference in which some of the arguments of this book were presented but also allowed me to read in advance the introduction to their conference volume; Michael Tsin read part of the manuscript on short notice; colleagues in the departments of History and Asian Studies at the University of British Columbia have been most supportive.

On more practical matters, funding for the initial research for this book was provided by the Chiang Ching-kuo Foundation and the China Times Cultural Foundation. A Mellon Fellowship from the Society of Fellows in the Humanities at Columbia University allowed time to draft the first of many versions of this book. In helping turn the manuscript into a book, Marigold Acland, Alison Powell, and Ken Karpinski have been most patient. Eric Leinberger drew the maps, and Paul Buell drafted the index.

Over the years, family members have provided crucial moral and material support. Although words are never enough, I want to thank my parents, sisters, and parents-in-law for offering nourishments and places to rest whenever I needed them, and I want to express my sincere appreciation for my wife, Stephanie Chang, for sharing the joy and grief of this project from start to finish. Nathan is right that this book has taken much time away from playing, but I hope the words here will one day help answer questions he has not begun to ask.

Finally, I acknowledge with great sadness that the late Professor Mote will not be able to see the fruit of the seed he sowed some twenty years ago in the classrooms in Jones Hall. He would have been my most trenchant and yet gentle critic.

Dynastic and reign periods

Shang	ca. 1700–ca. 1100 BCE
Zhou	ca. 1100–256
Qin	221–206
Han	206 BCE–220 CE
Three Kingdoms	220–280
Jin	265–420
Northern and Southern Dynasties	317–589
Sui	581–618
Tang	618–907
Five Dynasties	907–960
Song	960–1276
Yuan	1271–1368
Ming	1368–1644
Hongwu	1368–1398
Jianwen	1399–1402
Yongle	1403–1424
Hongxi	1425
Xuande	1426–1435
Zhengtong	1436–1449
Jingtai	1450–1456
Tianshun	1457–1464
Chenghua	1465–1487
Hongzhi	1488–1505
Zhengde	1506–1521
Jiajing	1522–1566
Longqing	1567–1572
Wanli	1573–1620
Taichang	1620
Tianqi	1621–1627
Chongzhen	1628–1644
Qing	1636–1912
Republican China	1912–1949
People's Republic of China	1949–

Conventions

With a number of exceptions, I have transliterated Chinese names and terms using the *pin yin* system, especially according to the guidelines established by the Library of Congress. Although the results might appear unfamiliar, the practice of transliterating each Chinese character separately does have the benefit of compelling us to reexamine many of the key terms in the Chinese discourses on boundaries and identities. For translating Chinese official titles and for understanding the functions of the myriad government offices, I have found Charles Hucker's *Dictionary of Official Titles in Imperial China* indispensable.

To convert Chinese dates into their Western equivalents, I have relied on Keith Hazelton's *Synchronic Chinese–Western Daily Calendar, 1341– 1661 A.D.* In cases when only the year of an emperor's reign is mentioned in the source, I have followed the convention of rendering the lunar year to its closest Western counterpart. Hence, the tenth year of the reign of the Chenghua emperor, which lasted from 18 January 1474 to 5 February 1475, would be referred to in the text simply as 1474.

In preparing for the maps of Guangxi, I have made extensive use of volume 7 of the monumental *Historical Atlas of China* (*Zhongguo li shi di tu ji*) edited by the late Professor Tan Qixiang of Fudan University. To help the reader to locate a particular area mentioned in the study, I have, whenever necessary, indicated in parentheses the larger administrative unit of which the area was a part. Hence, "Quan Zhou (Guilin)" is shorthand for "Quan Zhou was located in Guilin prefecture."

In citing multi-chapter (*juan*) Chinese sources, I have in general followed the practice of placing a colon between the *juan* number and the page range. But if a modern edition of an early Chinese source is cited, I would in most instances replace the colon with a period. In such cases, the page range referred to is that of the pagination of the modern edition.

Abbreviations

Cangwu	Ying Jia et al., *Cangwu zong du jun men zhi*
DMB	Goodrich and Fang, *Dictionary of Ming Biography*
DYYZ	Yang Fang et al., *Dian Yue yao zuan*
GXTZ (1531)	Huang Zuo et al., *Guangxi tong zhi*
GXTZ (1599)	Su Jun, *Guangxi tong zhi*
GXTZ (1733)	Jin Hong et al., *Guangxi tong zhi*
jr.	*ju ren* (provincial graduate)
js.	*jin shi* (metropolitan graduate)
MHD	Shen Shixing et al., *Ming hui dian*
MS	Zhang Tingyu et al., *Ming shi*
MSL	*Ming shi lu*
pref.	prefaced
YJJW	Tian Rucheng, *Yan jiao ji wen*
YXCZ	Wang Sen, *Yue xi cong zai*
YXWZ	Wang Sen, *Yue xi wen zai*

1   History of the margins

One of the first things we must do in imagining a world without tribes is to try to realize that the seemingly solid evidence of tribes in historical accounts is largely illusory.

Morton H. Fried, "Tribe to State or State to Tribe"

China's expansion to the south in the imperial period has generally produced uncomplicated stories. Han migrants seeking opportunities beyond the central plains spread to the frontier through successive waves of migration and cultivated roots in the hostile but sparsely inhabited country. They transformed the landscape of the border zone with their agricultural tools and techniques, introduced to the territory their social and economic institutions, and disseminated throughout the region the beliefs and practices of Chinese culture. In their new surrounding, settlers found opportunities not only in farming but also in hunting, fishing, gathering, logging, mining, and trading. Many who migrated to the south did so to escape wars or natural calamities, but others were soldiers sent by Chinese rulers to establish control. Han settlement was almost always accompanied by the extension of the Chinese state: civil administration was organized in areas where the fiscal base was considered sufficiently stable, and garrisons were set up at strategic locations where military presence was deemed essential. China's "march toward the tropics" – as Herold Wiens suggestively titled his now-classic study published over half a century ago – has thus been regarded by many as a process of colonization, sustained by the economic needs of Han settlers, the political interests of the state, and the "urge to civilize" of Chinese rulers and elites.

The conventional historical narratives generated from this broad framework have ranged from ones of confrontation and assimilation to ones of accommodation and acculturation. The stories of confrontation, as told by both traditional and modern-day historians, invariably emphasize the tensions between Han settlers and the native population. Seen from this perspective, the narrative of Han expansion is not so much one of taming the wild land as one of concerted annexation. Over time, migrants from

1

the central plains, in trying to secure for themselves the most productive resources, are said to have had to frequently solicit help from the Chinese state to kill off or push further into marginal lands those natives who had stood in the way. The stories of assimilation, on the other hand, tend to focus on the roles of Han settlers in the transformation of the native population. While some historians have attributed the success of the project of sinicization to the presumably unifying and transformative power of Chinese civilization, others – among whom the still-influential Owen Lattimore – have pointed to the favorable natural environment of the south as the reason the Chinese state was able to extend to the border zone its administrative and cultural apparatuses.[1]

The narratives of accommodation, by contrast, treat as their focus not the tensions between Han settlers and the native population but the transformations both groups had to undertake to facilitate the creation of a new order. The essential story of China's expansion, according to many a historian, is the emergence and development in the borderlands of a variety of formerly non-existent political, social, and economic relationships. To extend its political reach to the southern border zone, the Chinese state for much of the imperial period is said to have had to embrace and promote the institution of native chieftaincy. The stories of acculturation, similarly, opt to emphasize the profound influences Han and non-Han peoples have had on one another. Rather than depict the settlement of Han migrants and the extension of the Chinese state as forms of colonization, however, the narratives of acculturation tend to portray China's expansion as an almost inevitable process through which Han and non-Han peoples would eventually join together to form a unified nation.[2]

---

[1] For a classic exposition of the confrontation and assimilation theses, see Wiens, *China's March Toward the Tropics*. Among the body of scholarship that forms the basis of Wiens's synthesis are Eberhard, "Kultur und Siedlung der Randvölker China"; Li, *Formation of the Chinese People*; Xu Songshi, *Yuejiang liu yu ren min shi*; She Yize, *Zhongguo tu si zhi du*. For recent studies that place particular emphasis on the demographic, economic, and environmental factors in China's expansion, see von Glahn, *Country of Streams and Grottoes*; Marks, *Tigers, Rice, Silk, and Silt*; Lee, "Political Economy of a Frontier." For the rhetoric, if not necessarily the practice, of assimilation, see Wang Gungwu, "The Chinese Urge to Civilize." For a recent exchange concerning the concept of sinicization, see Rawski, "Reenvisioning the Qing"; Ho, "In Defense of Sinicization." For Lattimore, see *Inner Asian Frontiers of China*.

[2] For the accommodation thesis, see, for example, Shepherd, *Statecraft and Political Economy on the Taiwan Frontier* (but see also the critique in Brown, *Is Taiwan Chinese?*). For an explicit effort to apply Richard White's idea of "the middle ground," see Giersch, "'A Motley Throng.'" For the concept of "unitary multi-national state," see Fei Xiaotong, "Zhonghua min zu duo yuan yi ti ge ju." For an application of Fei's framework to the history of south China, see Wu Yongzhang, *Zhongnan min zu guan xi shi*. For the institution of native chieftaincy, see my discussion in Chapter 3.

Such narratives do contain a measure of truth – wars did break out frequently, special political, social, and economic institutions did emerge, and natives of the southern border zone did come to share many cultural traits with settlers from the central plains – but most also leave unexamined some long-cherished assumptions in the writing of Chinese history. Of such firmly-held beliefs, perhaps the most entrenched is the conviction that binaries such as Chinese and non-Chinese, Han and non-Han, are self-evident. To be sure, historians are now less likely to speak of "the Chinese mind" (or the "essence" of Chinese culture) and more inclined to draw attention to the diversity of the geography and population of China. But even as scholars become more attentive to local differences as well as to the distinctions between "Chinese" and "Han" as categories (the so-called Han nationality, according to the official census of 2000, made up 91.59 percent of China's population), it remains the case that much of what was once deemed to constitute the essence of Chinese culture – textual traditions, social and religious practices, and so on – has simply been repackaged and reinterpreted as the core of Han ethos. And while historians are mindful that the boundaries between "Chinese" and "non-Chinese," "Han" and "non-Han," are necessarily fluid (members of one group could, in time, adopt the cultural or social markers of the other), many have continued to find it useful to explain the history of China's expansion as one of interactions – whether in the form of confrontation, assimilation, accommodation, or acculturation – between inherently distinct peoples.[3]

More fundamental, what such narratives have in common is what may be characterized as a primordialist approach to the concept of ethnicity. For many a historian, the notion of ethnicity is closely associated with the "essence" – whether it be engendered by a common language, a set of shared beliefs and practices, a sense of a common ancestry, or a combination of such and similar elements – of individual ethnic groups. Although scholars who subscribe to this view might differ in how and how strongly they would make a case for the existence of such primordial ties (and the full range of their arguments is certainly more complex and nuanced than is often acknowledged by their opponents), they do share the belief that ethnic identities are rooted in certain "givens" and should not be attributed solely to considerations for power, status, or material gains.[4]

[3] For efforts to distinguish between "Chinese" and "Han," see, for example, Xu Jieshun, *Han min zu fa zhan shi.* For population statistics, see Zhongguo guo jia tong ji ju ren kou tong ji si, *Zhongguo ren kou tong ji nian jian.*
[4] For an introduction to the debates concerning the concept of ethnicity, see Hutchinson and Smith, *Ethnicity.* For the case of China, see Crossley, "Thinking about Ethnicity in Early Modern China."

Just as clear, the narratives of China's expansion, not unlike those concerned more broadly with the history of China conceived over the past century, have also been shaped by the import of the concepts of nation and nation-state. On one level, the history of the *national* history of China could no doubt be traced to the emergence of scientific, nation-based historical writings in Western Europe toward the end of the eighteenth century. On another level, the desire among political leaders and intellectuals in the past century to construct a linear model of history for China – in which the Chinese nation as a self-evident and sovereign entity is seen as continuously evolving through a process of self-realization – has clearly been propelled by the need to create a modern nation-state following the collapse of the Qing dynasty (1636–1912). Although the languages they use to describe the nation have changed over time, most political leaders and intellectuals of modern China would agree that it is the inherent unity of the people (or, more precisely, that of Chinese civilization) that has been the nation's principal constitutive force. And although the narratives of expansion do differ in their focus, most share the assumption that the "Chinese nation," notwithstanding its internal multiplicity, is ultimately a meaningful unit for historical analysis.[5]

In retelling the story of China's expansion, my aim in this book is not to dismiss the conventional narratives but to incorporate them into a more satisfactory one. The story told here is anchored on the simple premise that labels such as "Han," "Yao," and "Lao" one encounters in the historical records are not to be taken to stand for self-evident, objectively constituted ethnic groups; rather, they should be understood as historically constructed categories whose precise contents shifted with time and space. Although the assumption here is hardly novel – the works by Dru Gladney and Pamela Crossley come immediately to mind – by explicitly structuring the story of China's expansion around the supposition, it is my hope that this study would encourage its readers to step outside the limited framework of "Han" versus "non-Han" and to approach the history of China with new questions. For example, if the categories "Han" and "non-Han" are not to be treated as building blocks for the history of China's expansion, how should one make sense of the real and imagined differences between people who are identified in the records as Han and those who are labeled as Yao, Lao, Ling, Zhuang, and so on? And how should one conceive a *new* history of China's expansion

---

[5] For the evolution of scientific, nation-based history in Europe and North America, see, for example, Breisach, *Historiography*, 199–267; Appleby et al., *Telling the Truth about History*, 53–90. For a critique and an explicit attempt to write against the grain of national history, see Duara, *Rescuing History from the Nation*.

without some of the *old* conceptual tools? I do not pretend I have fully answered these questions, but I believe this book has provided a useful starting point for further reflections.[6]

The arguments of this book are relatively straightforward. In China during the imperial period, the borderlands were at once full of perils and opportunities. Contacts between natives and settlers no doubt transformed the border zones – whether in terms of political and social organization, economic relations, environmental configuration, or a combination of such – but they also shaped the ways borderlands were imagined. This book is *not* about how Han people conquered, assimilated, or co-opted the non-Han; rather, it is about how interactions between populations with unequal claim or access to power led to the construction of boundaries and hierarchies in the border zones. As the centralizing state extended its reach to the south, this book argues, the political interests of the center, the economic needs of the settlers, and the imagination of the cultural elites all facilitated the demarcation and categorization of the population in the border region. In this process, not only did officials and other observers from the so-called central plains increasingly distinguish between people who were considered subjects of the state and those who were deemed "beyond the pale," they also became more and more interested in differentiating and categorizing the borderland "non-Chinese" populations. China's historical expansion to the south is no doubt a story of colonization and acculturation, but just as significant, it is also a story of demarcation and differentiation.[7]

Although this book is not explicitly comparative, its arguments are intended to contribute to several broad-ranging dialogues. By framing the history of China's expansion in terms of boundary formation and transformation, this study joins a substantial and growing body of scholarship – which can be traced to but has by now surpassed the pioneering works of Fredrik Barth – that treats as its focus not the presumed "contents" of individual groups but how particular populations, whether they are identified in racial, ethnic, national, or religious terms, have come to be defined and demarcated. Although there are clear differences among scholars who subscribe to this approach, one widely-accepted view is that identities are necessarily constructed. While this book is aimed primarily at offering a more theoretically informed narrative for China's historical

---

[6] For scholarship that shares the assumption of this book, see, for example, Gladney, *Dislocating China*; Crossley, *Translucent Mirror*.
[7] For recent works that emphasize demarcation and differentiation as an integral part of China's colonialism, see Hostetler, *Qing Colonial Enterprise*; Teng, *Taiwan's Imagined Geography*. See also the contributions in Crossley et al., *Empire at the Margins*. For comparative perspectives, see Dirks, *Colonialism and Culture*.

expansion, its approach and arguments, it is hoped, could also serve as an inspiration for historians of other parts of the early modern world. In particular, what this study underscores is that although identities were in many cases negotiated (a somewhat tired metaphor that implies both the *identifiers* and the *identifieds* were always actively engaged), such negotiations were almost never conducted on equal terms. Not only did people with greater claim or access to power have more opportunities to shape the contour of historical memory, they also had more resources to define the boundaries of collective identities.[8]

unequal terms

Second, by rejecting the categories "Han" and "non-Han" as the building blocks for China's history, this book also adds to a body of scholarship that renders problematic the concepts of majority and minority. To be sure, to be perceived as a member of a minority, whether it is defined in terms of race, class, ethnicity, nationality, gender, religion, or other criteria, has real-life consequences. But as the designations of majority and minority have repeatedly demonstrated their uncanny capacity for self fulfillment and perpetuation – one need only to consider the cases of the "minority nationalities" (*shao shu min zu*) in China or of the "First Nations" or "Native Americans" in North America for contemporary examples – it has become increasingly evident that majorities, as one scholar puts it, "are made, not born." Just as the idea of majority is based on a presumption of homogeneity, the notion of minority is founded on the desire to mark differences. As such, the two conceptual categories – and the people they represent – are clearly interdependent. And even though the claim that majorities and minorities are necessarily constructed is not particularly original, this study is a useful reminder that how majorities and minorities were constituted did vary across time and space and that the urge to classify and to differentiate is certainly not an impulse peculiar to the modern period.[9]

Finally, by focusing on the roles of the state and its agents in the processes of boundary formation, this book joins a substantial body of literature that calls attention to the intricate links between frontier expansion and state-building. For historians of other periods or other parts of the world, some of the arguments found in this study would no doubt seem familiar. In particular, the observations that the state often had to negotiate with local agents to maintain a semblance of control, that the

---

[8] For Barth, see his introduction to *Ethnic Groups and Boundaries*. Two other foundation texts for the approach discussed are Said, *Orientalism*; Anderson, *Imagined Communities*.

[9] For two collections of stimulating studies, see Gladney, *Making Majorities*; Burguière and Grew, *Construction of Minorities*. For the quotation, see Gladney, "Introduction: Making and Marking Majorities," 1.

limit of its reach was determined to a significant extent by logistics and by a sort of cost–benefit analysis, and that imaginations and representations were often as influential as events on the ground in shaping policies and strategies would undoubtedly find parallels in studies of the Roman empire, the Ottoman empire, the Russian empire, as well as the European empires in the Americas. But while how the centralizing state sought to incorporate its borderlands remains an important area of inquiry, what this book underscores is that the construction of group boundaries, not to mention the making of majorities and minorities, was not simply a by-product of state-building but must instead be viewed as an integral part of the processes of state formation and transformation.[10]

"March toward the tropics"

In many ways, the story told in this book is not unique to the Ming dynasty (1368–1644) but is part of a more general narrative of the history of China. Although what constituted the southern border zone has changed over time, ever since the founding of the first centralized polity of China – the Qin dynasty – in the third century before the common era, it has been the practice of the centralizing state to foster a semblance of order in its border regions by officially recognizing the rule of local magnates and chieftains. This can be seen in the early imperial period in the creation in present-day Guangdong, Guangxi, and northern Vietnam of a number of nominal administrative areas. And this can be observed even more clearly in mid-imperial times through the formal recognition by the state of a large number of "loosely reined" (*ji mi*) domains. Not only did such practices help bring about a degree of order in areas where local magnates or chieftains ruled, they also allowed the centralizing state to claim control of its southern borderland without having to expend its limited resources. Although the specific arrangements of such practices would change over time, it is evident that, for much of the imperial period, the ability of the state to maintain a semblance of political unity was founded not so much on its military prowess but – ironically – on its capacity to reinforce local distinctions and divisions.[11]

Nor is the story of demarcation and differentiation told here limited to the arena of political configuration. Although the historical records are

---

[10] For recent studies of the frontier or borderland histories of the empires mentioned, see, for example, Whittaker, *Rome and Its Frontiers*; Karpat and Zens, *Ottoman Borderlands*; Sunderland, *Taming the Wild Field*; Daniels and Kennedy, *Negotiated Empires*. For a reflection on the functions and limits of the state, see Scott, *Seeing Like a State*.

[11] For a history of the imperial practice, see Wu Yongzhang, *Zhongguo tu si zhi du*.

fragmented, it is evident that long before the establishment of the first centralized polity of China, there had already emerged in ancient times a general concept of political and cultural centrality. Not only did the earliest Shang (ca.1700–ca.1100 BCE) and Zhou (ca.1100–256 BCE) rulers, who claimed authority principally over the central and lower Yellow River regions, refer to their domains, respectively, as the "central lands" (*zhong tu* or *tu zhong*) and the "central dominion" (*zhong guo*), they also consciously distinguished between people who lived within *zhong tu* or *zhong guo* and those – such as the so-called Man, Yi, Rong, and Di – who populated areas beyond the core region. During the imperial period when China was ruled, on and off, as a centralized polity, just as it was the practice of the state to recognize the rule of local magnates and chieftains, it was apparently also in its interest to identify and categorize the peoples both at and beyond its borders. As a result, long before the Ming dynasty, one could find in historical records concerning present-day south China frequent references to the Yue, the Wuhu, the Li, the Lao, as well as a variety of other "non-Chinese" populations.[12]

That said, the story of this book is focused on Ming China (see Map 1.1) for at least two reasons. First, how we now think of the southern borderland of China has, to a significant extent, been shaped by the experiences of the Ming. Although Ming rulers and officials did not find it necessary to build a Great Wall – as they did in the north – to physically separate the "Chinese" from the "non-Chinese," it was in the late imperial period that many of the boundaries we now take for granted in relations to southern China came into being. In terms of the transformation of political boundaries, the region of Yunnan was officially incorporated into the "central dominion" during the Ming, the area of Guizhou was organized into a province in 1413, and the boundary between present-day China and Vietnam was more or less settled in its present form following the debacle in the early fifteenth century in which the Ming sought but failed to extend its rule to what was then Annam. In terms of the demarcation of borderland peoples, it was during the Ming as well that many of the categories we now use to classify the "minority nationalities" of China first appeared in the records. Although modern-day scholars have used the appearance of such categories to trace the history of individual nationalities to the Ming period, as I will explain, it is perhaps more meaningful

---

[12] For the etymology of the terms *zhong tu* and *zhong guo*, see Chen Liankai, "Zhongguo, Hua–Yi, Fan–Han, Zhonghua, Zhonghua min zu." For more sophisticated analyses of the relations between the people of the "central dominion" and their neighbors, see Wang Mingke, *Huaxia bian yuan*; Di Cosmo, *Ancient China and Its Enemies*. For a survey of the southern "peoples" identified in the historical records, see Wu Yongzhang, *Zhongnan min zu guan xi shi*.

Map 1.1. Ming China, ca. 1580. *Source:* Mote, *Imperial China*, Map 15.

to think of such labels not as references to self-evident *peoples* but as both political and cultural markers for demarcation and categorization.[13]

---

[13] For a survey of the Ming borderlands, see Mote, *Imperial China*, Chap. 27. For the building of the Great Wall, see Waldron, *Great Wall of China*. For China's expansion to Yunnan and Guizhou, see Lee, "Political Economy of a Frontier," and the forthcoming books by C. Pat Giersch and John Herman. For Vietnam, see Shin, "Ming China and Its Border with Annam." For the relations between Ming China and the polities in Southeast Asia, see Wang Gungwu, "Ming Foreign Relations"; Wade, *Southeast Asia and the Ming Shi-lu*.

Second, although historians have observed that the Ming was the only "native" or "Han Chinese" dynasty in the later imperial period, neither the assumptions nor implications of this claim have been adequately scrutinized. To be sure, that the rulers of both the Yuan (1271–1368) and Qing dynasties – which immediately preceded and succeeded the Ming, respectively – had come from beyond the "central plains" did profoundly shape the ways China was administered. But instead of reflexively framing the differences between the Ming, on the one hand, and the Yuan (or the Qing), on the other, in terms of native versus alien rule, it is probably more revealing to examine how the rulers of different periods chose to portray themselves as well as to compare and contrast the assumptions and implementation of their specific policies. Not only would understanding how Ming emperors and their representatives conceived and administered the southern borderland allow us to explain more satisfactorily what it meant then to be Chinese and non-Chinese, given the renewed interests in issues concerning identities in the Qing context, it would also enable us to recognize more readily the changes and continuities in the later imperial period.[14]

In this book, I focus on the province of Guangxi for also at least two reasons. First, unlike that of Yunnan and Guizhou, the region of Guangxi has been claimed by the centralizing state since almost the start of the imperial era. Following his conquest of all major rival states, the First Emperor of Qin (r. 221–210 BCE) apparently sought also to incorporate into his newly found empire areas corresponding to present-day Guangdong, Guangxi, and northern Vietnam. Not only did the Qin emperor order some half a million soldiers to the southern region, according to the records, in 214 BCE, he also decreed that three commanderies – Nanhai (Southern Seas), Guilin (Cinnamon Forest), and Xiang (Elephant) – be set up in the borderland. Although it was not until the founding of the People's Republic in 1949 that the centralizing state was able to claim something close to firm control of the region, the desire by successive dynasties to extend their rule to the southern border zone had from early on led to the establishment in Guangxi relatively elaborate administrative and military hierarchies. As a result of this considerable presence of the state in the region, as the central authorities sought to strengthen their rule in

---

[14] For a strong claim of the Ming as a Han Chinese dynasty, see, for example, Mote, "Introduction," 1. For an introduction to Yuan-dynasty rule, see Twitchett and Franke, *Cambridge History of China*. For the Qing period, see the discussion in Chapter 6. For recent studies that place the Ming dynasty in the broader context of later imperial China, see Smith and von Glahn, *Song-Yuan-Ming Transition*; Struve, *Qing Formation in World-Historical Time*.

the southern borderland in the Ming period, it was in Guangxi, rather than in Yunnan or Guizhou, that tensions between the state and the local population were most extensively documented.[15]

The second reason for focusing on Guangxi has to do with its geography. Although known to visitors mostly for its rugged landscape, the region of Guangxi is in fact endowed with an extensive and navigable river system (i.e., the West River) that has since the early imperial period facilitated the transport of both people and goods. Although it is impossible to tell how many of those half a million soldiers purportedly sent by the First Emperor actually went to Guangxi, over time, it is evident that people from the so-called central plains had migrated in significant numbers to the southern border region. Especially after the construction in the Qin period of the Ling (Numinous) Canal (which, essentially, links the Yangzi River to the West River system), not only did the centralizing state find it feasible to deploy a large army to the region if necessary, in time, it also found it possible to extract from Guangxi a variety of resources. Compared with other parts of the southern borderland such as Yunnan and Guizhou, the region of Guangxi thus offers a superior vantage point from which to examine the construction and perpetuation of cultural as well as political boundaries.[16]

To conceive an alternative narrative, I begin this study (Chapter 2) with an analysis of Guangxi as a real and imagined borderland. For Ming-dynasty travelers from the "central plains," to journey to the border region was to reach the end of the realm of civilization. Not only was its landscape intimidating and its climate forbidding, the southern border zone was also widely seen as plagued by diseases. To establish control, the Ming state had sought from early on to extend to the southern region both its administrative and military apparatuses. Not only did representatives and agents of the state encourage the creation and registration of permanent settlements (from which taxes and corvée duties could be extracted), they also sought to provide a semblance of order by setting up military guards and battalions at strategic locations. But as much as officials wanted to transform the southern border zone and bring it under the control of the

---

[15] For the history of Guangxi, see, for example, Huang Tirong, *Guangxi li shi di li*; Qin Yanhuan and Liao Guoyi, *Guangxi shi gao*; Zhong Wendian, *Guangxi tong shi*.

[16] For a brief history of the southern migration, see Marks, *Tigers, Rice, Silk, and Silt*, Chap. 2. For water transportation, see Qi Yi, *Guangxi hang yun shi*. I am mindful of William Skinner's macroregional approach, especially the utility of considering the bulk of Guangdong and Guangxi as an integrated region. But given my central concerns – and the ready availability of the works by Marks and others – I am comfortable in leaving unpursued in this book some of the implications of Skinner's model.

centralizing state, all would learn that there were limits imposed by the natural environment. My argument here is that just as the extension of the state (and the expansion of the population) in Guangxi would in time transform the environment of the region, it would also reinforce some of the actual and invented boundaries of the southern border zone.

reinforce actual & invented boundaries

Despite efforts by the centralizing state to extend control, it is argued in Chapter 3, its reach in the southern border zone remained limited. Caught between its "urge to civilize" and the high costs of frontier management, the Ming state had from early on adopted the practice of earlier dynasties of offering official titles and other privileges to native chieftains (referred to as *tu guan*) in exchange for their nominal submission. Although Ming rulers and officials would continue to frame this arrangement in terms of "using non-Chinese to control non-Chinese" (*yi yi zhi yi*), it was obvious to all concerned that just as the chieftains found the recognition by the state desirable, the Ming also considered the services offered by such *tu guan* indispensable. From time to time, the centralizing state would seek to rein in some of the more intractable chieftains. But what Ming rulers and officials would realize was that the solution to the problems of *tu guan* was not to eliminate the institution of chieftaincy but to instead recognize an ever greater number of chieftains. The position Ming rulers and officials found themselves in was thus a peculiar one: as they sought to impose an order on the southern border zone, they had to divide the region into a patchwork of native domains and to create a political landscape that, to some degree, would persist to the early part of the twentieth century.

In spite – or because – of the efforts by the centralizing state to impose order, the southern borderland remained a violent place (Chapter 4). In Guangxi, as in other southern border provinces, it is evident that Ming officials had to contend with a variety of peoples who neither conformed to the image of tax-paying subjects nor desired to be brought under the control of the state. In areas in Guangxi where Ming authorities had instituted regular administrative units (instead of domains led by native chieftains), the competing political and economic interests of officials, settlers, and the native population (concerning primarily but not exclusively land and other natural resources) meant that warfare was seldom a distant concern. But the story told here seeks to go beyond the familiar tales of confrontation and assimilation. It explains how, over time, the increased interactions and conflicts among the borderland population had prompted Ming officials to reinforce – rather than erase – the distinction between *min* and *man*, or between people who were considered subjects of the state and those who were "beyond the pale." More significant, this book shows how, by the end of the Ming period, such distinctions

Violent place

reinforce distinction b/w 民 / 蛮

would be codified not only in textual records but also in striking visual representations.

Just as Ming officials and observers considered it necessary to reinforce the distinction between *min* and *man*, they also deemed it increasingly desirable to identify and categorize peoples they referred to as "non-Chinese" (Chapter 5). As more and more representatives and agents of the centralizing state traveled to the southern border zone (both for work and for pleasure) – a result, in part, of the increased commercialization and mobility of Ming society – they also had more opportunities to leave behind records of their observations. Although most of these records remain what may be called "sedan-chair" ethnographies, based primarily on hearsay and imagination, some do emphasize the empirical nature of the observations offered. And even though it is difficult to gauge the popularity of such writings, the long lists of titles found in various late-Ming bibliographies clearly testify to the presence of an intellectual if not commercial demand for works of such genres. The story told here is not simply the exoticization or demonization of "the other"; it is, rather, about how Ming elites constructed a cultural hierarchy and how, in doing so, they helped lay out an "ethnic landscape" that has perpetuated to the present.

The practice and process of demarcation, this study shows, have continued through the Qing period to the present (Chapter 6). Although the impetus behind such acts of demarcation has changed over time (from the urge to civilize to the need to project an image of a unitary multi-national state), their mechanisms and functions have been remarkably consistent. The affirmation of the presence of five major nationalities (*min zu*) in China in the nationalist discourse of the early twentieth century as well as the official classification of fifty-five minority *min zu* by the People's Republic are both considered here essentially a continuation of the exercise of demarcation in imperial times. In both the imperial and modern periods, the practices seem to have served not only to define and objectify the "minority" populations but also, as Dru Gladney, among others, has suggested, to project an image of homogeneity among the majorities. By way of conclusion, I offer also in Chapter 6 some reflections on the potentials and limitations of a history of the margins. I argue that although we may not be able to recover the so-called native voices, it is still possible to write a useful history of the borderlands by viewing the past not as a constant contest between self-evident peoples but as a continuous process of identity and boundary formation.[17]

---

[17] The *making* of the Han majority is a central theme in Gladney, *Dislocating China*.

Boundaries of imagination

To reconstruct this history of China's expansion, I have consulted a wide range of fascinating if under-used materials. In addition to standard sources such as the officially commissioned *Veritable Records of the Ming* (*Ming shi lu*), which are compiled from the administrative diaries of the imperial court, and the *Collected Statutes of the Ming* (*Ming hui dian*; 1511/1587), in which many of the rules and regulations concerning the border regions are cataloged, I have also made extensive use of local gazetteers, military handbooks, campaign chronicles, travel accounts, geographical treatises, encyclopedias, family genealogies, and various other writings (especially those of the *bi ji*, or "informal jottings," genre) by Ming observers who had firsthand knowledge of the southern border zone. In addition, I have drawn on a vast corpus of transcriptions and rubbings of Guangxi-related stone inscriptions, much of which has become accessible only in recent years.[18]

Of the sources examined, three sets are especially noteworthy. The first are the local gazetteers (*fang zhi*) of Guangxi. As it is well known, local gazetteers in the context of imperial China were essentially a cross between local history and administrative records. Compiled by officials and sometimes by prominent native sons, local gazetteers were in general intended as convenient references for both newly arrived administrators and occasional travelers. For many an observer, the compilation of the first gazetteer of an area was indeed a sign of the area's coming of age. Although local gazetteers had long existed for some parts of the southern border zone, it was in the Ming period that many administrative areas in Guangxi had their first *fang zhi* compiled. In fact, the first provincial-level gazetteer of Guangxi was not put together until some time in the mid-Ming. And while this compilation boom no doubt reflected a more general country-wide trend especially in the latter half of the Ming period, it was also a clear testimony to the increased presence of the centralizing state in the southern borderland.[19]

The second set of materials that deserves attention are the three anthologies compiled by the early-Qing scholar Wang Sen (1653–1726). Known collectively as the *General Anthologies of Guangxi* (*Yue xi tong*

---

[18] My use of the voluminous *Ming shi lu* has been facilitated immeasurably by the following guides: Taniguchi Fusao and Kobayashi Takao, *Mindai seinan minzoku shiryo*; Guangxi min zu yan jiu suo, *"Ming shi lu" Guangxi shi liu zhai lu*; Li Guoxiang, *Ming shi lu lei zuan*.

[19] For two useful catalogs of the gazetteers of Guangxi, see Guangxi tong zhi guan, *Guangxi fang zhi ti yao*; Chen Xiangyin and Qin Yongjiang, *Guangxi fang zhi yi shu kao lu*. For a discussion of the significance of local gazetteers as a source, see Franke, "Historical Writing During the Ming," 777–80.

zai; ca. 1704), this trilogy of collected writings – one each devoted to poetry, belles-lettres, and "miscellanies" – is essentially a literary record of Guangxi from the Han (206 BCE–220 CE) to the Ming periods. Begun perhaps as a project of diversion while Wang Sen was a minor official in the border province, the anthologies were intended, as the compiler explained, for both officials who had been appointed to Guangxi as well as other interested readers who might never set foot in the southern region. As a literary record, Wang Sen's anthologies are obviously far from comprehensive. Despite his search both within and outside Guangxi, Wang explained, many important titles that should have been included in his compilations were simply not available to him. (Some of the texts Wang Sen identified as missing have in fact survived and been consulted for this book.) As a historical document, however, Wang's trilogy is significant for at least two reasons: not only does it enable historians to trace how Ming and earlier writers imagined the southern borderland, its existence also demonstrates the increased interests officials and travelers in the late imperial period had in the region of Guangxi.[20]

The third set of sources that warrants special mention are the stone inscriptions that have been found throughout the southern province. As it is well known, in the imperial period, inscribing on stones (whether on cliff or rock surfaces or on stand-alone stelae) was a popular means of commemoration. Not only were stone inscriptions used routinely to memorialize the deceased or to honor the talented or the virtuous, they were also used regularly to celebrate the conclusion of military campaigns or the completion of public works such as city-walls, official buildings, bridges, and so on. In the case of Guangxi, although the majority of the inscriptions that have been preserved is of the genre of travel commemoration (the temptation to leave behind poems or other marks in scenic spots was too much for most visiting officials and scholars to resist), there are some of which the contents are rather unusual. Among the latter are ones that were commissioned by native chieftains, many of whom, as we will see, were eager to trace their genealogies to ancestors from the "central plains." Also among the more uncommon ones are inscriptions that commemorate military campaigns against the "non-Chinese" in the border region. Even though the transcriptions of many of such stone inscriptions can be found in the gazetteers and anthologies discussed earlier, a great number more have only been recovered in the past century. While I have made an effort to draw on these materials, given the

---

[20] For the general preface for the trilogy, see Gui yuan shu lin bian ji wei yuan hui, *Yue xi shi zai jiao zhu*, 4–7. For Wang Sen's objectives, see his introduction to the anthology of poetry in ibid., 8–9.

size of the corpus, I have been able to realize only a small part of their full potential.[21]

In thinking through the available sources, I am certainly mindful of their limitations. Not only are there major gaps in the records – even as basic a piece of information as the population of Guangxi, to borrow Martin Heijdra's term, can only be "guesstimated" – almost all our sources are left behind by representatives and agents of the centralizing state. Some of the limitations associated with such materials are well recognized. Even though they did not always agree with one another, the authors of these records did write from a position of privilege and power, and most did share the assumptions behind the civilizing mission of the state. Other limitations are more specific to a study of the southern border zone. Most of the officials and travelers who left behind writings on Guangxi had spent relatively little time in the province (and had at best come to be familiar with only a small part of it), and most who did so invariably compared and contrasted what they saw with what they perceived as the norms of the "central plains." Not only did many of such visitors have a hard time getting used to the life on the borderland, they also sometimes found it difficult to describe what they encountered. But even though these sources may not tell us what it was really like to be living in Guangxi in the Ming period, together they do offer historians a remarkable picture of how representatives and agents of the centralizing state perceived the southern border zone.

In retelling this story of expansion, I have in general refrained from extrapolating from local oral and textual traditions to reconstruct what may be conceived as the native perspective. Over the past decades, scholars have collected a vast body of ethnographic materials from the so-called minority areas in China. These materials include not only songs and stories that have been transmitted orally but also various genres of texts and epigraphic data. As part of their efforts to reconstruct the history of individual "minority nationalities," some overly enthusiastic scholars have even made use of the collected materials to trace the literary history (*wen xue shi*) of specific *shao shu min zu*. But such an enterprise is inherently fraught with intellectual perils. This is so not only because what is considered minority literature is often written or recorded in Chinese (a major exception is the large corpus of Yi-language documents) but also because the majority of the materials found cannot be dated with

---

[21] For transcriptions or rubbings of stone inscriptions in Guangxi, see, for example, Hu Renzhao et al., *Zhongguo xi nan di qu li dai shi ke*, vols. 4–13; Guangxi min zu yan jiu suo, *Guangxi shao shu min zu di qu shi ke*; Dang Dingwen, *Guangxi li dai ming ren ming sheng lu*; Taniguchi Fusao and Bai Yaotian, *Zhuang zu tu guan zu pu.*

any certainty. In the context of south China, the problem of authenticity is particularly evident in the case of the *guo shan bang* ("certificates of mountain crossing"), which purportedly explain the origins and migration routes of the so-called Yao people from their own perspective. Although some scholars have traced the appearance of these documents, which are recorded in Chinese, to the sixth century, I have, in view of the evidence, opted to treat them as products of much more recent times.[22]

Similarly, I have avoided in this study the practice of "downstreaming," the mapping of populations identifiable in textual or archaeological records to present-day ethnic groups. Although it is tempting to assume that people who are identified in the historical records as Yao or Zhuang – to name two examples – were direct predecessors of the "minority nationalities" now officially recognized by similarly sounding labels, even a cursory look at how such *shao shu min zu* came to be categorized in post-1949 China (Chapter 6) would show that many of the presumed continuities are more illusory than real.

In this book, I use the term "China" to refer to both the polity of *zhong guo* (literally, "central dominion") and the territory under its actual and apparent rule. And I use the term "central plains" (for *zhong yuan* or *zhong zhou*) to denote what was in general considered by Ming observers to be China's core territory. Although rulers and officials of the Ming period often appeared certain what constituted China and what it meant to be Chinese (*hua*, *xia*, or *huaxia*) – according to the circular logic, to be a constituent of *zhong guo* was to be *hua*, and to be *hua* was to subscribe to the beliefs and practices of *zhong guo* – it is the ambiguities (and contraditions) inherent in these critical labels that we will reflect on in this book.[23]

I have used the term "state" or "centralizing state" to refer to both the administrative and military apparatuses of the Ming ruling house. I have tried throughout the text to be specific about which constituent or constituents of the state (the emperor, the imperial court, local officials, military forces, etc.) I happen to be discussing, but such precision, as it would become clear, is not always attainable. In addition, I have from time

---

[22] For an introduction to the documentary records of various "minority nationalities," see Li Jinyou et al., *Zhongguo shao shu min zu gu ji lun*. For the literary histories of individual *min zu*, see, for example, Ouyang Roxiu et al., *Zhuang zu wen xue shi*; Huang Shuguang et al., *Yao zu wen xue shi*. For transcriptions and discussion of *guo shan bang* (also known as *Ping huang juan die* [certificates from Emperor Ping]), see Huang Yu, *Ping huang juan die ji bian*; Faure, "Lineage as a Cultural Invention," 12–14.

[23] For a survey of the historical usages of some of the critical terms discussed, see Chen Liankai, "Zhongguo, Hua–Yi, Fan–Han, Zhonghua, Zhonghua min zu."

to time referred to the "representatives" and "agents" of the centralizing state. Although I obviously include among them the regular civil and military officials of the Ming, I also place in these categories people who did not formally belong to the bureaucracy (such as individual settlers and travelers) but whose activities or writings did much to further the interests of the state in the borderlands. I am mindful that these representatives and agents did not necessarily recognize themselves as such nor always share the same objectives. My claim is that even though they were far from homogenous, such representatives and agents were united by both their recognition of a centralized polity and their general assumption of the superiority of Chinese beliefs and practices.

In reconstructing this history of demarcation and categorization, I have variously used the term "borderland," "border zone," or "border region" to refer to the province of Guangxi and, sometimes, to that of Yunnan and Guizhou (as well as parts of Sichuan, Huguang, and Guangdong), where the reach of the state was limited by the presence of native chieftains. I have refrained from referring to the southern borderland as a frontier except when I need to draw attention to the perspectives of particular observers. While this book is primarily about the words and actions of the representatives and agents of the state, it is important to keep in mind that what might appear to Ming officials and travelers as a perilous frontier was for many others a place called home. Nor have I attempted in this study to explicitly compare and contrast China's northern and southern borderlands. Even though the southern border region was never as serious a military concern for the Ming state as the northern border zone, it should be self-evident that recognizing how boundaries were formed and transformed in the south would help us better understand the challenges the Ming faced in defining and defending its other borders.

Finally, I use the labels "Han" and "non-Han" to refer to the borderland population only when my sources allow me to do so. For Ming rulers and officials, this study argues, the most important criterion for differentiating between the populations in the southern border region was not whether the latter were Han or non-Han (although we will encounter such arguments); rather, the most frequently cited criteria were whether or not the people in question were registered subjects (*min*) of the state and whether, by extension, they were "civilized" (*hua*). I have on occasions referred to people who were considered *min* as "settlers" and those not as "natives." I do so *not* because I find the distinction particularly helpful but because the terms do correspond to the concepts of *ke* ("guest") and *zhu* ("host"), respectively, found in Ming-dynasty records. I have referred to the chieftains and their soldiers in the southern border region as "native" (*tu*), but I do so simply to convey the terms *tu guan, tu si,* and *tu bing* in Chinese sources. And although in the following pages I will refer to the "non-Chinese" as *man, yi,* or *man yi* (and sometimes specifically as Yao, Lao, Ling, Zhuang, etc.), I do so not to reify the people in question but to show how borderland populations are categorized in the records of later imperial China.[24]

As it should be clear, this book is far from a comprehensive study of China's expansion to the south. Many questions that deserve to be answered more fully – especially those concerning local economic relationships – would have to await another study with a different aim. Nor should this book be mistaken an example of what is sometimes referred to as new frontier history. As I will explain in greater detail in the concluding chapter, I make no pretense that I have recovered the voices of "the natives." But if this book is not intended to be all-encompassing, it does aim to reorient how we think about China and its history. This is a study of the construction of borders, but more important it is a study of the making of the center. This book is about how representatives and agents of the state – officials, but also travelers and settlers – constructed and perpetuated distinctions, and it is about how they, in doing so, reinforced what it meant to be civilized and – by extension – to be Chinese. But this study is not about imaginations and representations alone; whenever possible, it also shows how people who lived at China's edge, in order to survive, had to continually reconfigure their relations with their natural environment, with one another, and with the centralizing state. This book is about the formation and transformation of boundaries on a particular borderland in Ming China, but the story it tells, I believe, would find resonance with many other dimensions of the human past.

---

[24] Although the terms *tu guan* and *tu si* are often used interchangeably in Ming-dynasty records, they do have different connotations. For our purpose, I will use *tu guan* to refer to chieftains who were recognized by the Ming court as "native officials" and *tu si* to refer to both the offices they held and the territories (domains) they controlled.

> The northeastern part [of Guangxi] is civilized. Its air is pure and fine.
> As a result, its people are refined and cultured. The southwestern part
> is uncivilized.... Its air is malarial. As a result, its people are ferocious
> and crude.   *General Gazetteer of Guangxi* (1531)

Some time during the tenth year of the reign of the Chenghua emperor
(1474 in conventional rendering), a certain Li Zongxian of Changzhou
prefecture (Southern Metropolitan Region) was handed the unenviable
assignment of serving as prefect of Xunzhou in central Guangxi. Unless Li
was exceptionally brilliant or especially unfortunate, the prefect-designate
was probably in his late twenties or early thirties in 1460 when he obtained
the much-esteemed metropolitan graduate (*jin shi*) degree. It is unclear
what Li's earlier appointments had been or how well he had performed in
those capacities, but as he was ranked a middling 62 (out of 156) in the
metropolitan examinations, it was unlikely he would have been placed on
a career fast track in the Ming officialdom. Although the post of prefect
was accompanied by a respectable rank of 4a (on a descending scale from
1a to 9b), it is not difficult to imagine how disappointed Li Zongxian must
have been, especially when one realizes that the prefecture of Xunzhou
had been the site of major clashes between the Ming military and the
local "Yao" population less than a decade earlier and that neither his predecessor nor successor for the position even possessed the *jin shi* degree.
In terms of career advancement, the transfer to Guangxi was clearly not a
very promising move. As it turned out, prospect in the officialdom would
be the least of Li's concerns.[1]

Li Zongxian's misfortunes had begun even before he stepped foot
in Guangxi. His wife, according to our source, was so terrified by the
prospect of living in a country of "miasma and poisons" that she would

---

[1] For the ordeals of Li Zongxian, see Zhang Ning, *Fangzhou za yan*, 13b–15a. For Li's
ranking in the metropolitan examinations, see Zhu Baojiong and Xie Peilin, *Ming Qing
jin shi ti ming bei lu*, 1256. For his appointment to Xunzhou, see *GXTZ* (1531), 8:19a.
For official ranks, see Hucker, *Dictionary of Official Titles*, 158.

not accompany him. Neither, apparently, would his servants. Undeterred, Li Zongxian took in a concubine and a new attendant as he prepared to travel to the south. As it happened, Li passed away just two years into his term in Guangxi. Although the cause of his death is not recorded, to Li's family back home the culprit was no doubt the inhospitable environment of the border region. Nor did Li Zongxian's death mark the end of his ordeal. The concubine he left behind fell ill in Xunzhou as well, and the attendant he had brought with him turned out to be a scoundrel who wanted nothing more than to take over Li's possessions. Fortunate for the Li family, a junior official named Yi Hai had just been appointed to Xunzhou as the assistant prefect. On learning of the situation, Yi Hai offered to help. Li's concubine was nurtured back to health and was in time accompanied back to Changzhou. Li Zongxian's coffin, which for months had lain in the open in his official residence, was eventually also brought back to his native place for proper burial.

To Zhang Ning (js. 1454), who has recorded this episode in his *Miscellaneous Words*, a collection of *bi ji* or informal jottings, what was noteworthy about the case was not so much Li Zongxian's ordeal but Yi Hai's generosity. As Zhang explains toward the end of his account, he had first come across the case of Li through word of mouth within the literati circle. He later became acquainted with Yi Hai, who had in time been transferred to Jiaxing prefecture (Zhejiang), where Zhang Ning's hometown was located, and was able to confirm many of the story's details. Not only did Yi Hai take it as his responsibility to look after Li's concubine and to ensure her safe journey home, Zhang remarks, he was also able to do so without jeopardizing propriety. "In the case of [Li] Zongxian," Zhang Ning concludes, "[Yi's] actions could be set as an example for all gentlemen."[2]

For others who took an interest in the story – members of the "literati circle" (*jiang hu shi da fu*), but also the early-Qing scholar Wang Sen as well as the compilers of the 1733 edition of the *General Gazetteer of Guangxi* (*Guangxi tong zhi*), both of whom have included a version of Zhang's account in their works – the episode of Li Zongxian must have confirmed many of their worst impressions of the southern border zone. Not only was the region miasmic and poisonous (as indicated by the premature death of Li Zongxian), it was also where family relationships (such as the bonds between husbands and wives, masters and servants) were tested and where the most sordid human instincts surfaced. It was of course the decision of the appointed official whether to bring along his

---

[2] For the quotation, see Zhang Ning, *Fangzhou za yan*, 15a. Zhang's own biography can be found in *MS*, 180.4765–67.

family while he was on assignment. But even though an official would sometimes choose to leave his family behind, it is difficult to imagine it was commonplace for family members to refuse to accompany the patriarch. That Li Zongxian's wife, not to mention his servants, would violate the norm thus underscores the real and perceived danger of the southern borderland. For Li's wife at least, it was evidently preferable to be deemed unvirtuous than to be dead.[3]

Finally, to visitors who had traveled to the southern border region, Li's ordeals might seem atypical but were far from improbable. For officials from the central plains, the southern province might turn out to be less treacherous than they had imagined. But just as evident, for many of them, the main concern was to survive their terms and to quickly move on to more desirable assignments. To such veterans, the episode of Li Zongxian was in part a curious anecdote and in part a reminder of the perils of the southern border zone. (To the same veterans, the story of Li also served as a reminder of the well-known ordeals of Liu Ren of Guizhou province. Not only would Liu Ren, who was appointed in 1521 to the post of vice prefect of Wuzhou, succumb to illness before he could reach his destination in southeastern Guangxi, family members who accompanied him to his assignment would in time also fall victims to local "Yao bandits.") Guangxi might not be a country of poisonous vapor as some assumed, but its precipitous landscape and harsh climate were certainly not for the faint-hearted.[4]

Moral geography

To visitors from the central plains in the imperial period, the geography of Guangxi had almost always inspired both awe and fear. As early as the Tang dynasty (618–907), the noted scholar, official, and essayist Liu Zongyuan (773–819), for example, was full of admiration for the landscape of Liuzhou (present-day central Guangxi), where he was exiled from 815 to the time of his death. In his characteristically simple but elegant prose, Liu wrote of the presence in the area of large and beautiful mountains, "many [of which] are of singular appearance." During the Song dynasty (960–1276), Fan Chengda (1126–93), prefect of Jingjiang (present-day Guilin in northeastern Guangxi) from 1173 to 1175, even suggested that of all the mountains under heaven, those in Guilin were the most extraordinary. Countless observers would in time echo Fan's sentiment. One such commentator was the judicial commissioner Wang Zhenggong (1133–1203), who opined in 1201 that "the mountains and

---

[3] The story of Li Zongxian is found also in *YXCZ*, 6:17–18a; *GXTZ* (1733), 127:49–50a.
[4] For the episode of Liu Ren, see Wei Jun, *Xi shi er*, 5:10; *YXCZ*, 7:24b–25a.

waters [i.e., landscape] of Guilin are the most splendid of all-under-heaven" (*Guilin shan shui jia tian xia*), an utterance that would in time be immortalized in countless references to Guangxi. During the Ming, travelers to the southern province almost always quoted the words of Fan Chengda and Wang Zhenggong approvingly. But even visitors such as Xie Zhaozhe (1567–1624), a provincial administration commissioner who believed Fan and others had overstated their case, would concede that although the mountains in Guangxi might not be the most "gracious" (*ya*) and the waters the most "tranquil" (*xun*), the landscape of the southern province was indeed "extraordinary" (*qi*).[5]

Awed as visitors might be by the landscape of Guangxi, for many, to travel to the southern borderland was to journey to the end of heaven-and-earth. During the Ming, to approach Guangxi from the central plains, one would travel upstream along the Xiang River – which flows from the south through part of Huguang province – until one crossed into Guangxi and reached the start of the Ling Canal. From there one would make his or her way through the all-important water channel and arrive at the head of the Li River. From the Li River it would be a short downstream journey to the city of Guilin, the provincial capital (see Map 2.1). Just how long such a trip would take depended on the nature of the journey. In 1406, when the minister Huang Fu (1363–1440) was dispatched on an expedition against Annam, he noted in his journal that it took the army twenty-four days to travel from one courier station to another to cover the distance between Yingtian (present-day Nanjing), the Ming capital then, and Guilin. In contrast, when Yue Hesheng (b. 1569) was assigned to Qingyuan prefecture in north central Guangxi in 1611, it took him more than twice as long (fifty-two days) to travel about the same distance. Despite his apparent equanimity about his new appointment ("How do we know [Qingyuan] would not turn out to be a heaven [*tian tang*]?"), Yue was clearly in no hurry to reach Guangxi. Along the way, he took time to travel to scenic sites and made special efforts to visit friends. Qingyuan might or might not turn out to be a heaven, but Yue Hesheng, not unlike many in his situation, seems to have prepared himself never to be able to return home (as it happened, Yue would be recalled in just over three months).[6]

Alternatively, to approach Guangxi from the east, one would travel against current along the West River – which flows from Guangxi into

---

[5] For Liu Zongyuan's essay, see *YXWZ*, 19:2–3; for a discussion and translation, see Schafer, *Vermilion Bird*, 143–44. For Fan Chengda's descriptions, see his *Gui hai yu heng zhi*, 83. For Wang Zhenggong's inscription, see Hu Renzhao et al., *Zhongguo xi nan di qu li dai shi ke*, vol. 10, p. 59. For Xie Zhaozhe (Hsieh Chao-che), see *YXCZ*, 17:13a; *DMB*, 546–50.

[6] For Huang Fu's journey, see *YXCZ*, 3:6–17. For Yue Hesheng's, see *YXCZ*, 4:1–44a; the quotation is from 4:2b.

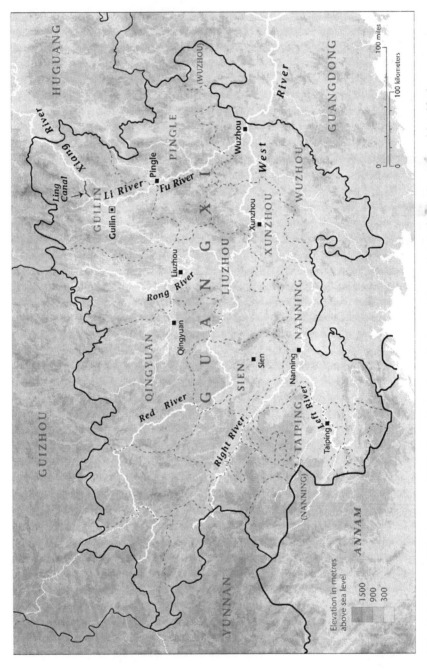

Map 2.1. Guangxi Province, ca. 1580. Note that only prefectures with regular prefectural seats are identified.

Guangdong – until one reached the prefectural seat of Wuzhou. From there to Guilin, one would sail upstream along what is present-day Gui River (part of which was known in the Ming as the Fu River) and arrive at the prefectural seat of Pingle. From Pingle it would be a short journey up the river to the provincial capital. Compared with the northern approach, the journey to Guilin from Wuzhou was apparently even more hazardous. In 1506, in a memorial pleading – for the second time – for retirement, Zhang Ji (1451–1518), a provincial surveillance vice commissioner, reports that he had nearly been drowned twice while trying to carry out his duties along the Fu River. "Having taken these painful experiences to heart and having all hopes [of bringing order to the Fu River area] dashed to pieces," Zhang writes, he would be most grateful if the emperor would let him return home to live out his remaining years. For his part, Tian Rucheng (js. 1526), who was appointed in 1538 as an assistant administration commissioner of Guangxi, once recalled he had had to put on a brave face to convince his parents that he would be just fine being posted to the "strange country" (*yi yu*) in the south. According to a diary Tian kept, traveling upstream from Wuzhou to Pingle was indeed a major challenge. Not only do the waterways become more and more rapid as one travels north, Tian Rucheng observes, on both sides of the banks are countless bandits who await to ambush innocent travelers. In making one's way through the 200 *li* (100 kilometers) between Wuzhou and Pingle, Tian reports, "one could travel for days without encountering another person." Just as in the evening "one could hear the howling and shrieking of apes and monkeys," during the day "one could spot the movements of tigers and leopards." The landscape along the Fu River is "a most impressive scenery on this side of the [Southern] Range," Tian concludes, but it is also most precipitous.[7]

As much as they found the landscape along the Guilin–Wuzhou corridor both breathtaking and intimidating, visitors who chose (or were compelled) to venture further into Guangxi would report an even more hostile environment. In the 1531 edition of the *General Gazetteer of Guangxi*, it is noted that whereas the northeastern region of the province, where Guilin is located, is relatively "civilized" (*chu*), the southwestern area, with its proximity to Yunnan province and Annam, is "uncivilized" (*mo*). And whereas in the northeast the air is "pure and fine" and the people are relatively "refined and cultured" (*xiu er wen*), in the southwest, the air is malarial (*zhang li*) and the people are "ferocious and crude" (*han er zhi*).

---

[7] For Zhang Ji's memorial, see his *Gucheng ji*, 1:20b–23a; *YXWZ*, 5:46–48. For Tian Rucheng's journey, see *YXWZ*, 1:25–31a; *YXCZ*, 3:17–29; the quotations are from 3:27b–28a.

In the case of the prefecture of Liuzhou, where Liu Zongyuan was once exiled, "even though it is located adjacent to Guilin, its atmosphere [*feng qi*] is different from that of the central plains [*zhong zhou*]." Not only was its climate unusual (its winter was warm and its spring was cool), according to the gazetteer, the area was afflicted also by violence associated with the "non-Chinese" (literally, *yao lao*) population as well as by miasma and malaria. As for the prefecture of Xunzhou, where Li Zongxian was once assigned, "although the mountains and waters are extraordinary and beautiful," the presence of a large population of *man* and *lao*, the congregation of a variety of venomous birds and snakes, and the confluence of conditions favoring the growth and spread of miasma had all contributed to the area's inhospitality.[8]

Concerns of Ming visitors about the inaccessibility of Guangxi were not entirely misplaced. Although some observers no doubt exaggerated the difficulties of traveling around the province – Huo Tao (1487–1540), a native son of Guangdong, remarked for instance that some mountains in Guangxi were so high that even "birds could not cross" – they were correct in noting the region's mountainous terrain. According to modern-day surveys, while about 75 percent of the area in Guangxi, which now incorporates the relatively level coastal region, may be considered "mountainous" (the ratio for the country as a whole is 66 percent), only less than 15 percent may be classified as "plains." The rest is made up of lakes, rivers, and so on. What is striking about the physical geography of Guangxi is of course not only its rugged terrain but its karstic topography – spectacular limestone formations fashioned by erosions – that is most notable in the greater Guilin area but in all makes up a third of the province's territory. And even though Guangxi is endowed with more than fifteen hundred rivers each with a surface area of 50 square kilometers or more, given the region's topography, traveling in the province in the imperial period must have indeed been quite a challenge.[9]

Not only were travelers to Guangxi intimidated by its landscape, as we have seen, they were also apprehensive about its tropical climate. Such concerns are to some extent supported by present-day data as well. The average temperatures in Guangxi, which range from 17 degrees Celsius in the north to 23 degrees in the south, are among the highest in the country. In terms of rainfall, although the southern province generally

---

[8] For descriptions of the geography of Guangxi, see *GXTZ* (1531), 1:4a, 10b–11a, 23b–24a.

[9] For Huo Tao, see *YXWZ*, 8:19. For an overview of the physical geography of modern Guangxi, see Guangxi Zhuangzu Zizhiqu di fang zhi bian zuan wei yuan hui, *Guangxi tong zhi: zi ran di li zhi*; for the statistics cited, see pp. 3–5. For a historical perspective, see Marks, *Tigers, Rice, Silk, and Silt*, Chap. 1.

receives more than 1,500 millimeters per year (compared with just above 600 millimeters for the national average), the concentration of precipitation in the spring and summer, when the province would typically receive about 75 percent of its annual intake, and the uneven distribution of rainfall across the region (with a great deal more in the east than in the west) have led to not only frequent floods but also periodic droughts in different parts of the province.[10]

To Ming observers, the unusual climate of Guangxi was not the result of happenstance but was closely linked to the geography (*di li*) and the configuration of *qi* (variously translated as pneuma, ether, vapor, air, energy, etc.) of the southern province. In his *Record of Extensive Travels* (pref. 1593), in which the one-time assistant administration commissoner of Guangxi reflects broadly on the geography of the Ming, Wang Shixing (1547–98) observes that the temperature in the south is in fact not a function of season but of sunshine. Because the "veins of the earth" (*di mo*) in Guangxi are coarse (*shu li*), Wang explains, the warm or male (*yang*) *qi* that would otherwise be contained inside the earth has been able to escape. As a result, when the sun is out, the *qi* would rise, and the area would warm up. "Thus [a day] in the middle of winter would be no different from a day in the spring or summer." By contrast, because the mountains surrounding Guangxi are mostly stony (and not covered with vegetations), Wang Shixing observes, when it rains, the chill or female (*han*) *qi* associated with rocks would rise alongside the mists and fogs of the forests. As a consequence, "even though it is in the middle of summer, [the temperature on a rainy day] is no different from that in the middle of winter." Similarly, in the 1599 edition of the provincial gazetteer, it is noted that while the regular release of warm *qi* from the earth has enabled plants in Guangxi to bloom year round, the cyclical rise of chill *qi* – which could suddenly bring down the temperature – has also rendered the daily weather unpredictable.[11]

As much as visitors to the southern province were awed by its landscape and climate, they were apparently even more concerned about the threats posed by the seemingly omnipresent miasma (*zhang*). According to Chen Lian (1370–1454), a native son of Guangdong who served from 1392 to 1401 as Instructor of the Confucian school of Guilin prefecture, *zhang* was formed when the poisonous haze of mountains coalesced with the foul air of forests. Not only was *zhang* present everywhere in Guangxi (except around Guilin), Chen observed, it was especially potent in the

---

[10] Guangxi Zhuangzu Zizhiqu di fang zhi bian zuan wei yuan hui, *Guangxi tong zhi: zi ran di li zhi*, 4.

[11] Wang Shixing, *Guang you zhi*, shang.215–16; *GXTZ* (1599), 3:43–44.

southern province because of the unpredictability of the weather. As Chen
Lian explained, just as there were different types of *zhang* for different
seasons, there were various degrees of illnesses. Whereas the symptoms of
the mild form of *zhang*-induced sickness resembled that of malaria (*nüe
ji*), the most severe type, known as *ya zhang*, would render its victims
both unable to speak and unable to orient themselves. In the case of
ya zhang, according to Chen, death was a certainty. To cope with the
threats posed by *zhang*, travelers to the southern borderland had in time
devised a variety of strategies. Almost as soon as he arrived in Guangxi in
the early seventeenth century, for instance, Yue Hesheng was cautioned
by his fellow officials to be watchful of his diet as well as of what they
euphemistically referred to as "the boundary between men and women."
Not only should Yue be mindful not to indulge in wine or sex, he should
pay attention to the weather and adjust his clothing throughout the day
lest the poisonous *zhang* had a chance to seep through his skin.[12]

To Ming travelers, the *di li* (literally, "coherence of the earth") of
Guangxi was not simply a random collection of physical and climatic
traits; to them, both the configuration of the landscape and the timing
of the development of the region had their own logic. In the 1531 edition of the provincial gazetteer, for instance, it is observed that because
Guangxi is located "at the end of heaven-and-earth" and is "where ten
thousand things return" (*wan wu zhi suo gui*), not only are its mountains
and waters both extraordinary and beautiful, it is also home of a wide variety of unusual minerals and animals. Although it has been suggested by
some commentators that the geography of the southern province might
have favored the creation of things over the cultivation of human talents,
the gazetteer argues, it would be just a matter of time before the province
would become populated with talented people.[13]

To others, the *di li* of Guangxi was best understood in connection with
the general circulation of *qi*. In his *Record of Things Heard on the Torrid
Frontier* (*Yan jiao ji wen*; pref. 1558), a collection of personal and secondary observations concerning the southern border zone, Tian Rucheng
surmises that the "current of civilization" (*wen feng*) necessarily travels
in a cyclical fashion. Of the four quarters of the Chinese (*xia*) realm,
according to Tian, the northwest, the northeast, and the southeast, in
that order, were the first to be touched by the current. Although it might
not be obvious, Tian argues, the southwest (of which Guangxi is a part)
would in time be reached by the same *wen feng*. Similarly, in his *Record of*

---

[12] For descriptions of various types of *zhang*, see Chen Lian, *Qinxun ji*, 7:33b–35a; *GXTZ*
(1531), 17:8b–11a; *GXTZ* (1599), 3:43b–44a. For Yue Hesheng, see *YXCZ*, 4:23.
[13] *GXTZ* (1531), 12:1a.

Extensive Travels, Wang Shixing notes that of the three "dragons" (*long*) –
systems of mountains and ridges that provide visual clues to the flow
of *qi* – present in the central dominion, the one in the middle, which
runs roughly parallel to the Yellow River, was the first to manifest (*fa*)
the "kingly" *qi*. By contrast, the southern dragon, which covers Guangxi,
among other southern provinces, has been the last one to do so.[14]

Reach of the state

Despite the challenges posed by the geography of Guangxi, rulers of
the Ming had from early on extended to the southern border zone the
state's administrative and military apparatuses. Although the configurations in Guangxi did share many of the features of provincial administration found in the central plains – notably the setting up of three provincial
agencies with overlapping jurisdictions (the administration commission,
the surveillance commission, and the military commission), the establishment of the position of the grand coordinator (*xun fu*) to coordinate
the civil and military affairs of the province, and the eventual creation
of the position of the supreme commander (*zong du*) to take charge of
cross-provincial military matters – some arrangements were clearly particular to the border region. In Guangxi as in other parts of the southern borderland, not only did the Ming state have to contend with the
limits of its administrative and military apparatuses, it also had to confront a large "non-Chinese" population. As a result, in Guangxi, as in
Guizhou, Yunnan, and parts of Sichuan, Huguang, and Guangdong,
whereas some areas were (at least nominally) under the direct control of
the state, others were considered native domains under the jurisdiction
of local chieftains.[15]

Of the imperial and state institutions established by Ming rulers in
Guangxi, one of the most symbolically significant was the princely estate
(*wang fu*). As early as 1370, the Hongwu emperor (r. 1368–98), the Ming
founder, decided to adopt the practice of earlier dynasties to enfeoff imperial princes. Although an ostensible reason for the arrangement was to
allow such princes to help secure the Ming territory, the primary impetus was the emperor's desire to minimize opportunities for succession
struggles. It is unclear why Guilin, among other potential cities in the

---

[14] *YJJW*, 4:22–23a; Wang Shixing, *Guang you zhi*, shang.210–12, 214. For "dragons" and
the theories of siting, see, for example, March, "An Appreciation of Chinese Geomancy";
Clunas, *Fruitful Sites*, 179–89.

[15] For an overview of the structure of Ming provincial administration, see Hucker, *Dictionary of Official Titles*, 75–78.

southern border provinces, was chosen as a destination for enfeoffment. In any case, the scale of the estate in Guangxi was impressive. According to reports from present-day fieldworks, before it was burned down during the Ming–Qing transition, the princely estate at Guilin might have occupied as much as 19 hectares of land (or the equivalent of twenty-five standard soccer fields). The massive stone wall that surrounded the compound is said to have been nearly 8 meters in height, almost 6 meters in thickness, and close to 2 kilometers in length. Inside the walled compound, in addition to a large number of buildings and structures, land was apparently set aside also for an imperial garden complete with a freshly dredged pond for boating and other pleasures. Also enclosed within the princely estate – and standing tall above all – was the Peak of Singular Beauty (Duxiu Shan), the 66-meter pinnacle that had long been a landmark of Guilin.[16]

But while the princely estate at Guilin was an obvious symbol of imperial reach, it would also come to associate with some of the major problems the Ming faced in establishing order in the southern border region. In theory, the cost of maintaining a scattered network of princely estates would be a small price to pay for avoding fraternal strife. But not only did the arrangement fail its first major test – the fourth son of the Hongwu emperor would eventually usurp the throne – given the generous provisions set out by the Ming founder, the imperial clan (with as many as one hundred thousand stipend-collecting members by the final years of the Ming) would also become a major drain on the state finances. In the case of the princely estate in Guangxi, the fiscal problems were evidently exacerbated by the province's limited resources. Even though a significant portion of the tax revenues was already routinely diverted to pay for the stipends and operating expenses of the imperial clan, to sustain their lifestyle, members of the princely estate at Guilin – who would number more than two thousand by the end of the sixteenth century – were said to have had to resort to salt smuggling and other illicit transactions. Thus what had begun by the Hongwu emperor as an effort to maintain order and to extend control turned out to be a source of much trouble in the southern border zone.[17]

---

[16] For the princely estate at Guilin, see *MSL*, *Taizu shi lu*, 51.1000–1002; *MS*, 118.3612–14; *GXTZ* (1531), juan 11; *GXTZ* (1599), juan 6; Xu Hongzu, *Xu Xiake you ji*, 3A.291–342 passim; Dang Dingwen, *Guangxi li dai ming ren ming sheng lu*, 150–51; Zhang Zimo, *Ming dai fan feng ji Jingjiang wang shi liao*. For more general studies, see Satō Fumitoshi, *Mindai ōfu no kenkyū*.

[17] For a discussion of the burden imposed by the imperial clan, see Hucker, "Ming Government," 24–28. For the troubles associated with the princely estate at Guilin, see *GXTZ* (1599), 6:3b–5a.

In addition to the princely estate, Ming rulers had from early on also established in Guangxi an administrative structure similar to that found in other provinces. At the top of the hierarchy was the Provincial Administration Commission (*bu zheng shi si*), an agency responsible for conducting censuses, collecting taxes, and handling communications between the central government and local administrative units, among other essential tasks. Placed in charge of the agency in Guangxi were two commissioners (rank 2b), two vice commissioners (3b), and two assistant commissioners (4b). To facilitate administration, four branch offices, each headed by a vice or assistant commissioner, and each given the jurisdiction over a specific part of the province, would in time be set up, respectively, at the prefectural seats of Guilin, Wuzhou, Xunzhou, and Liuzhou. The commission in Guangxi was supported also by the usual range of staff, including a registrar (6b), a judicial secretary (6b), an office manager (7b), a record keeper (8b), a proofreader (9a), and a storehouse commissioner (9b). Of these, the positions of the record keeper and the proofreader were eventually abolished in 1530. In 1473, an additional vice commissioner was appointed to Guangxi to take charge of tax collection (and, in time, salt administration). By 1580, however, the post was deemed redundant and the duties associated with it were turned over to one of the administration commissioners.[18]

In Guangxi, although officials had sought at the start of the Ming period to simplify the existing (Yuan-dynasty) administrative structure, over time they would find it advantageous to expand the number of regular administrative seats (see Map 2.2). According to the Ming administrative scheme, areas under the jurisdiction of the provincial administration commission were divided into units of prefectures (*fu*), subprefectures (*zhou*), and counties (*xian*). Whereas some of the newly established units, such as Yongan Zhou and Zhaoping county (both in Pingle prefecture), were carved out of existing regular administrative areas, others were former native domains (see Chapter 3) that had as a result of rebellions (e.g., Chongshan Xian, Yangli Zhou, Yongkang Xian, Sien Fu) or internal power struggles (e.g., Zuo Zhou, Shangshixi Zhou, Shangsi Zhou) come under the jurisdiction of the provincial authorities. But although the creation or conversion of such administrative seats did to an extent mark the expansion of the state, not all newly established units would come under the actual control of the provincial administration commission. In the case of Shangshixi Zhou, for example, even though it had by 1479 been designated as a regular administrative area, powerful native chieftains would continue to dominate it. As a result, officials who

---

[18] For the structure of provincial administration in Guangxi, see *GXTZ* (1599), 7:24–25a.

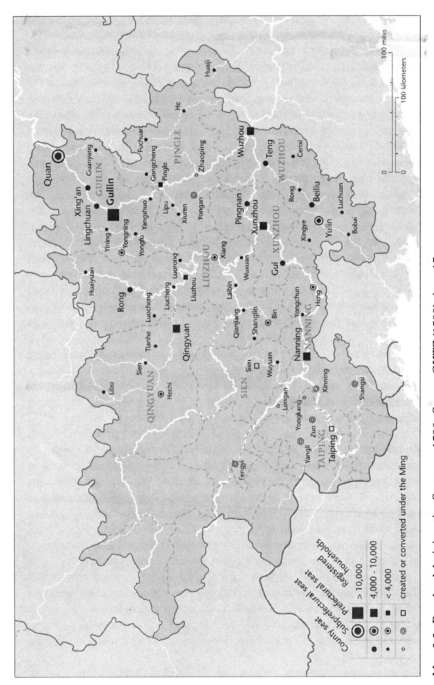

Map 2.2. Regular Administrative Seats, ca. 1590. *Source: GXTZ* (1599), juan 17.

had been assigned to the area were forced to take up residence in a nearby regular administrative seat. It was not until 1591, according to the records, that Ming officials were able to set up in the area an administrative office. Similarly, in the case of the conversion of the Sien domain, even though officials did manage to establish in the newly converted prefecture an administrative apparatus, as we will see, control of the region by the Ming authorities would remain tentative at best.[19]

In addition to increasing the number of regular administrative seats, Ming officials also sought to extend the reach of the state by restoring and expanding the infrastructure in the southern province. An example of such efforts was the periodic renovation of the centuries-old Ling Canal, a vital link not only between the Xiang and Li rivers in northeast Guangxi but also more generally between the central plains and the southern border region. During the Ming period, the Ling Canal, which had come to serve both transportation and irrigation needs, was said to have undergone at least four major restorations, twice during the Hongwu reign and twice in the fifteenth century. Another example of Ming officials' attempts to expand the infrastature in Guangxi had to do with overland transportation. In the 1580s, a major effort was undertaken to carve out a state route (guan lu) alongside the all-important Fu River. As part of the project, 40 post houses, 13 ferry crossings, and 625 bridges were reported to have been constructed as well. Over time, a large number of public works did appear to have been carried out in the southern border region. Although one must treat official statistics with skepticism, a memorial dated 1625 does make a point of noting that, in the previous year alone, there were in Guangxi 3,583 major water-control projects completed.[20]

Although the Ming state did succeed in extending its administrative reach and expanding the infrastructure in the southern border zone, it also encountered major obstacles. One set of problems had to do with the threats, both real and imagined, posed to the representatives and agents of the state. In the southern province, not only did officials have to learn

[19] For the creation of Yongan Zhou and Zhaoping county, see Chapter 4. For the conversion of native domains, see GXTZ (1531), 50:14b–23. For Shangshixi Zhou, see GXTZ (1599), 32:53–54. Another indicator of the efforts by Ming officials to extend the reach of the state was the periodic restoration and construction of city walls; see GXTZ (1599), juan 8; YXWZ, juan 23–24 (for a selection of commemorative essays); Wu Xiaofeng, "Ming dai Guangxi cheng shi xu shi," esp. 91–93.

[20] For the renovation of the Ling Canal, see MSL, Taizu shi lu, 60.1191, 247.2583; Taizong shi lu, 28.2509, 266.2417. For the construction of the state route, see the commemorative essay by Guan Daxun (js. 1565) in YXWZ, 44:38b–41; Wang Shixing, Guang zhi yi, 5.379–80. For more on the development of communication and transportation in Guangxi during the Ming, see Wu Xiaofeng, "Ming dai Guangxi jiao tong"; for broader contexts, see Su Tongbing, Ming dai yi di zhi du; Brook, "Communications and Commerce," esp. 582–619. For the 1625 memorial by Dong Yuanru (js. 1601), then grand coordinator of Guangxi, see MSL, Xizong shi lu, 65.3061.

to adjust to an unfamiliar physical environment, they also had to confront various forms of violence. Even if they managed to arrive at their posts and survive the tropical climate, Ming officials might – as in the case of Ye Zheng, a vice prefect of Qingyuan in the mid-fifteenth century – still find their lives in jeopardy just by performing their duties. As a result of such actual and apparent threats, according to Ming observers, many officials would avoid either traveling to or staying long in the border region. What this meant was that many who did take up local administrative posts in the southern border zone were not necessarily the most qualified or competent. Another set of problems had to do with the relatively limited tax base in Guangxi. Over time, it was not uncommon for the Ming state to have to eliminate offices and positions within the bureaucracy in the southern province. This can be observed, for example, in the abolition of two of the five local commercial-tax offices (*shui ke si*) by the mid-sixteenth century, and this can be seen also in the closure of all six of the region's fishing-tax offices (*he po suo*) by the late Ming.[21]

To extend its military reach in Guangxi, the Ming state had from early on continued the Yuan-dynasty practices of organizing regular military officers and soldiers into units of guards (*wei*) and battalions (*suo*) (see Map 2.3) and carrying out the policy of "military colonization" (*jun tun*). According to this so-called *wei suo* system, which was implemented in most parts of the Ming realm, regular officers and soldiers (and members of their immediate families) were assigned to settle in designated areas where they were expected to farm in times of peace and defend in times of war. In theory, the system not only would ensure the state a steady source of abled bodies but would do so also without imposing onto the government a serious financial burden. Such a system, it was hoped, would also allow officers and soldiers to bring to the border regions the beliefs and practices of the central plains and to facilitate the process of "civilization." In practice, however, the *wei suo* system, at least as it was implemented in Guangxi, was a failure. In time, not only did local authorities have to continue to finance a largely defunct military structure, they also had to keep up with the costs of a variety of defense arrangements that had sprung up in its stead.[22]

Although the Ming military had scored some important early successes, the problems with its organization would become apparent by the

---

[21] For the case of Ye Zheng, who was apparently killed along with a number of family members as he led an effort to confront some local *man* bandits, see *YXWZ*, 2:29–30a. For the lack of competent officials, see, for example, *YJJW*, preface:1. For the elimination of tax offices, see *MHD*, 35.254, 36.264; *GXTZ* (1599), 19:10b–11.

[22] For an overview of the Ming military organization, see Hucker, "Ming Government," 54–72. For the implementation of the *wei suo* system in Guangxi, see Su Jianling, "Ming dai Guangxi de wei suo."

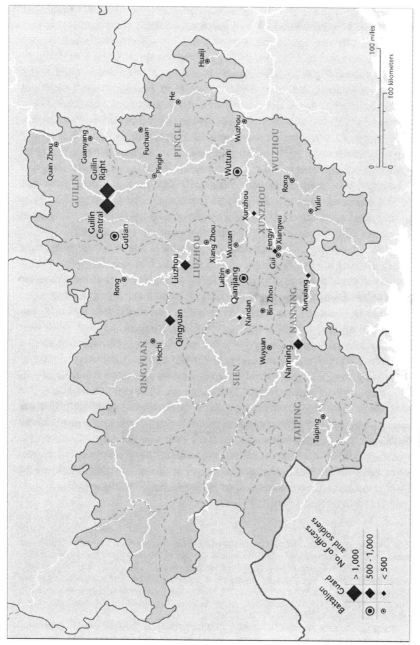

Map 2.3. Guards and Battalions, ca. 1580. *Source: Cangwu*, 7:5b–8a.

decline in regular soldiers

mid-fifteenth century. One major concern for the state was the decline in number of its regular soldiers. In Guangxi, whereas the original number (*yuan e*) of officers and soldiers in the *wei suo* system might have been as high as about 120,000, by 1450, the actual number had apparently fallen to below 45,000. (The figure would have been even lower if the so-called housemen [*she ren*] and surplus men [*yu ding*], who were not part of the regular force, were excluded from the count.) In 1466, Han Yong (1422–78), an assistant censor-in-chief who would help establish in the capital of Wuzhou a permanent headquarters for the office of the supreme commander, offered an even more sober assessment: the total number of officers and soldiers in the twenty-eight guards and battalions in Guangxi was just over twenty thousand. The decline would continue into the sixteenth century. In a 1546 memorial, Feng Bin (js. 1529), a regional inspector, observes that although the bandits in Guangxi number in the tens of thousands, "the number of soldiers is not even 10,000." By 1599, according to the provincial gazetteer, the number of regular officers and soldiers in Guangxi would stand at just 9,836.[23]

disappearance of military farms

The decline of the regular military force was attested to also by the disappearance of military farms (*tun tian*). Whereas the "original acreage" of *tun tian* in Guangxi was reported to have been more than 590,000 *mu* (about 330 square kilometers), by 1587, the "actual acreage" had evidently decreased to just above 290,000 *mu*. Although the disappearance of military farms from the official registration can be attributed in part to the conversion of a large portion of such *tun tian* into private holdings – in 1577, the supreme commander Ling Yunyi (js. 1547) was moved to order a new audit so as to uncover such illicit conversion – the deterioration of the institution of "military colonization" must in part be explained by the actual decline of the regular military population. As early as 1435, for instance, Tian Zhen, an assistant regional military commissioner, was said to have recommended that the size of some of the military farms in Guangxi be scaled back because, as he explained, "many who had been conscripted have fled."[24]

---

[23] For the early- and late-Ming military population figures, see *GXTZ* (1599), 21:2b; for the size of individual guards and battalions at the end of the sixteenth century, see 21:2b–10a. For the 1450 figure, see the memorial by Yu Qian in *YXWZ*, 5:2a. For "housemen" and "surplus men," see Hucker, "Ming Government," 57, 64. For the 1466 figure, see the memorial by Han Yong in *Cangwu*, 23:3b. For the position of supreme commander, see *GXTZ* (1599), 7:1. For Feng Bin, see *MSL, Shizong shi lu*, 312.5844. For a discussion of the decline, see *GXTZ* (1599), 21:1, 10.

[24] For *tun tian* figures, see *GXTZ* (1599), 21:13a; *MHD*, 18.119. For observations concerning the decline, see *GXTZ* (1599), 21:12–13a, 18b–19a. For Ling Yunyi, see *MSL, Shenzong shi lu*, 59.1357. For Tian Zhen's memorial, see *MSL, Yingzong shi lu*, 12.218. For a discussion, see Wang Yuquan, *Ming dai de jun tun*, esp. 98–113.

Two related factors seem to have contributed to the decline of the regular military force in Guangxi. The first had to do with the scale of warfare and the environment in the southern border region. By most accounts, a turning point for the Ming military in Guangxi was the annexation of Annam in the early fifteenth century. According to the 1599 edition of the provincial gazetteer, as a result of the war, "no more than two or three of every ten officers and soldiers [who had been deployed] had survived." Even when their lives were spared in combat, soldiers who were not used to the tropical climate of the southern border zone were often victims of plagues and other diseases. In the case of the Hechi battalion (in Qingyuan prefecture), it is noted in an essay that by the early fifteenth century, as a result of plagues (*yi li*), only "two of every ten" soldiers had remained. In another account dated to 1430, it is reported also that as a result of *zhang*, the number of officers and soldiers in the Wuxuan battalion (Liuzhou) had been reduced from 1,582 to only 47. The relatively hostile conditions in the southern border region evidently also affected the ability of the state to conscript replacement soldiers. In 1445, Liu Pu (d. 1461), a regional commander, noted that many of the conscripts from the lower Yangzi region would not travel to Guangxi because of their fear of its climate.[25]

The second factor had to do with the desertion or conversion of military households. Over time, while a large number of military families in Guangxi managed to disappear from the records by becoming tenants of well-to-do landlords, others were apparently able to transform themselves into registered civilian households. An example of the latter may be found in the case of a certain Zhang clan of Guilin. According to our sources, the Zhangs in question were originally from Yangzhou prefecture in the lower Yangzi region. In the second half of the fourteenth century, a certain Zhang Li was said to have served as an officer in the early Ming army. Following the founding of the dynasty, Zhang Li was first assigned to Guangxi but was in time commissioned to fight in Annam. Upon his death, his only son, Zhang Fu, was supposed to inherit the father's officer position in Guilin but died unexpectedly en route to the imperial capital. It happened that Fu also had only one son, who was then only a child. The Zhangs had apparently by this time fallen into financial hardship. For reasons not entirely clear, Fu's widow decided to leave the family

[25] For comments on the impact of the annexation of Annam, see *GXTZ* (1599), 21:1a; *MSL, Taizong shi lu*, 104.1650. For Hechi, see the commemorative essay by Tang Geng (jr. 1396) in *YXWZ*, 23:1b. For Wuxuan, see *MSL, Xuanzong shi lu*, 72.1692. For problems associated with conscription, see *MSL, Yingzong shi lu*, 131.2604–606. The Hongwu emperor once specifically sent a message to remind his officers in Guilin to be watchful of their food and drink so as not to fall prey to illnesses; see *YXWZ*, 2:20b–21a.

so that Fu's younger sister could stand a better chance raising the child. How the Zhang clan eventually parted way with its military registration we are not sure. What is evident is that when Fu's son finally grew up, Fu's sister had to plead with him to give up his claim to the hereditary officer position. By the 1430s, according to our sources, the Zhangs had "renounced [their] military registration" and chosen instead to concentrate their efforts on "farming and learning." Over the course of the Ming, not only did the Zhang clan manage to transform itself into one of the most prominent lineages in Guilin, it was apparently able also to produce at least three holders of the *jin shi* degree. Although the case of the Zhangs might not be typical, at least two other prominent officials from Guangxi, Wu Tingju (js. 1487) of Wuzhou and Lü Tiaoyang (1516–80) of Guilin, who once served as censor-in-chief and grand secretary, respectively, were said to have also descended from military households.[26]

To supplement the depleted ranks, Ming officials had from very early on been forced to look for other sources of abled bodies. In addition to conscripting replacement soldiers (an exercise known as *qing jun*), authorities in Guangxi had also come to depend on a steady supply of troops from the neighboring provinces. From the mid-fifteenth century on, arrangements were made to station in Guangxi five thousand soldiers from Huguang (a total of ten thousand were allotted for rotations) and fifteen hundred from Guangdong. The dwindling of the regular force also necessitated the employment of civilian militias (*min bing* or *min zhuang*) and mercenary soldiers (*mu bing*). As early as 1426, the censor Zhu Hui was said to have recommended that all regular civilian households in the southern province be organized into units of *bao* ("watches") and *jia* ("tithings") and that selected abled men of such units be trained to provide local defense. In time, efforts were apparently made to expand the *bao jia* system so that each regular county or subprefecture in Guangxi would have its own civilian militia. But because most of the men who did report for service were physically unfit to serve, according to the 1599 edition of the provincial gazetteer, officials in Guangxi were forced to increasingly rely on mercenary soldiers. By the end of the sixteenth century, the size of the *mu bing* population in the southern province (more than twenty-four

---

[26] For the case of the Zhang clan, see *GXTZ* 1599, 30:8; *YXWZ*, 72:4b–7b; *Guilin Zhang shi jia cheng*, 6:9–10. For education of students from military household, see *MHD*, 78.452; for alteration of household registration, see, *MSL, Yingzong shi lu*, 214.4615. For reports on desertion, see, for example, *MSL, Xuanzong shi lu*, 104.2331–32; *Yingzong shi lu*, 12.218. For Wu Tingju, see *GXTZ* (1531), 44:25b–28a; *YXWZ*, 69:47–51a. For Lü Tiaoyang, see *DMB*, 1013–14.

thousand) was evidently far larger than that of the *wei suo* force and civilian militia combined.[27]

In addition to mercenary soldiers, officials in Guangxi had also come to rely on the so-called farmer-soldiers (*geng bing*). Numbering nearly sixteen thousand by the end of the sixteenth century, "farmer-soldiers" were native soldiers who had been sent by native chieftains to assist the Ming in its warfare and who had subsequently been assigned to settle in the newly secured areas. As early as 1437, the regional commander Shan Yun (d. 1438) was reported to have recommended that a group of native soldiers from western Guangxi be transferred to Xunzhou prefecture to help protect the area from local banditry. In 1518, the censor-in-chief Chen Jin (1446–1528) was also noted to have suggested that three to four thousand native soldiers, together with their families, be relocated to the Fu River region to help fend off local bandits. Over time, although some of these *geng bing* would remain under the jurisdiction of their original chieftains, others, especially those whose new settlements were far away from their native domains, would form relatively autonomous units.[28]

One consequence of the breakdown of the *wei suo* system was the escalation of the financial burden on the centralizing state. Rather than be able to rely on an hereditary, self-sufficient army to defend its territory, the Ming had to devise alternative strategies to accomplish its military objectives. In the case of the southern border region, the high cost of sustaining an increasingly complex military apparatus had by the middle of the Ming period clearly become a major concern for officials. In 1493, Li Dongyang (1447–1516), who would in time serve as a grand secretary, reported in a memorial that the grain supply in Guangxi had dropped to such a level that soldiers there had become restless. He recommended that local officials be ordered to take preemptive measures lest the problem turned into a crisis. In 1600, Yang Fang (js. 1577), the grand coordinator of Guangxi, apparently also found it necessary to submit a special request to the central government to withhold certain taxes so that local soldiers could be paid. Although what is generally perceived as the "decline" of the Ming military since the mid-fifteenth century might have indeed been exaggerated, in the context of Guangxi at least, the

[27] For soldiers from Huguang and Guangdong, see *GXTZ* (1599), 21:22–27. For *min zhuang* and mercenary soldiers, see *GXTZ* (1531), 31:20–25a; *GXTZ* (1599), 22:1–42. For Zhu Hui, see *GXTZ* (1599), 22:1a; for the incompetence of *min zhuang*, see 22:1b.

[28] For *geng bing*, see *GXTZ* (1599), juan 23. For Shan Yun, see *MSL, Yingzong shi lu*, 35.673. For Chen Jin, see *MSL, Wuzong shi lu*, 162.3187–88. For more on the commission of native soldiers, see the discussion in Chapter 3.

variety, and persistence, of testimonies by officials does seem to point to the limited effectiveness of the *wei suo* system in the southern border provinces.[29]

Demographic patterns

If the official records were to be trusted, not only had Guangxi remained a hotbed of miasma and poisons, its registered population had also declined sharply over the course of the Ming period. Whereas at the end of the fourteenth century there might have been in the southern province some 1.5 million registered individuals, according to the 1599 edition of the *General Gazetteer of Guangxi*, by the late Ming, the population would fall to just over eight hundred thousand (see Table 2.1).

But official statistics, of course, should not be taken at face value. Although it had been the policy of the Ming state since 1381 to conduct a country-wide census every ten years, efforts to bring up to date the population records were largely unsuccessful. Even the few sets of data historians have considered reliable – namely, the official enumerations of 1381 and 1391/1393 – are in fact of only limited value for the study of Guangxi and other border regions. Not only did officials in Guangxi lack the logistical support to provide an accurate count of the people under their watch, their efforts, as we will see more clearly in Chapter 4, were also complicated by the presence in the region of a sizable "non-Chinese" population.[30]

Several reasons should give us pause in taking too seriously the census figures presented in Table 2.1. The first has to do with the quality of the data. Consider the person-per-household ratios as reported for 1391/1393, 1522, and 1594. If we assume – as it seems reasonable – that the family structure of the registered population in Guangxi had remained relatively stable throughout the Ming period, it would follow that the average household size should also remain more or less constant across time and space. A glance at the table would reveal however that such was not case. At the provincal level, the average number of persons per household had evidently fallen from 7.0 in 1393 to 5.7 in 1522 to 4.4 in 1594, a decline too dramatic, it seems, to be reasonable. Meanwhile, at

---

[29] For the financial burden imposed by the *wei suo* system, see Waldron, *Great Wall of China*, 81–84. For Li Dongyang's memorial, see *MSL, Xiaozong shi lu*, 76.1451–63. For Yang Fang's request, see *MSL, Shenzong shi lu*, 349.6527. For cautions against dismissing the Ming military system, see, for example, the discussion in Robinson, *Bandits, Eunuchs, and the Son of Heaven*.

[30] For a recent evaluation of the early Ming censuses, see Cao Shuji, *Zhongguo ren kou shi*, 18–56.

Table 2.1. *Registered population in Ming Guangxi, 1391–1594*

Prefecture	li[a]	1391			1522			1594		
		Households	Persons	Ratio	Households	Persons	Ratio	Households	Persons	Ratio
Guilin	343	...	...	...	59,789	307,787	5.2	64,012	241,252	3.8
Liuzhou	205	35,963	231,926	6.5	23,046	161,645	7.0	21,969	113,979	5.2
Qingyuan	146	17,272	82,417	4.8	17,128	93,698	5.5	12,465	87,463	7.0
Pingle	20	...	...	...	5,093	32,377	6.4	7,352	28,743	3.9
Wuzhou	220	43,407	248,538[b]	5.7	32,832	181,067	5.5	38,659	158,986	4.1
Xunzhou	96	...	...	...	13,348	78,473	5.9	19,919	63,217	3.2
Nanning	93	...	...	...	11,986	96,061	8.0	12,250	53,946	4.4
Taiping	3	4,859[c]	49,040[c]	10.1	4,859	40,940	8.4	1,536	15,947	10.4
Sien	20[d]	...	...	...	1,886	12,705	6.7	3,960	43,583	11.0
Total	1,146	211,263[e]	1,482,671[e]	7.0	186,090	1,054,752	5.7	182,122	807,219	4.4

Source: GXTZ (1599), 17:2–17. Ellipsis dots indicate no data is available. Note that numbers do not add up to the total.

[a] Data is drawn from GXTZ (1531), juan 1–2 (for essentially identical figures, see also Li Xian et al., *Da Ming yi tong zhi*, juan 83–85). For fiscal as well as control purposes, all registered civilian households in Ming China were, in theory, grouped into units of *li* ("hundred") and *jia* ("tithing"). Although a *li* was supposed to be made up of 110 households, in practice it was seldom the case. For Guangxi, a quick calculation using the 1391 household figures for Liuzhou, Qingyuan, and Wuzhou would show that the number of households per *li* in the three prefectures in the early Ming were 175, 118, and 197, respectively. For an overview of the *li jia* system, see Cao Shuji, *Zhongguo ren kou shi*, 57–77; Brook, "Spatial Organization," 32–35.

[b] Figure is from Xie Junwei et al., *Wuzhou fu zhi*, 7:2a.

[c] Figure is from Cai Ying'en and Gan Dongyang, *Taiping fu zhi*, 1:37a.

[d] Figure is from GXTZ (1531), 50:14b. Sien became a regular prefecture in 1505.

[e] Figure is for the year 1393.

Table 2.2. *Male–female ratios, ca. 1522*

Prefecture	Male	Female	Ratio
Guilin	171,413	136,343	1.26
Liuzhou	91,125	70,521	1.29
Qingyuan	61,211	42,486	1.44
Pingle	19,534	12,843	1.52
Wuzhou	90,862	82,464	1.10
Xunzhou	40,350	35,122	1.15
Nanning	58,566	37,495	1.56
Taiping	21,600	18,340	1.18
Sien	7,575	5,130	1.48
Total	600,819	453,933	1.32

Source: GXTZ (1531), 18:1–12, 50:16a. Note that numbers do not add up to the total.

the prefectural level for the year 1391 (for which we do not have all the data), the average household size appears to have varied from 4.8 in Qingyuan to 10.1 in Taiping – a range, again, too wide to be plausible. Although the ratio of five persons per household that was apparently quite common in the lower Yangzi region might not have been the norm in border regions such as Guangxi, it is likely that in areas where the average reported household size was especially high (such as Taiping in 1391), undercounting of the population was a serious problem.[31]

To gauge the quality of the available data, consider also the male–female ratios as reported for 1522, the only year such figures are available for Guangxi. Here the numbers are suspicious for two reasons. If one accepts the common assumption that, as a result of female infanticide, there were on average in Ming China 110 boys for every 100 girls, the reported ratio of 132 to 100 for Guangxi as a whole would seem unusually high, especially when there is no reason to suspect that the practice of female infanticide was particularly rampant in the southern border region. Furthermore, even if one accepts a higher male–female ratio for Guangxi, one would expect that variations within the province would be statistically insignificant. But such was not the case according to the official figures. As can be gleaned from Table 2.2, the reported numbers of males for every 100 females in Guangxi range from 110 in Wuzhou to an implausible 156 in Nanning. Following the same logic we used

[31] The discussion here follows some of the arguments in Cao Shuji, *Zhongguo ren kou shi*, esp. 24–39; for Cao's brief discussion of Guangxi, see pp. 143–46.

earlier, it seems reasonable to conclude that in areas where the reported male–female ratios were especially high (such as Qingyuan, Pingle, and Nanning in 1522), undercounting of the female population was a major problem.[32]

The second reason one should be cautious in using the official population figures has to do with the scope of the data. Set aside for now the problem of under-reporting. Even if one were to treat the official statistics as reliable, a careful examination of the data from 1522 and 1594 would reveal that the numbers in fact refer to different constituents. In the case of the data from 1594, the population figures for individual prefectures seem to have taken into account only people who were living under the direct control of the state; with occasional exceptions, people who were under the rule of native chieftains were not included in the enumerations. By contrast, in the case of the data from 1522, the population figures evidently include also people who lived in native domains. Consider the case of Qingyuan prefecture. A quick calculation using the data in the 1531 edition of the provincial gazetteer would show that of the reported population of nearly ninety-four thousand in Qingyuan in 1522, about sixty-five thousand were from the regular administrative areas, while close to twenty-nine thousand were from the native domains under its jurisdiction. What this means is that, at least from the perspective of the official book-keepers, the "regular" population in Qingyuan prefecture had actually increased over the course of the sixteenth century. And what this means for our understanding of the census data of Guangxi is that a simple comparison of the figures would yield very little insight into the demographic trends of the province.[33]

The third and most important reason one should be careful in using the official census figures has to do with the gaps in the data. In Guangxi as in other parts of the southern border zone, a significant portion of the population – people who are generically referred to in the records as *man, yi,* or *manyi* – was never registered with the state and was thus never included in the official enumerations. Although it is difficult to gauge the number of people who were left out, based on anecdotal evidence (see Chapter 4) – as well as the fact that 40 percent of the population in present-day Guangxi are classified as non-Han – it seems fair to assume that the

---

[32] For a discussion of male–female ratios, see Cao Shuji, *Zhongguo ren kou shi,* 39–43.

[33] For the population data for Qingyuan, see *GXTZ* (1531), 18:4b–6; *GXTZ* (1599), 17:5b–6. Another problem concerning the scope of the data has to do with changes in provincial boundaries. Because Quan Zhou and Guanyang county (both in Guilin) did not become part of Guangxi until 1394, information about their populations is most likely not reflected in the 1393 figure for the southern province.

actual population in Ming-dynasty Guangxi was at least 60 percent more than what was reported in the official records.[34]

But if historians are understandably suspicious of official census data they have nevertheless pointed to a number of demographic patterns in the southern province. One such pattern had to do with the expansion of population. Although direct evidence is difficult to come by, most historians would agree that the population in Guangxi – just as that of Ming China as a whole – had increased over time. For Robert Marks, who accepts the 1391 official figure of 1.39 million and assumes an annual growth rate of 0.3 to 0.4 percent, the population in Guangxi would by 1640 have increased to about 3.25 million. By contrast, for Martin Heijdra, who assumes a much larger population for early-Ming China (eighty-five instead of the officially reported sixty million by 1400) and, in one scenario, an annual growth rate ranging from 0.4 to 0.6 percent, the population in Guangxi would by 1600 have expanded to 6.5 million. It is worth noting that even if one accepts Heijdra's higher estimates, the population density in the southern province – 29 persons per square kilometer according to one calculation – would still be far below that of the provinces of Zhejiang (349) and even Guangdong (67), a state of affairs well corroborated by observers of the time.[35]

Another trend historians have pointed to is migration. Over time, a variety of people had traveled the distance to make the southern province their new home. Of them, the largest group was no doubt made up of officers and soldiers who had been assigned to the guards and battalions in the border region. But just how many officers and soldiers had migrated to Guangxi over the course of the Ming it is difficult to determine. On the one hand, the periodic references in the records have made it clear that efforts were continuously made by the Ming state to recruit soldiers from outside the province to fill the ranks in the *wei* and *suo*

[34] For an overview of the composition of population in modern-day Guangxi, see Guangxi Zhuangzu Zizhiqu di fang zhi bian zuan wei yuan hui, *Guangxi tong zhi: ren kou zhi*. The boundary of Guangxi in present-day China encompasses also the coastal area that was under the jurisdiction of Guangdong during the Ming. The rough figure of 60 percent (calculated from $1 \div 0.4$) is a conservative "guesstimate." Given the limited reach of the state, it is highly probable that there were at least as many people who were left out of the official enumerations as those who were included.

[35] For a discussion of population growth in southern China during the Ming, see Marks, *Tigers, Rice, Silk, and Silt*, 87–100, esp. 87 n. 3. For an alternative estimate, see Heijdra, "Socio-Economic Development," 436–40, esp. Table 9.2. Cao Shuji, who revises the 1393 official figure for Guangxi upward to 1.73 million and assumes an annual growth rate of 0.3 percent, would arrive at a population figure of 3.5 million by 1630; see Cao Shuji, *Zhongguo ren kou shi*, 143–46, 194–95, 281. Figures for population density are calculated based on the data found in Table 9.2 in Heijdra, "Socio-Economic Development," and Table 7.1 in Cao Shuji, *Zhongguo ren kou shi*.

[Margin notes: demograph patterns; expansion of population; migration; largest group – officers & soldiers]

units in Guangxi (soldiers who stationed at the Xunxiang Guard in Nanning prefecture in the early sixteenth century, for example, were said to have come from the lower Yangzi region). On the other hand, no doubt because of the inability of the state to fulfill its objective (the periodic imperial exhortations are telling indications), it is clear that relatively few officers and soldiers would actually migrate to Guangxi after 1400. To put the scale of military migration to the southern province in perspective, let us assume, for the sake of argument, that there had indeed at one point in the early Ming period been 120,000 officers and soldiers from the central plains stationing in Guangxi. Let us assume further that each of these officers and soldiers would bring with him two family members. In this admittedly highly improbable scenario, the total military migrant population in Guangxi would stand at 360,000. If we assume also that the actual population in the southern province at the end of the fourteenth century was at least 60 percent more than the 1.5 million cited in the official records (for a total of 2.5 million), it would seem that military migrants did constitute a significant though not overwhelming presence in Guangxi.[36]

In time, as many have pointed out, other types of migrants would also come to make their presence felt in the southern province. Among them were officials who had been banished to the border zone, once-itinerant merchants from as far north as the lower Yangzi region who had decided to settle in the south, desolate peasants from Huguang and Guangdong who had chosen to take up farming in the relatively sparsely populated Guangxi, and an assortment of questionable characters who, for a variety of reasons, had opted to seek a new life in the border region. Together, these groups constituted only a small portion of the population in Guangxi. But what they lacked in number they appeared to have made up by their influence.[37]

Yet another pattern historians have pointed to had to do with the distribution of the registered population. Although the official census data for Guangxi is mostly unreliable, some of the patterns found in Table 2.1 are corroborated by anecdotal evidence. One such characteristic is the relative concentration of the registered population in Guilin and Wuzhou

---

[36] For an overview of migration during the Ming, see Cao Shuji, *Zhongguo yi min shi*. For military migration to Guangxi, see Fan Yuchun, "Ming dai Guangxi de jun shi yi min." For the origins of the soldiers of the Xunxiang Guard, see Wang Ji, *Jun ji tang ri xun shou jing*, 2b. For the average size of a regular military household, see Cao Shuji, *Zhongguo ren kou shi*, 89–90.

[37] For an overview of different migrant groups, see Su Jianling, "Ming Qing shi qi Zhuang Han min zu," 33–37. For a discussion of the activities of some of these migrants, see Chapter 4.

prefectures. This is perhaps not surprising given the fact that the former was where the capital of Guangxi was located and the latter was home of the province's military headquarters. This pattern of distribution is also not unexpected given that of the prefectures in the southern province, Guilin and Wuzhou were the most accessible from the central plains. One corollary of this pattern is that, within Guangxi, it was in Guilin that one seems to find the highest concentration of prominent clans, at least as they are measured by the number of examination degree holders produced. Of the particularly notable lineages in Guilin, the most prominent were apparently the Jiangs and the Chens of Quan Zhou (located in the northeastern part of the prefecture) and the Lüs and the Zhangs of Lingui county (home of the prefectural and provincial seats). In the case of the Jiangs, not only did the clan manage to produce one of only two grand secretaries – one of the most powerful positions in the imperial court – to have come from Guangxi (the other grand secretary was a Lü of Lingui), over time, it also succeeded in turning out at least nine other *jin shi* and sixty-one provincial graduates (*ju ren*).[38]

Life in the borderland

By most accounts, the southern border region was a challenging place to make a living. Not only "are [its] mountains mostly barren," according to the 1599 edition of the *General Gazetteer of Guangxi*, "land that is productive makes up not even one tenth [of the area in the province]." For one reason or another, land that was left uncultivated could be seen tens of *li* (one *li* is about one half of a kilometer) at a stretch – a sight apparently particularly unsettling for visitors from the central plains. As a result, according to the compiler of the gazetteer, "the amount of wealth and taxes [that could be generated] from Guangyou [i.e., Guangxi] cannot even match that from a large county in eastern Wu [i.e., the lower Yangzi region]." But the troubles with the border region were not limited to the lack of productivity of its land, according to Ming observers. In the same gazetteer, it is noted that farmers in Guangxi "conduct irrigation at the wrong time, easily grow tired tilling land, and . . . often cannot tell beans from wheat." Not only "do [women] not practice women's work," people in the province "are ignorant about barter and trade." As a result, "from the stationery used by officials to the scissors and measuring sticks used by ordinary folks," much of what people need have to be brought in from other provinces.[39]

---

[38] For a partial list of prominent clans in Guangxi, see *YXCZ*, 9:4b–12.
[39] For observations, see *GXTZ* (1599), 4:1b, 17:1a, 3:47b.

Descriptions such as these do not lie, but neither do they offer the full picture. For Ming travelers writing about the material life of the people of Guangxi, the comparison was almost always with what the visitors understood to be the norms of the central plains. To such observers, the southern border region was almost always lacking in some measures – whether it be the proportion of fertile land, the productivity of its people, the variety of goods produced, and so on. Such comparisons were perhaps unavoidable, given the background of most of the officials and travelers who left behind written records. But such comparisons, ultimately, did more than just compare. By emphasizing the "lacks" of Guangxi, such writers – even as they added to the knowledge about the borderland – did help reinforce the perceived boundaries between the central plains and the southern border zone.[40]

For Ming visitors, what distinguished the southern borderland from the central plains was not only its geography but also its people. Consider the observations by Wang Ji (d. 1540). Although Wang spent only less than a year as an assistant magistrate in Heng Zhou (Nanning), his reports on life in the border zone are highly interesting. In his *Hand-held Mirror for Daily Inquiries in the Gentleman's Hall* (pref. 1522), a brief collection of informal jottings, not only is Wang Ji keen on pointing out the special flora and fauna in the southern region and comparing the different types of foodstuffs in the area with the ones back home – "in terms of fruits and melons, [what one can find in Heng Zhou are] in general far inferior to [those in] the Zhejiang region" – he is also interested in describing in detail what he considers the unusual customs of the people in the border zone (see Chapter 5 for more on the context of the composition of this work). In particular, in his descriptions of the farming practices in Heng Zhou, Wang Ji reports that farmers there generally put in much less work in cultivation than the people in his hometown in the lower Yangzi region. After they have transplanted the young shoots to the fields, Wang notes, farmers in Heng Zhou would largely leave the plants alone. Only when there is a drought would people irrigate the fields by breaching the walls of nearby ponds or the banks of adjacent streams, and only on occasion would farmers bother to get rid of wild vegetation. Although the land in Heng Zhou is sufficiently fertile to produce more, Wang Ji observes, people there are satisfied with a yield of two piculs for every *mu* (or 200 liters of grain for about every 570 square meters) of land. "This is because [people are] accustomed to being lazy and not working

40 Historians have just begun to explore the history of economic life in south China. For the late imperial period, see, for example, Marks, *Tigers, Rice, Silk, and Silt*; Zhou Hongwei, *Qing dai liang Guang nong ye di li*.

hard." Wang notices also that people in Heng Zhou have only limited knowledge of growing and handling wheat. Instead of allowing the crop to dry thoroughly before putting it away, he reports, they often let it rot in storage.[41]

For Ming observers, not only was Guangxi, agriculturally speaking, a notably unproductive region, it was also in many ways a death trap for unsuspecting itinerant merchants. In an anecdotal account collected in Wang Sen's *Anthology of Miscellanies of Guangxi* (and attributed to an undated gazetteer of Qingyuan prefecture), we are told that, in the eleventh year of the Chenghua reign (1475), a young man named Chen Xian from Jiangxi province was one day found lying unconscious on a roadside in Nadi Zhou in northern Guangxi. According to Chen, who was in time nurtured back to health by a fellow traveler, he had been traveling with his uncle as merchants in the area before he was overcome by illness (what their business was the account does not say). But rather than take care of his nephew, Chen's uncle apparently decided to leave the young man behind to die and return home to take over his nephew's property. In time, according to the account, Chen Xian would become well enough to travel back to Jiangxi to report his uncle's deeds to the authorities. The story, as we can see, actually has very little to do with Guangxi. In many ways, it is a celebration of the goodness of people (not the uncle but the traveler who saved Chen Xian's life) and of the triumph of justice. But it was not for no reason that the account was chosen to be included first in a gazetteer of Qingyuan prefecture (where Nadi Zhou was located) and later in Wang Sen's anthology. To the compilers of these two works, the story of Chen Xian, perhaps not unlike that of Li Zongxian recounted at the start of this chapter, was a reminder not only of the presence of people with kindness but also, in the first place, of the lawlessness of the border region.[42]

Consider also the story of Zhou Li. In an anecdote first recorded in a collection of informal jottings by Huang Yu (1426–97), a scholar-official from Guangdong, we are told that some time during the Zhengtong reign (1436–49) a man named Zhou Li from the Southern Metropolitan Region was engaged in trade in western Guangxi when he married into a local family. According to Huang's account, after having stayed in the southern province for more than twenty years, Zhou Li one day resolved to return home for a visit. Worried that her husband might choose not to come back, however, Zhou's wife decided to mix in his food a *gu* poison. When it was time for Zhou to embark on his journey, his wife sent

[41] Wang Ji, *Jun ji tang ri xun shou jing*, 7a, 18.
[42] For the story of Chen Xian, see *YXCZ*, 6:16–17a.

(marginal handwritten note: death trap for itinerant merchants)

their fifteen-year-old son along and taught him how to treat his father in case the latter was willing to return to Guangxi. As it happened, Zhou Li promptly fell sick upon arrival in his home town. It was only after Zhou had expressed desires to return to his wife, according to Huang's account, that his son intervened to make him well again. For Huang Yu, the ordeals of Zhou Li only confirmed what he had known from other sources: the use of *gu* was prevalent among the "non-Chinese" (*man*) in the southern border zone, and it was itinerant merchants who were reckless enough to marry the native women there who were most often victims of *gu* poisoning.[43]

Adventures in the southern borderland were hazardous for other reasons. In another anecdote apparently first recorded by Li Wenfeng (js. 1532), a scholar-official from Qingyuan prefecture and author of, among other writings, an informative work on Annam, we are told that Sicheng Zhou, a native domain in northwest Guangxi, was one of the places where mercury, a highly poisonous but useful metal, was in abundance. To extract mercury from its source, according to Li's account, people who stood to profit had devised a wicked scheme. First, unsuspecting victims were lured to the area by itinerant merchants and were fed with rice and wine for three days. Then, the still-unwary victims would be led to the ore pits where they would be buried by force, presumably with only their heads exposed. In time, the heads of such human conduits would be chopped off, but it would be a few more days before their mercury-soaked bodies would be dug up. According to Li Wenfeng, similar practices could also be found in Annam just across the border from Guangxi. There, merchants from Jiangxi province (in southeast China) were said to have routinely conspired with local scoundrels to lure hopeful hired-hands to the trap.[44]

In addition to the day-to-day challenges, people in the southern province also had to cope with a range of nature-induced disasters. One area of constant concern had to do with flooding. In 1522, for instance, severe floods were reported in at least three administrative areas in eastern Guangxi: in Quan Zhou (Guilin), hundreds of *qing* of land (a *qing* was about 6 hectares or the size of eight standard soccer fields) were said to have been flooded; in Yangshuo county (also in Guilin prefecture), the water level was reported to have remained high even after five days; and in Cangwu county (home of the prefectural seat of Wuzhou),

[43] For the story of Zhou Li, see Huang Yu, *Shuang huai sui chao*, 5.97; *YXCZ*, 14:12b–13a. For more on *gu* poisons, see the discussion in Chapter 5.
[44] For Li's account, see *GXTZ* (1599), 42:13b–14a; *YXCZ*, 19:3. For his biography, see *GXTZ* (1599), 29:30b–31a.

more than ten thousand homes were said to have been washed away as a result. Again, in 1586, major floods were reported in at least six of the ten administrative areas in Wuzhou prefecture. In the capital of Wuzhou, the water level was said to have at one point risen to as high as five meters, and a total of 816 homes were reported to have been swept away as a result. Floods were of course not the only form of nature-induced disasters. Of equal concern to officials were the droughts and famines that had afflicted the region periodically. In the summer of 1434, the prefect of Nanning was apparently sufficiently worried about the lack of rainfall that he held a special praying session in a local Buddhist temple. (The session worked, or so our record claims.) Other concerned (or desperate) officials would seek divine intervention through Daoist priests. Whether the region of Guangxi was more prone to nature-induced disasters than other parts of the Ming realm it is difficult to say. But judging from the available records – it has been estimated that, between 1470 and 1949, there were in Guangxi on average a major flood every seven years and a major drought every three – it seems clear that the threat of disasters must have been a persistent concern for people who lived in the southern border province.[45]

To gain a sense of the impacts of such disasters, consider the drought of Bin Zhou (Liuzhou) of 1618. According to Sheng Wannian (js. 1583), who was given the task of dealing with the crisis, the effects of the drought were devastating. As "barren land stretched for thousands of *li* and the homeless swarmed the countryside," two pressing problems were banditry and the shortage of grain. Although Sheng Wannian and other officials were able to secure military aid from elsewhere and import grain from as far as Guangdong province, in all "more than half of the population died of starvation." The drought of 1618, as it turned out, was only the beginning of Bin Zhou's problems. In 1619, the area was hit by a plague. According to Sheng Wannian, mountains of human bones could be seen piling up everywhere. The conditions in the area would become so deteriorated that Sheng had to instruct his subordinates to bring along spades on their inspection tours so that they could help bury the dead as they encountered them.[46]

Even to this day, nature-induced disasters have continued to impact the lives of the people of Guangxi. For example, in July 2001, a series of

---

[45] For a catalog of nature-induced disasters in Guangxi, see *YXCZ*, 15:4b–14; for the floods of 1522, see 15:12b; for the floods of 1586, see 15:14a; for Nanning, see 15:5b–6a. For the involvement of Daoist priests, see *YXCZ*, 11:33, 35b–36a. The statistic is cited in Guangxi Zhuangzu Zizhiqu di fang zhi bian zuan wei yuan hui, *Guangxi tong zhi: zi ran di li zhi*, 4.

[46] For Bin Zhou, see the account by Sheng Wannian in *YXCZ*, 17:8b–12.

typhoons apparently brought so much rain to the western part of Guangxi that the Yong River, which flows through the present-day provincial capital at Nanning, was flooded to a level – 5 meters above the official flood line – that had not been observed since 1913. Even with the aid of modern technology and the mobilizing capacity of all three levels of the Chinese government, the county of Yongning (which comprises the city of Nanning and its surrounding areas) was devastated. According to news reports, more than 75 percent of the population in the county were affected, and some 60 percent of the agricultural land was damaged. In all, the direct economic loss was estimated at 1.6 billion yuan, or about 200 million U.S. dollars.[47]

Boundaries of nature

Humans were of course not alone in the southern border zone. As Robert Marks has made clear in his pioneering study of the environmental history of south China, over time, people of Guangxi also had had to learn to coexist with other species. Although the expansion of human settlement would in time drive many of these species to extinction, the course of encroachment was neither wholly in one direction nor without resistance. During the Ming, as more and more people sought to make a living in the southern border region, they were also frequently reminded – by the elephants and tigers but also by the myriad other species of wild animals that populated the tropics – of the perils of their endeavor.[48]

To understand the impacts of human encroachment, let us consider the case of the elephant. By all accounts, elephants once roamed in what is present-day south China. It was probably not by coincidence that, during the Qin dynasty, one of the three commanderies set up in the southern region was given the name "Elephant" (Xiang). During the Hongwu reign, not only did the emperor encourage native chieftains in the southern border region to help hunt for elephants and to bring them to the imperial capital for use in ceremonies, he also approved in as early as 1369 the establishment in Nanning prefecture a military guard with the explicit objective of rounding up the elephants in the area. But if there had ever been a substantial elephant population in southwest Guangxi in the beginning of the Ming dynasty, it was no longer the case by the end of the fourteenth century. The last record we have of native chieftains from the southern province presenting elephants to the court was dated 1388, and the last record of the military guard in Nanning doing the same was dated

---

[47] Shi Wei and Luo Chang'ai, "Guangxi Yongning Xian shou zai 16 yi."
[48] My discussion in this section is much inspired by Marks, *Tigers, Rice, Silk, and Silt.*

1393. By 1531, rather than offer firsthand observations, the compilers of the provincial gazetteer would simply cite an earlier, ambiguously-identified source in which it is suggested that elephants "would appear occasionally in the valleys near the border with Jiaozhi [Annam]." Given the silence in the records after 1393, it seems reasonable to conclude that elephants had indeed been forced to make an early exit in south China.[49]

Let us consider also the case of the tiger. Although there exist no reliable estimates for the tiger population in Guangxi under the Ming, anecdotal reports seem to suggest there was a sizable one. In one anecdote recorded by Shen Zhou (1427–1509), the well-known poet, calligrapher, and painter, it is noted that at the time when Zhao Fu (d. 1486) led a military expedition in Guangxi in the 1460s, "many tigers" could be seen drinking from the streams. Other observations, especially those dated to the second half of the Ming period, tend to focus on the menace of the tiger population. For example, in an ode composed on the occasion of a sacrifice to a mountain god, Huang Fang (js. 1508), an administration vice commissioner of Guangxi in the 1520s, mentions specifically the threats posed by tigers on human settlements. "Numbering more than a hundred at times, [tigers] regard us people as [nothing more than] chicken and pigs." Other reports are more specific. In an account found in the 1599 edition of the *General Gazetteer of Guangxi*, it is noted that from 1518 to 1521 the prefectural seat of Qingyuan was constantly under attack. "Not a single night when a tiger [or tigers] did not enter the administrative seat to menace." Residents killed were "too numerous to count," and the death toll of livestock was "even higher." In another account found in the same gazetteer, it is reported that in one particularly tragic year (1587) in the area of Chang'an Zhen in Liuzhou prefecture, tigers entered into one of the villages and devoured more than thirty men and women, leaving behind only eighteeen survivors.[50]

Such reports on tiger attacks, as Marks suggests, can be read in two different ways. On the one hand, such reports are indicators of the extent of destruction of the tiger habitat in south China. Because tigers, especially

---

[49] For a discussion of elephants in south China from a historical perspective, see Marks, *Tigers, Rice, Silk, and Silt*, 42–46. For the use of elephants in court ceremonies, see *MSL, Taizu shi lu*, 188.2816. For evidence on the desire for elephants by the Hongwu emperor, see *MSL, Taizu shi lu*, 179.2704, 179.2713. For the presentation of elephants by native chieftains, see *MSL, Taizu shi lu*, 193.2905. For the history and functions of the Xunxiang (Taming Elephants) Guard, see *MSL, Taizu shi lu*, 188.2816, 192.2885, 226.3306; *Cangwu*, 7:7a. For the quotation, see *GXTZ* (1531), 21:5b.

[50] For Zhao Fu's encounter with tigers, see Wei Jun, *Xi shi er*, 7:8b; *YXCZ*, 14:17a. For Huang Fang, see *YXWZ*, 75.398. For the problems in Qingyuan, see *GXTZ* (1599), 41:14b–15a; for Chang'an Zhen;, see 41:18. For more reports on tiger attacks, see *YXCZ*, 15:22b–23.

the males, require vast expanses of forests (20 to 100 square kilometers for each adult tiger, according to estimates) to sustain them, reports on their attacks on human settlements are useful indicators of the disappearance of their food supply as well as of the destruction of their habitat. On the other hand, the continual appearance of tigers in Ming-period records means that their destruction was not complete. Despite the encroachment of human settlement, some tigers were able to occupy marginal forests and to emerge periodically from their habitat to attack livestock and human settlers. In fact, in the mid-seventeenth century when south China was plunged into a period of turmoil as a result of dynastic change, according to Marks, a significant decrease in human population and the return of forests in some parts of the region actually led to an expansion of the tiger population.[51]

To recognize the limits of human encroachment, let us consider two final anecdotes. According to an account found in the 1631 edition of the *Gazetteer of Wuzhou Prefecture*, some time during the Jiajing reign (1522–66), a battalion commander named Ma Feng was presented by one of his tenants a gift of a tiger cub. Not knowing what to do with the unusual creature, Ma at first tied the cub to an iron chain and fed it with meat bought from the market. In time, according to the account, the tiger grew to be so tame that, for Ma Feng's amusement, it would on his order "spin around and jump up and down." But the good time between the master and his pet did not last. One late evening when Ma Feng returned home drunk and made the mistake of shouting at his loyal pet, it became angry and attacked Ma in his face. Ma Feng eventually died from his wounds, and the aggrieved tiger, according to the story, could later be seen lingering around Ma's grave looking longingly for its former master.[52]

To Chen Jian (js. 1607), who as prefect of Wuzhou from 1617 to 1620 edited the first draft of the local gazetteer, the moral of the story could not be clearer: for his misfortune Ma Feng had no one but himself to blame. Tigers should never be brought into one's home, Chen argued in his commentary, just as inferior persons (*xiao ren*) should never be kept in the company of a ruler. In both cases, he asserted, the treacherous creatures in question were bound to wreak havoc. Mindful of the increased political power held at the Ming court by imperial relatives and the eunuch Wei Zhongxian (1568–1627), Chen Jian lamented that since ancient times it had been people similar to Ma Feng who, through their reckless pursuits of pleasure, had time and again brought harm to themselves and to the

---

[51] Marks, *Tigers, Rice, Silk, and Silt*, 43–44, 323–27, 344–45.
[52] For Ma Feng, see Xie Junwei et al., *Wuzhou fu zhi* (1631), 20:11; *YXCZ*, 14:16; *GXTZ*, (1733), 128:43.

country. Ma's death need not be mourned, Chen maintained, because Ma Feng offered "fine meat to fill not the stomachs of men but the stomach of a tiger." Chen Jian's message for the Ming emperor was none too subtle: "[I have] particularly recorded [this story] here to warn people not to rear tigers."[53]

Although to Chen Jian the episode of Ma Feng was a quintessential cautionary tale on politics, to the historian the primary story here is clearly one of encroachment and exploitation. Even though it is not explained in the account cited how the tiger cub came to be caught (did Ma's tenant go out of his way to hunt for the tiger or was the cub caught wandering near human settlements?) or how commonplace such an occurrence might be in that part of Guangxi in the sixteenth century (according to a different late-Ming source, the area of Rong county, where Ma Feng was based, was a relatively tranquil place: "Its hills and streams are flat and wide" and "its people work and rest accordingly"), it seems likely that by the time the tiger cub was captured, much harm to its habitat – demolition of forests, depletion of wildlife, and so on – had already taken place. Kidnapping a tiger as Ma Feng did was thus the last of a series of violent acts by humans against the species. By framing his outrage in political and moral terms alone then, Chen Jian seems to have missed a larger truth. Ma Feng might have acted recklessly, but what enabled him to do so, it appears, was the changing environment of the southern border zone.[54]

Finally, let us consider the story of Yang the optimistic. According to an anecdote first recorded in an early-seventeenth-century collection of informal jottings, an official named Yang Shubao apparently had a very particular idea about how to rein in the tiger population. Instead of hunting the big cats, as an official in Jingzhou (in northern Huguang), Yang had decided to order the carving onto a mountain slope a passage of admonition. Whether Yang Shubao was truly convinced of the power of the inscribed words it is difficult to say. In any case, Yang would in time be appointed to Yulin Zhou in Wuzhou prefecture and would seek to repeat his efforts there. In particular, he wrote to a fellow official in Jingzhou and requested that rubbings of the original inscriptions be made and brought to Guangxi. As it happened, the two craftsmen who would in time be sent to produce the rubbings never made it back; while they were at work, a tiger was said to have emerged from behind and killed them. As it turned out, no one – at least not among the tigers – was paying attention to Yang Shubao's admonition. Although it is unclear when (or if) this episode actually took place, to a seventeenth-century reader the

[53] For Chen Jian's commentary, see Xie Junwei et al., *Wuzhou fu zhi*, 20:11b.
[54] For a description of Rong county, see *DYYZ*, 2:50.

message was clear: one might seek to change the nature of things, but one must realize that neither nature nor Nature can be easily transformed.[55]

Just as the episodes of Ma Feng and Yang Shubao reveal the distance to which officials would go to extend the reach of the state (broadly conceived), Ma's eventual demise and Yang's (perhaps unsurprising) failure might also be read – ironically – as testimonies to the limits of state expansion. Although the stories of Ma and Yang are both indicative of the increased encroachment by humans on natural habitats (presumably Yang Shubao was interested in transforming the nature of tigers because they were threatening human settlements), for Ming observers, the deaths of Ma Feng and the craftsmen were clear testimonies that the south remained a perilous frontier. Over the course of the Ming, as we have seen, the centralizing state had sought to extend to the southern region both its administrative and military apparatuses. Not only did officials encourage the creation and registration of permanent settlements, they also sought to provide a degree of order through the establishment of guards and battalions in strategic locations. But as much as some officials would like to quickly transform the border region and bring it firmly under the control of the state, all would learn that there were limits imposed by the environment. And as much as agents of the state dreaded the dangers of miasma and strayed tigers, they would come to realize that mysterious vapor and hungry beasts were only some of the more minor problems they had to encounter in bringing order to the border zone.

[55] For the case of Yang Shubao, see Wei Jun's *Xi shi er*, 7:8b–9a; *YXCZ*,14:17b.

3   Politics of chieftaincy

The reason the people of Jiao [Annam] . . . dare not to encroach on the interior [of the Ming territory] is that the superior military force of the native chiefs is fully capable of placing a stranglehold on [any intruders]. If we were to weaken our defense and remove our buffer, it is feared that the troubles at the border of the central dominion [*zhong guo*] would be even greater than those brought by the native domains.

General Gazetteer of Guangxi (1599)

In the autumn of 1368, a special proclamation was sent by the Ming founder to the native chieftains and peoples of Guangxi. With this decree the Hongwu emperor obviously had two goals in mind: to affirm his claim over the border zone, and to confirm the allegiance of the region's chieftains. In the edict, the Ming ruler first compares himself to the "wise men and kings of the past" who, in his view, were able to induce "submission from far and wide" because they understood how to "dispense both fear and generosity." To demonstrate his own munificence, the Hongwu emperor expresses his appreciation for the "simple ways of life" of the borderland population and for those chieftains who have stepped forward to submit to the new dynasty. "The sincerity of your admiration [for the Ming]," the ruler declares, "indeed deserves high praise." The purpose of the decree is not to underscore the military prowess of the Ming, the emperor explains, but to exhort native chieftains to "rein in [their] heart-and-mind" and to exert themselves to uphold order in the border region. The edict concludes with the instruction that native chieftains should help convey the Ming ruler's desire for peace so that their people would be put at ease.[1]

The Hongwu emperor might have come from humble roots, but the one-time Buddhist monk and rebel chief turned out to be no less a

---

[1] *MSL*, *Taizu shi lu*, 36A.667–68; copied with minor changes in *MS*, 318.8229–30. A version of this decree is also found in Gao Xiongzheng, *Siming fu zhi*, 6:1. The entry in *MSL* is dated 19 December 1368, but the communication of the edict obviously took place earlier.

master of imperial rhetoric. In the "Proclamation of Accession," a self-important declaration he sent to various neighboring countries following his enthronement earlier in 1368, the emperor attributes the rise of the Ming not only to the decline of fortune of the Mongols, who had briefly ruled the central dominion as the Yuan dynasty, but also to the "bearing the favor of Heaven above" by the new ruling house. Because the Ming founder and his followers were able to "make a rigorous show of military might," the proclamation boasts, they managed to "suppress and settle the four quarters" and enabled people to once again "rest secure in their fields and villages." In an exchange with one of his most valued generals later in 1368, in which the latter expressed concerns about the trustworthiness of the "non-Chinese" population in the southern region, the emperor sought to assure his anxious lieutenant that even the most ferocious *man yi* would succumb to the universal appeal of the Ming rule: "The nature and customs of the *man yi* might be unusual, but their fondness for life and aversion to death are not dissimilar [to that of the norm]." If Ming officials could "pacify them with amity, treat them with sincerity, and exhort them with reason," the emperor asked without apparent irony, "how could they not be willing to transform and follow [our way]?"[2]

The Ming founder of course had his practical side. Much as he liked to claim to rule "all under heaven," he knew his reach was limited. In the area of foreign relations, for instance, the Hongwu emperor explicitly forbade his successors from invading what he derisively referred to as "the small countries of the southern *man*." This injunction came about not because the emperor had developed an affinity for the countries in "the southern seas" but because he was much more concerned with the threats posed by the Mongol remnants in the north. In the area of domestic control, the Ming ruler realized also that the state had only scarce resources. Rather than rely solely on its own military forces to maintain order in the borderlands, the emperor reckoned, it would be more beneficial for the state to contract out at least part of its border defense to local chieftains. This was the rationale behind the Ming ruler's decision to issue the 1368 edict to the chieftains of Guangxi, and it was the reason for his ready recognition of native domains in the border region in the south. An official from Huguang province, in a memorial dated March 1369, was no doubt correct in explaining this willingness of the Hongwu emperor to appoint

---

[2] For the "Proclamation of Accession," see Wang Chongwu, *Ming ben ji jiao zhu*, 107–108; for a slightly different version, see *MSL, Taizu shi lu*, 29.482–83; for a translation, see Langlois, "The Hung-wu Reign," 109–10. For the exchange between Yang Jing (d. 1382) and the Hongwu emperor, see *MSL, Taizu shi lu*, 34.613; copied with minor variations in *MS*, 318.8229.

native chieftains to official posts: "This way, the affairs of the *man* could be easily managed and the number of soldiers that need to be stationed [in the borderlands] could be reduced."[3]

Over time, the Ming court would apparently recognize some 340 native offices in Guangxi alone. (By contrast, in Yunnan, Guizhou, Sichuan, and Huguang – provinces where there were also significant "non-Chinese" populations – the numbers were about 430, 240, 340, and 80, respectively.) Obviously, not all native positions were significant. In the case of Guangxi, by the late sixteenth century, the number of major native domains (*tu si*) would stand at just under forty-five (see Table 3.1; Map 3.1). The Ming founder might genuinely believe in the efficacy of native chieftains, that they would help maintain order in the border region and lessen the burden on the Ming military. He might even accept as self-evident the civilizing power of the centralizing state, its prowess of transforming the practices of even the most recalcitrant of native chiefs. But what the Hongwu emperor had not anticipated was how the Ming state would grow to be so reliant on the institution of chieftaincy that it would not be able to do without it. Over time, the centralizing state had sought to rein in some of the more intractable native chieftains. But what Ming officials would realize was that the solution to the problems was not to eliminate all native offices or native domains. The answer was instead to expand the "chieftain system" and to rely on an ever greater number of native chiefs to preserve a semblance of order.[4]

The chieftain system

The practice of co-opting native chieftains was at first not so much part of a grand design as it was an ad-hoc measure adopted by the future Ming founder to maintain local order as he set out to consolidate power. Following his conquest of Huguang in 1364, the future Hongwu emperor was reported to have reappointed many of the chieftains there to the same posts they had held under the Yuan. In time, the practice was extended to all parts of the southern border zone. The rationale behind the so-called chieftain system is simple: in exchange for a semblance of order in the border region, the Ming emperor was willing, to a certain extent, to leave the chieftains alone and to let them rule as they desired. The Hongwu emperor once explained this mutual expectation to a visiting chieftain from Guizhou in 1376: "If on your return [to your native domain]

---

[3] For the Ming relations with Southeast Asia, see Wang Gungwu, "Ming Foreign Relations," esp. 311–12. For the 1369 memorial, see *MSL, Taizu shi lu*, 38.779; *MS*, 317.8207.

[4] For the provincial figures of native offices, see Gong Yin, *Zhongguo tu si zhi du*, 58, 61.

Table 3.1. *Major native domains, ca. 1580*

Domain	Family name	Year appointed	Reported population	Grain quota (picul)
Right River regon:				
Nandan Zhou	Mo	1370	12,358	729
Donglan Zhou	Wei	1379	18,311	1,014
Nadi Zhou	Luo	1374	8,931	1,367
Xincheng Xian	Mo	1496	1,480	321
Yongshun Si	Deng	1493	2,013	359
Yongding Si	Wei	1493	2,041	735
Zhen'an Fu	Cen	1369	12,147	678
Tianzhou	Cen	1369	30,329	5,000
Shanglin Xian	Huang	1377	1,783	225
Dukang Zhou	Feng	1400	1,293	241
Xiangwu Zhou	Huang	1369	5,310	869
Fulao Xian	Huang	1374	1,001	215
Sicheng Zhou	Cen	1369	11,678	1,647
Guishun Zhou	Cen	1419	1,905	150
Anlong Si	Cen	1403	7,014	142
Shanglin Si	Cen	1403	4,494	400
Left River region:				
Wujing Zhou	Cen	1468	. . .	2,391
Guide Zhou	Huang	1369	2,173	449
Guohua Zhou	Zhao	1369	869	140
Zhong Zhou	Huang	early Ming	4,572	150
Taiping Zhou	Li	1369	3,980	239
Encheng Zhou	Zhao	1368	1,740	187
Anping Zhou	Li	1369	3,486	191
Wancheng Zhou	Xu	1369	2,915	502
Shangxiadong Zhou	Zhao	1369	1,070	103
Zhenyuan Zhou	Zhao	1370	1,654	99
Dujie Zhou	Nong	1370	1,120	98
Quanming Zhou	Li	1369	2,180	120
Mingying Zhou	Li	1369	1,505	103
Sitong Zhou	Huang	1368	1,080	88
Longying Zhou	Li	1368	2,186	376
Jiean Zhou	Zhang	1369	1,035	78
Jielun Zhou	Feng	1369	1,310	101
Luoyang Xian	Huang	1369	872	156
Tuoling Xian	Huang	early Ming	3,384	246
Siming Fu	Huang	1369	11,822	76
Siming Zhou	Huang	1369	1,687	61
Xiashixi Zhou	Bi	1369	1,358	25
Jiang Zhou	Huang	1368	2,782	220
Luobai Xian	Liang	1370	391	15
Siling Zhou	Wei	1388	1,680[a]	30[a]
Long Zhou	Zhao	1369	15,418	462
Pingxiang Zhou	Li	1369	914	165

Sources: Tu guan di bu, juan 1–2; *GXTZ* (1531), juan 51–52; *GXTZ* (1599), juan 31–32; Gong Yin, *Zhongguo tu si zhi du*, 997–1158; Taniguchi Fusao, "Kōsei doshi seido no isshuku," Table 3; Taniguchi Fusao and Bai Yaotian, *Guangxi tu si zu pu ji cheng*. Unless otherwise noted, data for population and grain quotas (the latter rounded to the nearest whole number) is from *GXTZ* (1599), juan 31–32. Ellipsis dots indicate no data is available.

[a] *GXTZ* (1531), 52:14a.

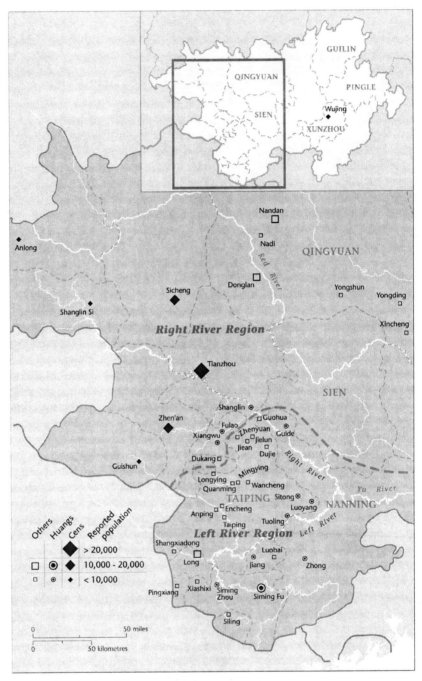

Map 3.1. Major Native Domains, ca. 1580. *Source:* Table 3.1.

you could pacify [your people] and make them content with their living,
you yourself would also enjoy wealth and honor for a long time to come."
In the case of Guangxi, the practice of co-opting native chieftains had
apparently begun even before the Ming forces officially settled the region
in the summer of 1368. But it was not until a year later – perhaps in
response to the special proclamation sent by the emperor mentioned at
the start of this chapter – that formal missions, complete with tribute
horses and specialty goods, were sent by the chieftains of Tianzhou Lu,
Laian Lu, Xiangwu Zhou, Taiping Lu, Siming Lu, and Long Zhou. In
return, the Hongwu emperor not only reappointed these chieftains to
their original posts but also granted them the right to hereditary rule.[5]

This formal recognition of native chieftains and domains, however,
did not mean that Ming rulers had given up their claims over the border region. To impose a measure of structure, the Ming court had from
the start continued the Yuan-dynasty practice of categorizing the chieftains and their domains. Native officials who commanded a large following of native soldiers or who controlled areas that were beyond the
military reach of the state were given titles ranging from the impressive-
sounding "pacification commissioner" (*xuan wei shi, xuan fu shi, an fu
shi, zhao tao shi,* etc.) to the more lowly "squad leader" or "chief" (*zhang
guan, man yi zhang guan,* etc.). To underscore their military functions,
the imperial court had chosen from early on to place such chieftains
under the authority of the Ministry of War. By contrast, native officials
whose duties were seen as mainly preserving local order or who were
otherwise considered "civil" were granted titles – native prefect (*tu zhi
fu*), native subprefect (*tu zhi zhou*), native county magistrate (*tu zhi xian*),
and so on – that mirrored those of regular local officials. To emphasize
the "civil" duties of such chieftains, the Ming court had from the outset
placed them under the jurisdiction of the Ministry of Personnel. Although
the distinction between "military" and "civil" chieftains would prove to
be more illusory than real – the well-informed Shen Defu (1578–1642),
for one, observed that the practice of categorizing native chieftains had
become by his time rather confused – the formal organizational structure did allow both the imperial court and the chieftains to project a
clearer image of order and control of the border region than they could
otherwise.[6]

[5] For the appointment of chieftains in Huguang, see *MSL, Taizu shi lu,* 15.196; *MS,*
310.7982. For the emperor's remarks, see *MSL, Taizu shi lu,* 108.1801; *MS,* 316.8168.
For the formal missions of the chieftains of Guangxi, see *MSL, Taizu shi lu,* 32.572,
43.852.

[6] For classifications, see *MHD,* 6.31, 118.613; *MS,* 76.1875–76, 310.7982. For confusions,
see Shen Defu, *Wanli ye huo bian, bu yi,* 4.926–27.

In addition to categorizing the native chieftains, the Ming court had from the beginning sought also to further formalize the institution of chieftaincy by conferring onto the *tu guan* a variety of symbolic gifts. Apart from his or her title (not a few chieftains were women), each native official was also offered a patent of appointment, an official seal, and a formal attire. Such symbols of recognition were evidently taken seriously by both sides. A "native prefect," for instance, would expect to receive a *chi* patent (but not a *gao* patent, which was reserved for officials of higher ranks), a square bronze seal 2.5 *cun* (about 8 centimeters) in length and 0.5 *cun* (1.5 centimeters) in height (the size was specified in the Ming statutes), as well as an attire featuring a cap with four horizontal spines (but not more) and a belt decorated with gold. During the Ming, both the imperial court and native chieftains seemed to consider the seals as the most important symbols of legitimacy. According to official records, from time to time Ming rulers would deny requests by individual chieftains to assume the position of *tu guan* because the latter had either lost or been robbed of their official seals. This formalization of the so-called chieftain system, however, did not extend to aspects concerning renumeration. Although native officials were, as a matter of practice, assigned the same ranks as those of their regular counterparts (A "native prefect," for instance, would in general be ranked 4a, just as in the case of a regular prefect), they received no regular stipends. Instead, chieftains had to derive their incomes from the taxes and fees they levied on the people under their rule as well as from the gifts and occasional military campaign payments they received from the Ming court.[7]

As part of the "system," the imperial court had from the start also required native chieftains to submit periodic tributes (*gong*). During the Ming, such tributary relations were evidently taken seriously by both the emperors and the chieftains. In principle, all major *tu guan* were required to send a mission to the imperial capital once every three years. Items they might bring as tribute goods ranged from horses, elephants, rhinoceros horns, and so on, to herbs, incense, and betel nuts. In the case of Guangxi, apart from horses (which most chieftains were asked to send, though not necessarily all the way to the capital), native chieftains were also asked to include in their tributes medicinal herbs, silver utensils (such as incense burners), and tin (a useful mineral found in abundance especially

---

[7] For patents of appointment, see *MHD*, 6.32–33; *MS*, 72.1736; for samples, see Gao Xiongzheng, *Siming fu zhi*, 6:2–7. For official seals, see *MHD*, 79.457–58; *MS*, 72.1747; for images, see Taniguchi Fusao and Bai Yaotian, *Zhuang zu tu guan zu pu ji cheng*, 606, 648. For formal attires, see *MHD*, 61.383–84; *MS*, 67.1634–35. For ranks and the lack of stipends, see Shen Defu, *Wanli ye huo bian, bu yi*, 4.926–27; *MS*, 72.1752.

in Qingyuan prefecture). On arrival at the capital, a mission party would as a matter of practice be granted an audience with the emperor, while the goods it brought would be inspected by representatives from the Ministry of Rites. According to regulations promulgated in 1522, the "tributes" in question would be rejected if they had not been sent through a provincial capital, if they were underweight or of insufficient quantity, if there was an excess number of envoys in the mission party, or if the mission did not follow the proper schedule. Otherwise, if all were carried out according to regulations, the party should expect a generous reciprocation of silver and silk, among other gifts, in accordance with the rank of the chieftain and the size of the "tributes" presented.[8]

The so-called tributary system functioned, no doubt, because both the imperial court and native chieftains found it beneficial. From the perspective of Ming-dynasty rulers, even though the costs of maintaining the system clearly far outweighed any potential financial gains – not only did the court have to bestow lavish gifts to the chieftains in return for their "tributes," it also had to entertain the mission parties during their stay in the capital – the arrangement did allow them to reaffirm from time to time their authority over native chieftains. For the *tu guan*, although their gains are not well documented, the financial benefits of such missions must have been substantial. This can be judged, indirectly, from the periodic official decrees that sought to limit both the frequency of tributary missions and the number of envoys sent. But even in the case of chieftains, the economic benefits of the *gong* system should not obscure its political functions: native officials who took time to submit "tributes" were seeking not only material gains but also a periodic affirmation by the Ming court of their legitimacy.[9]

Not only did Ming-dynasty ruler require native chieftains to submit *gong*, from time to time they also demanded such *tu guan* to supply native soldiers (*tu bing*) for government military operations. Whether or not the image is justified, soldiers from native domains were widely known in the Ming period for their ferocity. Those from Guangxi are often referred to in the records as *lang* ("wolf") soldiers. Because of their allegedly superior combat skills and familiarity with the borderland terrain, a large number

---

[8] For regulations, see *MHD*, 108.583–85, 109.587, 113.597–98. For the variety of tribute goods from Guangxi, see *GXTZ* (1531), juan 51–52. See also the reports on tributary missions collected in Guangxi min zu yan jiu suo, *"Ming shi lu" Guangxi shi liu zhai lu,* 793–831.

[9] For tributary relations in the context of native chieftaincy, see Wu Yongzhang, *Zhongguo tu si zhi du*, 185–87; Gong Yin, *Zhongguo tu si zhi du*, 88–91. For comparisons with the arrangements between the Ming court and the Mongols, see, for example, Waldron, *Great Wall of China*, 84–85.

of *tu bing* from the southern province were apparently recruited by the Ming court to fight in its war against Annam in the early fifteenth century. Over the course of the Ming, not only were the native soldiers of Guangxi frequently called on by the state to combat rebellions in native domains, they were also often asked to travel to regular administrative areas – even as far as the coastal province of Fujian – to help suppress local uprisings. Although the recruitment of *tu bing* did allow the Ming state to maintain a degree of order in its southern border region, as we will see, the increased dependence on native soldiers would in time become a major source of troubles.

As part of their efforts to extend the reach of the state, Ming rulers had also sought from early on to superimpose onto native domains the administrative structure of the central plains. In Guangxi, where most major native chieftains were given civil (rather than military) official titles, the Ming court also classified most major domains – just as it did with regular administrative areas – into prefectures (*fu*), subprefectures (*zhou*), and counties (*xian*). But although the level of a *tu si* was in general a reliable indicator of its size and its military capacity, there were major exceptions: Sicheng Zhou, located in the so-called Right River region in the northwestern section of Guangxi, was by all accounts a much larger and more powerful native domain than Siming Fu, in the Left River region. To enhance the presence of the state *within* native domains, Ming rulers had also sought from the start to establish in the *tu si* a bureaucratic structure similar to that found in regular administrative areas. In Siming Fu, for instance, apart from the position of the native prefect, the list of official posts at one point also included a vice prefect, an assistant prefect, a registrar, a record keeper, an administrative clerk, a proofreader, a courier-station master, and a Confucian school instructor (see Table 3.2). The regular (i.e., non-native) officials who took up such positions in Siming were nominally under the jurisdiction of the chieftain, but all were appointed (and apparently paid) by the Ming authorities. Our knowledge of how these offices functioned remains limited. In a rare glimpse of the life of someone who was once the vice prefect of Siming, we are informed that the man, Chen Sui (1457–1504), was a provincial graduate from Quan Zhou (Guilin). Not only was Chen Sui a conscientious official who had consistently refused gifts and bribes from native chieftains far and near, according to Jiang Mian (1463–1533), a relative and a one-time grand secretary at the Ming court, he was also a just and capable administrator, responsible for reforms concerning local conscription and taxation. It is difficult to say how truthful or representative this account of Chen's experiences might be. But based on the available sources, especially the 1690 edition of the *Gazetteer of Siming*

Table 3.2. *Regular officials in Siming Fu*

Office	Official	Native province	Status[a]	Appointed
Vice Prefect	Liu Yichang	Jiangxi	jian sheng	1452
	Zhu Gang	Huguang	ju ren	. . .
	Yao Bi	Zhejiang	jin shi	1475
	Wang Tiangui	Huguang	jian sheng	1492
	Wu Yuanzheng	Huguang	ju ren	1496
	Chen Sui	Guangxi	ju ren	1501
	Yao Cheng	Fujian	ju ren	1508
	Zhang Huan	Jiangxi	jin shi	1517
	Guo Shou	Guangdong	ju ren	1518
	Ou Rang	Guangdong	ju ren	1521
	Yu Shisheng	Guangdong	ju ren	1527
	Huang Tu	. . .	. . .	. . .
	Xia Chun	. . .	. . .	. . .
	Wang Yiyue	Guangdong	. . .	. . .
	Su Rideng	Guangdong[b]	. . .	1605
	Zhu Mingshi	Yunnan[b]	. . .	1609
	Xu Fengchun	Fujian	. . .	1611
	Lin Mengding	. . .	. . .	1616
	Li . . .	Yunnan	. . .	1619
	Liu Chaosheng	. . .	. . .	1632
	Li Qiaochun	Jiangxi	ju ren	1637
Assistant Prefect[c]	Deng Guanxian	. . .	ju ren	. . .
	Li Yong	Guangdong	jian sheng	. . .
	Zhou Ang	. . .	ju ren	. . .
	Dai Guang	Guangdong	ju ren	1475
	Zheng Lun	Sichuan	ju ren	1493
	Tan Ke	Huguang	jian sheng	. . .
Registrar	Peng Yan	. . .	jian sheng	. . .
	Tan Wenjing	. . .	jian sheng	. . .
	He Chaocong	. . .	. . .	. . .
	He Qian	. . .	jian sheng	. . .
	Wu Fengxiang	Guangdong	jian sheng	. . .
	Zhao Zhang	. . .	jian sheng	. . .
	Tao Kan	. . .	jian sheng	. . .
	Qin [Tan] Ning	Guangdong	jian sheng	. . .
	Yang Huaide	Sichuan	jian sheng	. . .
	Tan Ying	Guangdong	jian sheng	. . .
	He Bin	Huguang	jian sheng	. . .
	Wang Gong	Zhili	jian sheng	1514
	Chen Qian	Zhejiang	jian sheng	1518
	Lu Zhi	Guangdong	jian sheng	1520
	Wang Ximin	. . .	. . .	1609
	Wu Yingzhao	. . .	. . .	1611
	Cheng Sidao	. . .	. . .	1631
	Zhang Xuchou	. . .	. . .	1635

(*continued*)

Table 3.2 (*cont.*)

Office	Official	Native province	Status[a]	Appointed
Record Keeper[c]	Xu Jie	. . .	jian sheng	. . .
	Ling . . .	. . .	. . .	. . .
	Zeng Cheng	. . .	ju ren	. . .
	Kang Quan	. . .	jian sheng	. . .
	Luo Wen	Sichuan	jian sheng	. . .
	Mo Xun	Guangdong	jian sheng	. . .
	Wang Fu	Fujian	jian sheng	. . .
	Zhang Ao	Huguang	jian sheng	. . .
	Li Tingfang	Huguang	jian sheng	. . .
	Zhang Su	Shandong	jian sheng	. . .
	Yang Yuanxi	Zhili	jian sheng	. . .
	Lü Jin	Zhili	jian sheng	1521
	Ge Ziyun	Sichuan	jian sheng	1526
	Wang Jingzhou	. . .	. . .	. . .
Administrative Clerk[c]	Yuan Jixu	. . .	jian sheng	. . .
	Gao Ming	Guangdong	jian sheng	. . .
	Liang Su	Guangdong	jian sheng	. . .
	Yang Lun	Zhili	jian sheng	. . .
	Wang Hong	Zhejiang	jian sheng	. . .
Proofreader[c]	Xie Bao	. . .	jian sheng	. . .
	Li Wei	. . .	jian sheng	. . .
	Feng Jun	Guangdong	. . .	. . .
	Huang You	Guangdong	jian sheng	. . .
	Chen Qing	Guangdong	jian sheng	. . .
	Lu Rong	Guangdong	jian sheng	. . .
Courier-station	Zhou Li	. . .	jin shi	. . .
master	Wu Huan	. . .	. . .	. . .
Instructor	Jiang . . .	. . .	. . .	. . .
	Ding Shirong	. . .	. . .	~1621
	Yin Shengjun	. . .	. . .	1630
	Liao Benxin	. . .	. . .	1635
	Liang Yanyong	. . .	. . .	1639
	He Mengxiong	. . .	. . .	1642

Source: Gao Xiongzheng, *Siming fu zhi*, juan 5. Ellipsis dots indicate no data is available.

[a] *jian sheng*: Imperial Academy student; *ju ren*: provincial graduate; *jin shi*: metropolitan graduate.

[b] *Siming fu zhi*, 3:21a.

[c] Position likely to have been abolished during the Ming.

Prefecture, it is evident that regular officials in native domains did assume a variety of duties, among them the compilation of gazetteers and the operation of local schools.[10]

But this effort to strengthen the state's ties to native domains was on the whole unsuccessful because many of the "regular" positions were never created or filled. In most *tu si*, often the only non-native post the Ming was able to set up was that of the administrative clerk (*li mu*). In the case of Siming Fu, at least four of the eight positions listed in Table 3.2 would evidently have been left vacant by the last century of the Ming dynasty. Although this lack of success of the state might reflect the limited administrative needs in the border region, it also testifies to the difficulties of recruiting and retaining regular officials to serve in native domains. The fact that many who took up positions in Siming were Imperial Academy students (*jian sheng*) – for whom such appointments were probably their best and last chance to enter officialdom – demonstrates also how undesirable such posts must have been. An example of how far officials would go to avoid serving in *tu si* can be seen in the case of Xie Hu (js. 1487). When he was faced with the prospect of having to serve in the Tianzhou domain in the Right River region in the early sixteenth century, Xie Hu, then prefect of Pingle in eastern Guangxi, apparently decided to run in the opposite direction by claiming that he had to first accompany his mother home. Even when officials did show up for their assignments, according to the records, they preferred to stay at nearby regular administrative seats and entered the native domains only when necessary. In the 1531 edition of the *General Gazetteer of Guangxi*, for instance, the compilers observe that "the so-called circulating [i.e., regular] officials would often walk to and from the territories [of native domains] and not dare to enter." Xiao Tengfeng (js. 1568), a one-time vice prefect of Qingyuan, reported also that officials who had been appointed to the native domains in his prefecture had been unwilling to venture into the *tu si* areas. One reason, according to Xiao, was that the chieftains in his region had the frightful habit of poisoning visiting officials. Rather than have the officials sit idly by, Xiao Tengfeng recommended in a memorial that three of the regular positions be abolished.[11]

---

[10] For the structures of "regular" administration in native domains, see *GXTZ* (1599), 7:75–79. For Siming, see Gao Xiongzheng, *Siming fu zhi*, 3:1a, 13; *GXTZ* (1733), 56:23b–24b. For the tomb epitaph for Chen Sui, see Jiang Mian, *Xiang gao ji*, 28:14–17; *YXWZ*, 74:7b–11.

[11] For *li mu*, see *GXTZ* (1599), juan 31–32. For Xie Hu, see *MSL*, *Wuzong shi lu*, 32.795, 42.982–84. For the quotation, see *GXTZ* (1531), 5:3a. For the case of Qingyuan, see Xiao Tengfeng, *Liang Yue yi gao*, xia:22.

Table 3.3. *Subdivisions in Taiping Zhou*

Subdivision	Number of villages	Grain quota (picul)
Upper Jie	12	15.3
Middle Jie	20	11.8
Lower Jie	10	15.6
East Jia	8	22.2
South Jia	8	. . .
West Jia	6	. . .
Dali Jia	5	. . .
Xiaoli Jia	16	. . .
Jiling Jia	7	. . .
Zhujiang Jia	3	. . .

Source: Cai Ying'en and Gan Dongyang, *Taiping fu zhi*, 3:52–54. Ellipsis dots indicate no data is available.

Efforts to extend the Ming bureaucracy failed also because over time native chieftains had developed in their domains their own administrative arrangements. Although the *tu si* in Guangxi varied in size – the seat of Taiping Zhou, located in the Left River region, was home of "several thousand families," while the entire Anping Zhou, just up the river from Taiping, was merely "a giant village," observed a seventeenth-century visitor – they did have some common organizational features. To enhance control, chieftains of major domains seemed to favor the practice of dividing their territories into smaller units and appointing deputies or headmen (*tou mu*) to supervise them. One example was the case of Taiping Zhou. According to the 1577 edition of the *Gazetteer of Taiping Prefecture*, the native domain was subdivided into three units of *jie* and seven units of *jia*, of which the largest *jie* unit is said to comprise as many as twenty villages (see Table 3.3). Another example was Tianzhou. According to Yao Mo (1465–1538), who, as we will see, led a major military campaign against the domain in the early sixteenth century, it had been, at least until the war, the practice of the chieftains of Tianzhou to divide the territory outside the domain seat into six *zhou*. Each of the *zhou* was apparently made up of eight *jia*, and each *jia* was composed of four clusters of villages. To maintain order, according to Yao, it had been the practice of the chieftains of Tianzhou to assign to each *jia* unit two chief *tou mu* and two assistants to serve as supervisors.[12]

---

[12] For descriptions of Taiping and Anping, see Xu Hongzu, *Xu Xiake you ji*, 4A.472–73. For the subdivisions in Taiping Zhou, see Cai Ying'en and Gan Dongyang, *Taiping fu zhi*, 3:52–54. For Tianzhou, see Yao Mo, *Dongquan wen ji*, 4:55–56.

Our understanding of the inner working of native domains has been substantially enriched by the discovery in the mid-1950s of the tomb tablet of a certain Zhao Yangsu (1564–1629). According to the epitaph, dated 1633, Zhao came from a family whose members had for generations been "legs and arms" to the chieftains of Encheng Zhou in the Left River region. The Zhaos are said to have arrived in the south from the Shandong region in northeast China some time in the Song period (a claim, as we will see, that was widely shared among chieftain families in the southern border zone). Zhao Yangsu is noted to have studied the classics as a young man and have become skilled at both calligraphy and essay composition. Perhaps because of his literary talents, Zhao's first appointment was to the post of secretary (*wen fang*). In time, he was appointed as seal-keeper and as head of Dianhe Jia. Each of his subsequent promotions was accompanied by an assignment to a *jia* unit. Toward the end of his career, Zhao was given the title of senior advisor (*fu lao*) – "as a symbol of honor and respect" – and was placed in charge of Outer Jia. Among his many notable achievements, according to his eulogist, was his supervision of the construction of a bridge in the southern section of the domain seat, for which "a hundred generations" would be grateful. Most commendable of all, said his eulogist, was Zhao Yangsu's undivided loyalty to the chieftains of Encheng and his "utmost efforts" to contribute to the affairs of the domain.[13]

To extend the reach of the state, Ming rulers also sought to impose onto native domains a variety of rules and regulations. As early as 1393, the court decreed that in order to be formally recognized as a native official, a candidate had to first provide documentations that he – or occasionally she – was the rightful heir of the deceased or retired chieftain. Although Ming rulers generally favored the succession of chieftains by sons or brothers, they also accepted wives and sons-in-law as legitimate heirs so long as they were "whom the native people trust" (a requirement, one must add, that did not seem to have much impact). To avoid disputes among real or alleged kin, the Ming court had from very early on also required each chieftain family to prepare a genealogical chart in which it would record the biographical information of its designated heir. Copies of the charts were to be safeguarded at the provincial capital as well as the Ministry of Personnel. Such genealogical charts were required to be updated every three years and, following the decree of 1530, to include information not just on the designated heir but on all potential successors. Even after a candidate had been acknowledged as a lawful successor, the

---

[13] The tomb epitaph for Zhao Yangsu is found in Guangxi min zu yan jiu suo, *Guangxi shao shu min zu di qu shi ke*, 10–11.

imperial court would occasionally withhold its formal endorsement until he or she had reached adulthood or had performed certain services for the state. Chieftain-designates in the early Ming were obliged to travel to the imperial capital to receive their appointments, but the practice had by the mid-fifteenth century been largely abandoned. Instead, chieftains during the second half of the Ming period were sometimes asked to submit to the state grain payments on the occasion of their succession. But this practice, too, would prove unsustainable and was formally abolished in 1581.[14]

One impact such rules and regulations had on native chieftains was the increased importance of genealogies. Consider the case of Encheng Zhou (where Zhao Yangsu was a loyal headman). The genealogical record of the chieftain family we now possess comes from a stone inscription found in present-day Daxin county. The inscription is dated 1472, though information up to the early eighteenth century, when the Encheng domain was formally abolished, is also appended. Apart from the fact that it is the earliest surviving example of its kind from Guangxi, what is noteworthy about this inscribed genealogy is the obvious attempt by the chieftain of Encheng to embellish the family history. According to Zhao Fuhui, who was chieftain from 1432 to 1472,

Ancestor Zhao Renshou was originally a native of Yidu county, Qingzhou prefecture, in Shandong. A follower of Regional Commander Di Qing [1008–57] in his military campaign against the southern *man* Nong Zhigao [1022–55] of Yong Zhou, [Renshou] was meritorious in his actions and was granted an area of water and land [in Guangxi] in return for his submission. Ancestor Zhao Renshou was specially ordered to assume the hereditary post of native official of Encheng Zhou, and his descendants have since inherited the ancestral estate one generation after another without cessation.[15]

The Zhaos were of course not alone in claiming an illustrious past. The Cens of Sicheng Zhou, for example, also sought to pass themselves off as descendants of the Han-dynasty general Cen Peng (d. 35CE). Chieftains in Guangxi no doubt constructed such narratives to satisfy the Ming demand for genealogical records, but they did so also to enhance their legitimacy and standing among their fellow native officials as well as whom they ruled.[16]

[14] For rules on succession, see *MHD*, 6.31, 121.626; *GXTZ* (1599), 32:72–73. For actual practices, see *Tu guan di bu*, xia:19b–58a; Wu Yongzhang, *Zhongguo tu si zhi du*, 168–78.
[15] Taniguchi Fusao and Bai Yaotian, *Zhuang zu tu guan zu pu ji cheng*, 405; also quoted with minor variations in Guangxi Zhuangzu Zizhiqu bian ji zu, *Guangxi Zhuang zu she hui li shi diao cha*, 4:125.
[16] For a discussion of the foundation myth of the Zhao clan, see Taniguchi Fusao and Bai Yaotian, *Zhuang zu tu guan zu pu ji cheng*, 403–18, 659–61. For the Cens, see *MSL*, *Xiaozong shi lu*, 222.4198; Wei Jun, *Xi shi er*, 8:13b.

Efforts by the imperial court to regulate native domains had their limits, however, as succession struggles among potential chieftains continued to plague Guangxi throughout the Ming period. The fundamental problem, according to contemporary observers, was that despite its periodic exhortation and promulgation of regulations (many of which can be found in the official *Collected Statutes*), the Ming court was simply unable or unwilling to enforce its rules against native domains. Shen Defu, for example, notes in his *Random Gleanings from the Wanli Period* (1619) that despite the benefits of doing so, native chieftains often failed to submit in advance their genealogical charts to the Ming administration. One apparent reason was that many chieftain families were too splintered to agree on a single genealogical chart. As a result, when a *tu guan* passed away, contenders to the chieftaincy would often have to scramble to present their own versions of the family tree.[17]

Not only was the Ming court far from successful in regulating succession in native domains, its attempts to "civilize" the native population also met with mixed results. Efforts to educate the children of native domains evidently began soon after the founding of the dynasty. As early as 1382, the Hongwu emperor was said to have ordered chieftain Zhe E of Puding Fu (in Guizhou) to instruct his people to send their children to study at the Imperial Academy (*Guo zi jian*). In 1395, perhaps to relieve the burden on the Academy, the emperor further decreed that Confucian schools (*ru xue*) be established in individual native domains so that children would be taught "the proper relations between rulers and subjects, fathers and sons." Those who excelled in these local schools would be sent to the Imperial Academy as "tribute students" (*gong sheng*) for more advanced education. Efforts were also made by the court, in 1444 and again in 1503, to require the designated heirs of chieftains to study at Confucian schools (so that they could "gradually be influenced by public morals and learn to rectify their obstinacy"), although records show that this mandate was at best only loosely enforced. Such attempts to transform the native population were in some cases successful. In Guangxi, a Confucian school was set up in Sien Fu in the Right River region in 1447 (the native domain would in time be coverted into a regular prefecture); by the beginning of the sixteenth century, a member of the chieftain family, Cen Ye, was said to have risen to the post of assistant administration commissioner (rank 4b) of Shandong province. Anecdotal evidence from the Ming period – the cases of Zhao Fuhui and Zhao Yangsu of Encheng included – also shows that some chieftains and members of their domains did acquire at least a basic level of cultural literacy. But the impact of the

[17] Shen Defu, *Wanli ye huo bian, bu yi*, 4.934.

Ming efforts was ultimately limited. Despite the exhortation by the state
and frequent pleadings by local officials – in 1605, the supreme commander Dai Yao (js. 1568) still found it necessary to include in his list of
recommendations for Siming Fu the creation of a Confucian school – the
number of schools that were set up in native domains was actually quite
small. In Guangxi, there were evidently never more than a handful.[18]

Just as the Ming court had limited success in regulating succession
and education in native domains, it also experienced mixed results in
collecting taxes. As other historians have noted, in the early Ming period,
extracting taxes from *tu si* was necessarily an ad-hoc affair. As early as
1374, the Hongwu emperor was said to have rejected the recommendation that the chieftain of Bozhou (in Sichuan) be required to deliver
an annual grain payment of 2,500 piculs. Because Bozhou was "first to
come forward to submit [to the Ming]," the emperor decreed that the
chieftain be allowed to deliver any amount the latter desired. But if the
Ming founder had at first been relatively unconcerned with issues surrounding taxation in the southern border zone, he would in time see to it
that native domains were assigned tax quotas. This can be attested to, in
the case of Guangxi, by a memorial dated to 1394, in which the chieftain
of Zhen'an Fu (in the Right River region) requested that the 3,000 piculs
of grain the native domain was responsible for annually be commuted
to a payment in silver. This request came about apparently because the
people of Zhen'an had been required to deliver their grain taxes to a faraway military guard in Yunnan province. The allotment of tax quotas is
also evident from a request submitted in 1412 by the *tu guan* of Dujie
Zhou (in the Left River region), in which the chieftain sought to change
the destination for the domain's grain taxes from a battalion station more
than 400 *li* (200 kilometers) away to a military guard nearby. But if it
seems clear that the native domains of Guangxi had from quite early on
been assigned tax quotas (see Table 3.1), how such quotas came about is
far from obvious. Unlike in regular administrative areas where, at least in
theory, periodic censuses and occasional land surveys provided the basis
for the assignment of tax quotas and service levies, in native domains, no

---

[18] For the Ming efforts to educate native chieftains, see Huang Kaihua, "Ming dai tu si zhi
du," esp. 166–205; Wu Yongzhang, *Zhongguo tu si zhi du*, 198–203; Gong Yin, *Zhongguo
tu si zhi du*, 100–104. For Zhe E, see *MSL, Taizu shi lu*, 162.2517; *MS*, 316.8186. For
the setting up of Confucian schools, see *MSL, Taizu shi lu*, 239.3475–76, 241.3502. For
"tribute students," see *MHD*, 77.446. For compulsory education, see *MSL, Yingzong shi
lu*, 119.2410–11; *MS*, 310.7997. For Sien, see *MSL, Yingzong shi lu*, 150.2994; *YXWZ*,
27:15b–17a. For Cen Ye, see *MSL, Xiaozong shi lu*, 149.2622, 206.3829, 222.4196;
MS, 318.8241. For Dai Yao's recommendation, see *MSL, Shenzong shi lu*, 415.7780.
For information on the Confucian school in Siming, see Gao Xiongzheng, *Siming fu zhi*,
4:4–17a.

such centrally directed efforts have been noted. In the case of Zhen'an, according to the records, the quota of 3,000 piculs was decided in the 1380s by the commander Fu Youde (d. 1394), who was at the time in need of grain supplies to sustain the Ming military operation in Yunnan. For other *tu si*, it seems possible that the tax quotas were assigned on the basis of the size of the populations as reported by the chieftains (as they were first formally recognized by the Ming court) or by the regular officials who had been posted to the native domains. In the epitaph for Chen Sui mentioned earlier, the vice prefect of Siming Fu is noted to have worked hard "to register the population and to catalog people's land" (*li ji zhi min tian*). But what Chen Sui's actions actually entailed our source does not say.[19]

Despite the allotment of tax quotas (however they were derived), Ming emperors had learned over time that tax collection in native domains could only be loosely enforced. Not only did the imperial court have to routinely grant tax exemptions to areas (such as part of Guizhou in 1388) where nature-induced disasters had struck, it also had to periodically adjust the tax quotas for individual *tu si* (such as in the case of the domain of Anlong Si in the Right River region in 1446) after local warfare had led to changes in territorial boundaries. But perhaps the more fundamental reason the Ming court had difficulties collecting taxes from native domains had to do with the increased dependence by the centralizing state on native soldiers. In 1520, in response to a request by Cen Meng (1490–1526), chieftain of Tianzhou Fu, it was decreed that soldiers who had been away from the *tu si* for an extended period be granted tax relief or exemption. Although it is unclear how long such exemptions were meant to last and whether they were meant to be extended to other native domains that had provided soldiers for government military operations, it seems clear that so long as the Ming state was dependent on native chieftains for troop supplies, it was unlikely that it would have much success in extracting taxes from the *tu si*.[20]

What is remarkable about the so-called chieftain system is that it was not so much a *system* – as the myriad official rules and regulations implied – as it was a form of alliance. The institution of chieftaincy was not

---

[19] For the Ming efforts to collect taxes from native domains, see Wu Yongzhang, *Zhongguo tu si zhi du*, 187–91; Gong Yin, *Zhongguo tu si zhi du*, 91–94. For Bozhou, see *MS*, 312.8039–40. For Zhen'an, see *MSL, Taizu shi lu*, 232.3391. For Dujie, see *MSL, Taizong shi lu*, 124.1656; *GXTZ* (1531), 51:23b. For Fu Youde (Fu Yu-te), see *DMB*, 466–71. For Chen Sui, see Jiang Mian, *Xiang gao ji*, 28:16a; *YXWZ*, 74:10a. See also Wei Dongchao, "Ming dai Guangxi tu si di qu de bian hu yu fu yi."

[20] For Guizhou, see *MS*, 318.8168. For Anlong Si, see *MSL, Yingzong shi lu*, 147.2897. For Tianzhou, see *MSL, Wuzong shi lu*, 194.3636.

wholly a creation of the centralizing state but the result of the confluence of two historical currents. On the one hand, the practice of recognizing native chieftains was an effort by the rulers of the central dominion to project onto the border regions a semblance of political order. As such, the practice may be perceived as a top-down imposition. On the other hand, the institution of chieftaincy could not have taken root in the border zones without the participation of the chieftains themselves. In this respect, the arrangement was a reflection of the evolution of the organization of borderland peoples, from one based primarily on kinship ties to one based increasingly on political and military power. These two currents were intertwined: just as the centralizing state depended on native chieftains to provide a degree of order, local chieftains who had consolidated power also sought formal endorsement from the imperial court to bolster their positions. The result was a strategic alliance, an expedient arrangement by which both the Ming court and native chieftains could claim control and an implicit contract based on which both could construct their respective political orders.

Fragile alliance

This alliance we speak of between the state and native chieftains was necessarily unstable. Not only did Ming rulers and officials remain ambivalent about the institution of chieftaincy, in native domains where the power and prestige of a chieftain often depended on the size of his or her dominion, native chieftains frequently waged wars against one another or formed alliances among themselves. Throughout the Ming period, one can find abundant examples of powerful domains taking over weaker ones, ambitious deputies seizing control from reigning chieftains, and ruthless kinsmen of chieftain families stabbing each other in the back. Violence in native domains evidently reached its height in Guangxi between the mid-fifteenth and mid-sixteenth centuries. By then, the facade of cooperation that had underlain the relations between the state and chieftains had apparently been replaced by a more open display of friction. Even though the Ming did succeed overall in containing the influence of the most powerful domains, the continual dominance – some would say belligerence – of some of the chieftains into the final years of the Ming period demonstrates clearly the enduring power of established clans and the limits of the state in the border region.

One reason this alliance was fragile was that native domains in Guangxi, as they were elsewhere, were dominated by a relatively small number of native clans. Even the Ming founder was apparently mindful of this entrenched power of major clans. "Since the Tang and Song periods, generations of Cens and Huangs have lived in the midst [of Guangxi]," the

Hongwu emperor was noted to have once remarked. "When at war they defend their territories; when in peace they offer tributes [to the court]." A popular saying dated to at least the sixteenth century – "in Sizhou [Guizhou] and Bozhou [Sichuan] there are the Tians and the Yangs; in Guangxi and Guangdong there are the Cens and the Huangs" – also testifies to the perceived, if not actual, power of the clans in question. Indeed, by the late Ming, of the forty-three major native domains in Guangxi, eleven were reported to be led by the Huangs, seven by the Cens, six by the Lis, and five by the Zhaos (see Table 3.1). Although chieftains who shared a family name need not have actually descended from a common ancestor – consider for instance the case of the Zhaos, whose forbearers were said to have been granted the use of the family name of the Song ruling house because they had chosen not to take part in an early-eleventh-century rebellion – given the rules and regulations on succession stipulated by the Ming court, many chieftains did take advantage of such real or imagined ties to defend their claims of jurisdiction or to encroach on one another's territories.[21]

An example of the dominance of such native clans can be seen in the case of the Huangs of Siming Fu. Located in the Left River region in southwest Guangxi just across from Annam, the domain of Siming (see Figure 3.1), as we have noted, was one of the first *tu si* in the province to be recognized by the Ming court. Although the early history of Siming is not well-documented, it is evident that the area had been recognized as a "loosely reined" (*ji mi*) domain in as early as the Tang dynasty. During the early Ming, not only was Siming designated by the court as a prefectural-level domain, it was also at first given jurisdiction over a dozen lower-level *tu si* (the number would dwindle to three by the mid-Ming). Although the territory of Siming was said to extend some 200 *li* (100 kilometers) from east to west and 130 *li* (65 kilometers) from north to south, its domain seat – which would by 1465 be surrounded by an earthen wall measuring just under 3 kilometers in circumference – was actually relatively small. The people of Siming were said to be by nature simple: they offered sacrifices to gods when people fell sick, and they played music when someone died. But since the early Ming, people there were reported to have followed the chieftains in "welcoming a sense of propriety and distancing [themselves] from the unorthodox."[22]

---

[21] For the remarks by the Hongwu emperor, see *MSL, Taizu shi lu*, 36.667–68. For the popular saying, see *YJJW*, 3:6a. For the adoption of "Zhao" as the family name, see Fan Chengda, *Gui hai yu heng zhi*, 135.

[22] For a history of the Siming domain, see Taniguchi Fusao and Bai Yaotian, *Zhuang zu tu guan zu pu ji cheng*, 321. For the size of its territory, see Gao Xiongzheng, *Siming fu zhi*, 2:1b–2a; for the city wall, see 2:5b; for the customs of the people, see 1:20b–21.

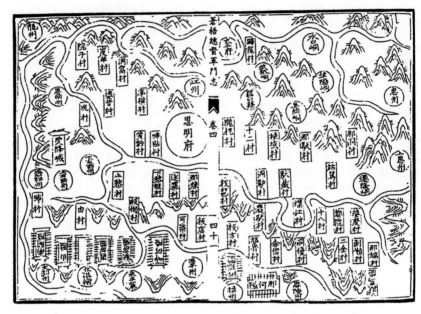

Figure 3.1. The Native Domain of Siming Fu. *Source: Cangwu,* 4:41.

Relations between the Ming court and the Huangs of Siming had from the start been founded on mutual benefits. This can be seen readily from a series of imperial orders that have, fortunately, been preserved in the 1690 edition of the *Gazetteer of Siming Prefecture.* The first of these, dated 1368 and issued by the Hongwu emperor to the chieftain Huang Hudu (1347–89), is almost identical to the decree found in the *Veritable Records* cited at the beginning of this chapter. It praises the Huangs for "being observant of the time and having a good sense of what is to come" and promises the chieftain that the emperor would not be miserly in rewarding jobs well done. Another imperial order, dated 1406, was issued by the Yongle emperor (r. 1403–24) to the chieftain Huang Guangcheng (1383?–1413) to offer him an honorific title in recognition of his service. The timing was hardly fortuitous: by 1406 the Ming court had clearly exhausted its patience with Annam and had decided to launch a major assault against the unruly kingdom. Because of its earlier territorial disputes with Annam, Siming was fully expected to contribute to the military campaign (a letter from a Ming official to Huang Guangcheng challenges the chieftain to actively participate in the attack lest the "good name of the family" be sullied). Yet another imperial decree, dated 1428, was issued by the Xuande emperor (r. 1426–35) to promote Huang Hong

(1401?–57), a son of Guangcheng, to the post of assistant military commissioner (rank 3a). This time the ruler was seeking a way out of Annam, which the Ming had occupied unsuccessfully for twenty years, and was looking at Siming again for help. In time, Huang Hong would be given the even more powerful post of regional military commissioner (2a) and assigned to Xunzhou prefecture. There he would help combat the so-called Yao bandits, who, as we will see in the following chapter, had been a major source of troubles for the Ming.[23]

To maintain dominance, the Huangs of Siming (see Table 3.4) had relied also on other real or imagined ties with the centralizing state and on their alliances with major chieftain families. One strategy for the Huangs was to claim to be descendants of some illustrious officials from the central plains. This tactic is most evident in a pair of tomb epitaphs commissioned by Huang Guangcheng. In one, for his father, Huang Hudu, the history of the Huangs is said to be traceable to as early as the ancient Zhou dynasty to an area named Huang (allegedly in present-day Hubei). In this version of the family history, it was during the reign of Renzong (1022–63) of the Song dynasty that a certain patriarch Huang was recommended by the commander Di Qing to be the administrator of Siming (in another tomb epitaph, for Guangcheng's mother, the Huangs are said to have come from the Shandong region instead). Since the Song period, according to their own account, the Huangs had been able to strengthen their rule over Siming not only through official appointments – Hudu is said to have stepped forth to pledge allegiance to the new ruler almost as soon as the Ming forces entered Guangxi – but also through intermarriages with other major clans in the south. Hudu's grandfather was apparently married to the Xus of the native domain of Wancheng Zhou in the Left River region, his father to the Zhaos of Long Zhou, and Hudu himself (by his second marriage) to the Huangs of the domain of Shangsi Zhou. Much of what is recorded in this pair of tomb epitaphs, especially concerning the early history of the Huangs, is no doubt embellished or outright fabricated, but such artful reconstructions are no less telling of the sources of power of the chieftains in Siming.[24]

---

[23] For the imperial orders, see Gao Xiongzheng, *Siming fu zhi*, 6:1–4; quotation is from 6:1a. For recent accounts of the Ming war against Annam, see Chan, "The Chien-wen, Yung-lo, Hung-hsi, and Hsüan-te Reigns," 229–31, 289–91; Wang Gungwu, "Ming Foreign Relations," 315–18; Tsai, *Perpetual Happiness*, 178–86. For relations between Siming and Annam, see *MS*, 318.8234–35; Shin, "Ming China and Its Border with Annam." For the letter to Huang Guangcheng, see *YXWZ*, 54:12b–14b. For Huang Hong's assignment to Xunzhou, see *MSL, Yingzong shi lu*, 35.673.

[24] For the tomb epitaphs by Xie Jin (1369–1415) for Huang Hudu and his second wife, see *YXWZ*, 73:11–13; Gao Xiongzheng, *Siming fu zhi*, 6:32–33. For a discussion, see Taniguchi Fusao and Bai Yaotian, *Zhuang zu tu guan zu pu ji cheng*, 321–33.

Table 3.4. *The Huangs of Siming*

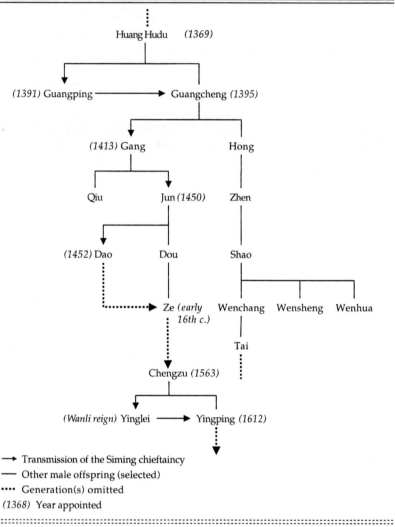

→ Transmission of the Siming chieftaincy
— Other male offspring (selected)
···· Generation(s) omitted
(1368) Year appointed

Sources: Taniguchi Fusao and Bai Yaotian, *Zhuang zu tu guan zu pu ji cheng*, 349–50; GXTZ (1599), 32:40–41a, 50–51a.

How this entrenched power of native clans came to destabilize the chieftain arrangement can be seen clearly through the case of Huang Hong. Despite nearly a century of relative stability, troubles in Siming erupted in 1451 after chieftain Huang Gang, who in 1413 had succeeded his father, Guangcheng, had decided to retire and hand over the chieftaincy to a son by a concubine. Huang Qiu, a son by Gang's principal wife, resented the decision to bypass him and sought help from his uncle Huang Hong – who, with his firm control of the native soldiers of the domain, was a potential king-maker. Unfortunate for Qiu, Hong apparently had his eyes set on the chieftaincy as well. Seizing this unexpected opportunity, Hong quickly dispatched his son Zhen to Siming under the pretense of troop recruitment. There, one evening, according to the records, Zhen and his followers quietly entered into the compound of Huang Gang and murdered the entire family. Feigning innocence, Zhen returned to the compound the next day and ordered that news of the murder be reported to his father so that Hong could start hunting for the perpetrators. Hong's sordid act might not have been caught by the Ming if not for a young servant who had managed to survive and report the killing to the authorities. Once exposed, Qiu and Hong were quickly imprisoned, while Zhen and his own son were able to escape.[25]

The worlds of court politics and chieftaincy collided in unexpected – and, to many, disturbing – ways following the capture of Huang Hong. Just as the disgraced commissioner was set to be executed, a memorial was submitted on his behalf to the Jingtai emperor (r. 1450–56), who had ascended the throne less than three years earlier after his half-brother, the Zhengtong emperor, had been abducted by the Mongols. In the memorial, Huang Hong surprises almost everyone by weighing in on the highly sensitive issue of imperial succession. Citing the need to abide by "the order of Heaven" and to solidify "the foundation of the state," Huang recommends that the emperor's own son – rather than the son of the Zhengtong emperor – be installed as the heir apparent. How Huang Hong, an otherwise unremarkable chieftain from the south, came to formulate an opinion on this highly divisive issue we cannot be certain (it is speculated in the *Veritable Records* that it was the vice minister Jiang Yuan [js. 1430], who was known to have supported a firm stand against the Mongols, who had given Huang the advice). In any case, Huang Hong's gamble paid off, at least in the short term. Not only did the Jingtai emperor decide not to punish Huang Hong for his transgressions in Siming, he even promoted the chieftain to a higher rank. Huang Hong was again sent off to Xunzhou prefecture on military duties, and in 1453, in recognition of his contributions in "exterminating bandits" and in the deliberation of "significant state matters," Huang was given the prestigious title of vice commissioner-in-chief (rank 1b).[26]

---

[25] For the events in Siming, see *MSL, Yingzong shi lu*, 215.4629; *GXTZ* (1531), 55:8; *MS*, 318.8235–36.

[26] For Huang Hong's memorial, see *MSL, Yingzong shi lu*, 215.4629–31. For speculation on Jiang Yuan, see *MSL, Yingzong shi lu*, 215.4631. For discussion, see Taniguchi Fusao and Bai Yaotian, *Zhuang zu tu guan zu pu ji cheng*, 337–39. For Huang Hong's promotion,

The family fortune of Huang Hong, not surprising, declined sharply following the restoration of the Tianshun – formerly Zhengtong – emperor (r. 1457–64). Huang Hong, realizing his life-saving memorial would come back to haunt him, committed suicide. But the erstwhile all-important chieftain was not allowed to rest in peace: unable to punish the two-faced scoundrel while he was alive, the Tianshun emperor ordered Huang's corpse be exhumed and flogged. In 1468, Huang Hong's son, Zhen, was in turn captured and executed. Huang's grandson, Shao, was able to put off his own demise by actually managing to briefly take control of the domain of Siming Fu. By 1505, the Ming emperor had had enough. Huang Shao was forced to commit suicide, and his son Wenchang, who would resist for several more years, would also be captured and executed. But despite the downfall of Huang Hong and his immediate family, his descendants apparently remained influential in Siming. Hong's great-great-grandson, Tai, would in time take over the native domain of Siming Zhou (a smaller *tu si* under the nominal jurisdiction of Siming Fu), and Tai's descendants would remain chieftains there until 1719 when the domain was converted into a regular administrative seat.[27]

What is remarkable about the case of Huang Hong, and of the Huangs of Siming Fu in general, is not so much how chieftains had to constantly fight for their survival or how infighting among them could influence – or be influenced by – dynastic politics. What is remarkable is how deeply rooted individual clans had become. To be sure, by the late Ming, the grip of the Huangs on Siming was no longer as firm as it had been under Huang Hudu or Huang Guangcheng. At the turn of the seventeenth century, two of the headmen (*tou mu*) of the chieftain Huang Yinglei – Lu You and Huang Shang – were reported to have effectively taken control of the domain of Siming Fu. But even in this case, according to the records, the Huangs were able to hang on to power following the intervention of the Ming military forces. To restore order in the domain and in the region, Ming officials did demand reforms (the incompetent Huang Yinglei was forced to step down to make room for his six-year-old brother). But in the end the Ming seemed to have no choice but to continue to support the Huangs of the troublesome domain.[28]

see *MSL*, *Yingzong shi lu*, 226.4926; Gao Xiongzheng, *Siming fu zhi*, 6:6a. For politics in mid-fifteenth-century China, see de Heer, *Caretaker Emperor*; Twitchett and Grimm, "The Cheng-t'ung, Ching-t'ai, and T'ien-shun Reigns."

[27] For the downfall of Huang Hong, see *GXTZ* (1531), 55:8; *Cangwu*, 18:10; *YJJW*, 1:18b; *GXTZ* (1599), 32:40–41, 50–51.

[28] For Lu You and Huang Shang, see *MSL*, *Shenzong shi lu*, 415.7780; Wei Jun, *Xi shi er*, 8:32–34a; *MS*, 318.8236–37.

The Ming court continued to recognize the Huangs as the chieftains of Siming Fu not because it considered them powerful allies but because it regarded them the least undesirable alternative. The Huangs might be dysfunctional, but the Ming had treated them as the rightful chieftains of the Siming domain since at least the Hongwu reign. To replace the Huangs without a just cause would be unthinkable for many Ming officials, not only because it would engender more disorders, as some believed, but also because it would also endanger the much cherished notion of legitimacy. The Ming reacted swiftly against the usurpation of Lu You and Huang Shang not only because their actions threatened the stability of Siming but also because their success would set a wrong example and place the institution of native chieftaincy in jeopardy. Likewise, the Ming (at first) responded quickly to Huang Hong's attempt to usurp power because his victory too would weaken the already fragile alliance between the state and native chieftains. The case of Siming thus illustrates an inherent tension in the so-called chieftain system. Ming rulers opted for the *tu si* arrangement because they thought it would bring about a degree of order. What they had not anticipated was how fiercely people of native domains would battle for the chance to be chieftains. And what Ming rulers had not expected as well was how chieftains, even after they had secured their own domains, would continue to try to expand their territories.

Limits of the state

Alliances between the state and native chieftains were inherently fragile in part because of the desires of chieftains to expand their domains. Whether it was to incorporate land and population previously under the jurisdiction of regular officials or to encroach on territories that belonged to other native domains, expansion by chieftains inevitably put a strain on their relations with the centralizing state. Although such desires to expand were almost always motivated by fiscal and military concerns – the larger the domain, the more the resources, and the stronger the fighting force – in many cases they were also prompted by local politics: it was not uncommon, for instance, for ambitious chieftains to take advantage of the internal power struggles in other native domains by either sending their soldiers to prop up some puppet *tu guan* or by seizing the *tu si* in question outright. Chieftains claimed ties with one another, and they especially liked to do so when they wanted to take control of each other's domain. The Ming did seek to deter such expansions – after all, it was not in the court's interest to see the rise of overly powerful native domains – but it did so only with limited success. Not only did the claims

and counterclaims of legitimacy prove baffling for Ming rulers and officials, the resources needed by the state to curb such incursions would
also turn out to be highly burdensome.

An example of this tension between the state and native domains can
be found in the case of the Cens of the Right River region. As the Huangs
of Siming Fu, the Cens were said to have stepped forward to submit to the
new regime almost as soon as the Ming military forces entered Guangxi.
In the summer of 1368, the chieftain of Tianzhou Lu, Cen Boyan, was
reported to have submitted his official seal to the Ming authorities as a
sign of submission. In the summer of 1369, the chieftain of Laian Lu, Cen
Hanzhong (a cousin of Boyan), was one of several *tu guan* from Guangxi
formally recognized by the Ming court. But even in the early Ming period,
rifts among chieftains can be detected. In 1372, for instance, Cen Boyan
was said to have falsely accused his nephew Cen Langguang, who had
just assumed the chieftaincy of Laian, for plotting against the Ming. As
a consequence, in 1376, areas that had been under the control of Laian
were placed under the rule of Tianzhou Fu (the unit *lu* would in time
be replaced by that of *fu*). As well, in 1395, Cen Yongchang, chieftain
of Sien Zhou (later elevated to Sien Fu), was accused by a neighboring
chieftain for withholding taxes from the state. Ming officials were asked
to prepare an attack against Sien, but for reasons unclear, the mission
was never carried out.[29]

Despite their internal squabbles, until the mid-fifteenth century, the
Cens of the Right River region (see Table 3.5) had fostered a relatively
close alliance with the centralizing state. Among their more notable leaders was Cen Ying (son of Yongchang), who, as chieftain of Sien, probably came closest to what Ming rulers would consider a model *tu guan*.
In 1438, for instance, Cen Ying was granted the honorary title of native
prefect of Tianzhou (even though he was not actually given jurisdiction
over the domain) in recognition of his contribution to a Ming military
campaign in the southern region. Similarly, in 1453, Cen was awarded
an honorific title of grand master (*da fu*) in exchange for having personally led native soldiers to station at the provincial capital. And in 1455,
on learning his son Bin – who was standing in for him as chieftain of
Sien – was causing havoc at home, Cen Ying not only reported his son to
the Ming authorities but also actually led an army home to restore order

---

[29] For Tianzhou, see *MSL, Taizu shi lu*, 32.571. For Laian, see *MSL, Taizu shi lu*, 43.852.
For abolition of the Laian domain, see Taniguchi Fusao and Bai Yaotian, *Zhuang zu tu
guan zu pu ji cheng*, 216–17. For accusation against Sien, see *MSL, Taizu shi lu*, 241.3505.
One may add to the list the territorial disputes between Cen Bao of Sicheng Zhou and
Cen Yan of Li Zhou; for a synopsis, see *MS*, 319.8257–58.

Table 3.5. *The Cens of Tianzhou and Sien*

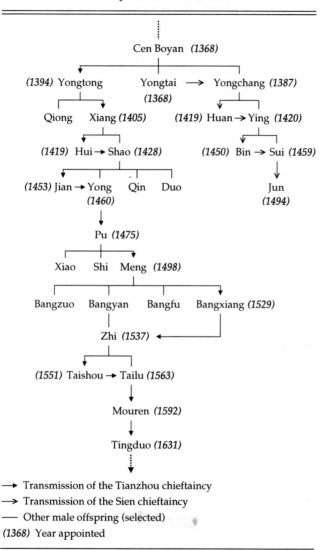

→ Transmission of the Tianzhou chieftaincy
→ Transmission of the Sien chieftaincy
— Other male offspring (selected)
(1368) Year appointed

Source: Taniguchi Fusao and Bai Yaotian, *Zhuang zu tu guan zu pu ji cheng*, 297, 319–20.

(Cen Bin would later hang himself). For this display of loyalty and his other services, Cen was promoted in 1455 to the rank of administration vice commissioner (3b) and in 1459 to that of military vice commissioner (2b). Finally, upon his death in 1478, Cen Ying was bestowed by the Ming

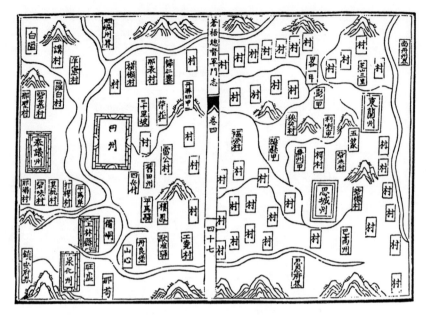

Figure 3.2. The Native Domain of Tianzhou. *Source: Cangwu,* 4:47.

court a posthumous title, just as he would be if he had been a "regular" official. The chieftain of Sien was of course not beyond self-interests. Over time, Cen Ying would seek constantly to expand his domain. In 1444, the chieftain was reported to have tried to incorporate into the Sien territory a number of villages from the nearby regular county of Yishan (home of the prefectural seat of Qingyuan). In all, over the course of Cen Ying's career (which spanned more than half a century), more than fifteen hundred additional households – twice as many as the original number of reported households in Sien – were said to have been brought under the control of the domain.[30]

By the latter half of the fifteenth century, intra- and inter-domain warfare had apparently significantly destabilized the Right River region. At the center of contention was Tianzhou (see Figure 3.2), a *tu si* that had been recognized (albeit under different names) by the centralizing state since at least the Song dynasty. According to a gazetteer quoted in the

[30] For Cen Ying's career, see *MSL, Yingzong shi lu,* 38.738, 230.5031, 259.5559, 305.6442; *Xianzong shi lu,* 175.3163; *MS,* 318.8239–40. For Yishan, see *GXTZ* (1531), 55:8b–9a; *MSL, Yingzong shi lu,* 115.2318. For the increase of households, see *GXTZ* (1531), 56:14b.

Union Gazetteer of the Great Ming (1461), in Tianzhou, "the hills are flat and the land is open." Although people "have only a rudimentary notion of decorum," their "[practices of] farming and weaving are quite close to that of the central plains." In 1505, Jiang Wan (1452–1507), a vice surveillance commissioner, reported also that not only was the land in Tianzhou (as well as in the neighboring Sien) rich and fertile, it was also densely populated (by 1531, according to the *General Gazetteer of Guangxi*, Tianzhou boasted three times the registered population of Siming Fu but eight times the latter's annual tax quota). Commercial activities were so lively that just east of the city-wall of Tianzhou, according to Jiang, the number of market places "exceeds a hundred." Although such descriptions must be taken with a grain of salt, the domain of Tianzhou probably did come under attack during the mid-Ming in part because of its perceived advantageous geography.[31]

Troubles in Tianzhou began soon after Cen Shao, who had inherited the chieftaincy in 1420, decided to pass on his post to his son Yong. Whether Cen Jian, Yong's half-brother, was himself eager to become chieftain or was a victim of manipulation by the headman Lü Zhao, as some sources suggest, we cannot be certain; what is clear is that even after Cen Jian had finally come to be recognized as the chieftain of Tianzhou in 1453 (the sources are silent on the fate of Cen Yong), the level of confrontation both outside and inside Tianzhou did not abate. Over time, native soldiers from the domain were sent in the name of the chieftain to attack various nearby *tu si*. The level of violence evidently reached a new height in 1459 when Cen Jian was murdered by Lü Zhao, who would in time try to pass his grandson off as a Cen descendant. The fortune of the Cens of Tianzhou was temporarily restored when both Ming officials and other chieftains in the region came to recognize the threats posed by Lü Zhao and rallied to suppress the usurpation.[32]

The intervention by the Ming state did provide a respite, but troubles in Tianzhou resumed soon after Cen Pu, a nephew of Cen Jian, assumed the post of chieftain. The new round of violence was apparently precipitated by the rebellion of yet another local headman. But even though chieftains from nearby domains would again come to the rescue of Tianzhou, in time

---

[31] For descriptions of Tianzhou, see Li Xian et al., *Da Ming yi tong zhi*, 85:21a. For Jiang Wan's observations, see *MSL, Wuzong shi lu*, 8.238–9. For the registered population (30,329 [6,389 households]) and annual tax quota (some 5,000 piculs), see *GXTZ* (1531), 52:6b. See also descriptions in *GXTZ* (1531), 2:10b–11a.

[32] For Lü Zhao's usurpation, see Ye Sheng, *Ye Wenzhuang gong liang Guang zou cao*, 6:3b–7; *Cangwu*, 17:13b–14a; *MS*, 318.8245–46.

some would seek to take over the troubled *tu si* themselves. It was not until 1490, according to the records, that such efforts to seize Tianzhou were crushed and that Cen Pu was finally accompanied back to the domain by Ming officials. As if there was not sufficient trauma in the ill-fated chieftaincy of the hapless Cen Pu, in 1493, the chieftain of Tianzhou was murdered by his eldest son, who evidently wanted to seize power before Cen Pu could designate his third and favorite son, Meng, to be the heir. The scheme failed, however, and the usurper was promptly captured and executed.[33]

Despite efforts by Ming officials to restore order, the domain of Tianzhou remained highly contested following the death of Cen Pu. In 1498, prompted by a new round of infighting in the troubled *tu si*, the chieftain of Sien, Cen Jun, along with others, decided to launch a take-over bid for Tianzhou. At least five thousand people were said to have been killed by Cen Jun's soldiers alone. Undeterred by the intervention of the Ming authorities, in 1503, Cen and his allies redoubled their efforts. In response, Ming officials concluded that in spite of the alliance the court had forged with the Sien domain, the belligerent grandson of Cen Ying would need to be punished. More than a hundred thousand government soldiers were reported to have participated in the military campaign of 1505. As a result, Cen Jun was forced to commit suicide, and both Sien and Tianzhou were ordered to be converted into regular administrative areas. Because of his incompetence (the official charge was "continuously abetting transgressions"), Cen Meng, the teenage *tu guan* of Tianzhou, was demoted to the rank of battalion commander and was given an assignment to the coastal province of Fujian.[34]

But the conversion of Tianzhou remained in theory only. For reasons that are unclear (some sources, without offering evidence, claim that Cen Meng was able to bribe his way through to the powerful eunuch Liu Jin [d. 1510]), the chieftain of Tianzhou was at the end allowed to stay put. But instead of assisting the Ming state to restore order, Cen Meng was said to have become more and more belligerent as time went on. In 1518, he was at the center of a plot to overthrow the chieftain of Long Zhou in the Left River region. In 1521, he co-coordinated an attack against the native

---

[33] For Cen Pu's ordeals, see *MSL, Xianzong shi lu*, 199.3495; *Xiaozong shi lu*, 38.816; *GXTZ* (1531), 56:6–7; *MS*, 318.8246. For his eventual demise, see *GXTZ* (1531), 56:8.

[34] For Cen Jun's campaigns, see *MSL, Xiaozong shi lu*, 156.2798, 187.3441, 210.3908; *GXTZ* (1531), 56:13b–15; *MS*, 318.8246–47. For the aftermath, see *MSL, Wuzong shi lu*, 4.129, 8.238–41.

domain of Sicheng Zhou, killing, according to the records, at least seven thousand people. Ming officials found it alarming also that when Cen Meng did send his troops to assist in government military operations – as he did in 1512 for a campaign in Jiangxi province – his soldiers would turn out to be just as unruly and destructive as the local rebels. As Cen Meng became increasingly dominant in the Right River region, the pressure to curb his power also intensified. By 1525, the tide had decidedly turned against Cen Meng as the Ming court began to discuss the possibility of waging a war against the unruly chieftain of Tianzhou.[35]

In a series of memorials dated to the fall of 1525, Yao Mo, who had been appointed supreme commander of Guangdong and Guangxi just a few months earlier, confirmed what the Ming court had known for some time: the thirty-five-year-old chieftain of Tianzhou had grown increasingly belligerent and had become "gradually uncontrollable." Over the course of two decades, soldiers under Cen Meng's rule were said to have murdered more than thirty native officials (and stolen at least seven official seals), slaughtered over twenty thousand people, seized in excess of 230,000 taels of silver, and confiscated vast areas of land from nearby domains. "More than half of the chieftains in Guangxi have fallen prey to him." Even more serious were Cen Meng's crimes against the Ming. Not only did he routinely poison regular officials who had been appointed to Tianzhou, the chieftain had also for over a decade resisted submitting taxes to the centralizing state and providing soldiers for its military operations. To Yao Mo, the case against Cen Meng was overwhelming: "Just as the Yao and Zhuang [and other "non-Chinese"] in the Guang region in the south [i.e., Guangdong and Guangxi] could not be reined in without native officials, the evils of native officials could not be vanquished without first punishing Cen Meng." By 1526, unbeknownst to Cen, the stage was thus set for a clash between the Ming military and one of the most powerful chieftains in the southern border zone.[36]

By July 1526, the one hundred thousand troops that had reportedly been assembled at Bin Zhou (some 200 kilometers southeast of the Tianzhou seat) had apparently completed their preparation. The Ming

[35] For Cen Meng's efforts to remain in Tianzhou, see *MSL*, *Wuzong shi lu*, 22.607, 32.795, 42.982–84. For the Liu Jin connection, see *YJJW*, 1:1b; *MS*, 318.8247–48. For Long Zhou, see *Wuzong shi lu*, 171.3310; Wang Ji, *Jun ji tang ri xun shou jing*, 22; *GXTZ* (1531), 56:17; *YJJW*, 1:12b–14. For Sicheng Zhou, see *MSL*, *Shizong shi lu*, 25.726; *GXTZ* (1531), 56:18a. For Jiangxi, see MSL, *Wuzong shi lu*, 87.1866–67; *YJJW*, 1:1b–2a. For war preparation, see *MSL*, *Shizong shi lu*, 57.1377.

[36] Yao Mo, *Dongquan wen ji*, 3:63–83a; quotations are from 67b, 74b, 69, respectively.

military forces were made up of not only regular armies and mercenary soldiers but also a significant contingent of native soldiers from Guangxi and Huguang. In Yao Mo's plan, the government forces would be divided into five columns, each of which was to converge on Tianzhou from a different direction. For his part, in anticipation of the war, Cen Meng was said to have gathered also more than one hundred thousand soldiers (the numbers in the records are impossible to verify). Groups of four to five thousand fighters were reported to have been sent by the chieftain to station at strategic passes around the domain. The first serious skirmish, fought between two auxiliary forces at Fort Dingluo (about 100 kilometers southeast of Tianzhou), was an easy victory for the government. The decisive battle, which took place on the fourteenth of July at Gongyao (about 50 kilometers southeast of Tianzhou), where Cen Meng had stationed more than twenty thousand troops, was also won by the Ming forces following a day of intensive fighting. There the government forces were assisted by the chieftain of Guishun Zhou, whose daughter was married to Cen Meng but who had apparently long resented Cen's ill treatment of her. After the fall of Gongyao, the march toward Tianzhou was met with little resistance. Cen Meng, who had meanwhile fled to Guishun en route to Annam, was eventually captured and forced to commit suicide.[37]

From the point of view of Ming officials, the campaign against Tianzhou was (at first) a complete victory. By the end of the war, 95 "stockades" (*zhai*) had been destroyed, 4,838 rebel heads had been taken, 1,752 women and men had been captured, and some 10,800 local families (more than 58,000 people) had been brought under the rule of the Ming. In addition, the Ming authorities also confiscated more than 900 taels of gold, nearly 6,000 taels of silver, 1,225 heads of oxen, 134 horses, 4,345 pieces of weapons, and a variety of miscellaneous items. For Yao Mo, the commander-in-chief, from whose reports these numbers are drawn, the war against Cen Meng was more than just another campaign against a recalcitrant chieftain; for Yao, the defeat of Tianzhou was the beginning of the end of the institution of chieftaincy, at least as it was configured in the Right River region.[38]

But the war against Tianzhou, as it turned out, did not fundamentally alter the balance of power between the Ming state and its native chieftains.

---

[37] For government preparation, see Yao Mo, *Dongquan wen ji*, 4:30–2; for Cen Meng's preparation, see 4:2b, 14; for an account of the campaign, see 4:32–34a. For the battle of Gongyao and the death of Cen Meng, see *YJJW*, 1:2, 9–12a; Tang Shunzhi, *Guang you zhan gong lu*, 3–5a.

[38] For the aftermath, see Yao Mo, *Dongquan wen ji*, 4:24, 4:36b–38a.

By the time Cen Meng was captured and forced to commit suicide in 1526, he had, along with Tianzhou, survived a coup d'état, withstood several attempts of invasion, and resisted a government takeover. At the height of his power, Cen Meng was known to wield unsurpassed influence over many of the native domains in both the Right and the Left river regions. According to an early-sixteenth-century local official, when the chieftain of Tianzhou, for whatever reasons, chose not to provide troops for government military operations, no *tu guan* would dare to defy him by mobilizing their own soldiers. Even regular officials "dare not to breathe a word" to offend Cen Meng "for fear that he might harm them with his insect poisons and the like." At the nadir of his reign, when the chieftain of Tianzhou was steadfastly pursued by the Ming military forces, however, neither his earlier influence nor his suspected use of poisons was able to save him. Alliances between the centralizing state and native chieftains were necessarily fragile not only because of the seemingly incessant power struggles within individual domains (as in the case of Siming) but also because of the almost inevitable rivalries among chieftains (as in the case among the Cens of the Right River region). But contrary to what Yao Mo once hoped, the war against Tianzhou did not diminish the dependence of the Ming on native chieftains (after all, even Yao Mo had found it necessary to rely on native soldiers from Huguang in his campaign against Cen Meng). As a result of the war, Ming rulers and officials were no doubt made more aware of the price of maintaining order in the southern border zone, but most seem to have remained just as convinced of the need for the institution of chieftaincy.[39]

Indeed, as in the example of the Huangs of Siming, what is equally striking about the case of the Cens of the Right River region is the entrenched power of native clans. Even after Cen Meng had been forced to commit suicide and the domain of Tianzhou "pacified," the Cens would continue to rule the area – albeit less belligerently – well into the Qing period. Despite talks among Ming officials to convert Tianzhou into a regular administrative unit, as we will see, it was decided at the end that the interests of the centralizing state would be best served by leaving the Cens alone. But if the Huangs of Siming were able to hold on to power in part because of their perceived function as a buffer against Annam, the Cens of Tianzhou were able to do so because of their apparent military prowess. The fragile alliances between the Ming court and native chieftains no doubt reflected the persistent rivalries both within

[39] For the observations by Wang Ji, see his *Jun ji tang ri xun shou jing*, 21b–22a.

and among native domains, but perhaps more significant, they reflected the limits of power of the centralizing state.

In search of buffer

Despite its many successes, the Ming never resolved the fundamental tensions in its military arrangements. Given the political and fiscal constraints the state faced, the task was perhaps impossible. To overhaul the military structure, the Ming court would have had to transform its procedures for recruiting and retaining soldiers as well as its approaches to collecting and distributing revenues. More significant, Ming rulers and officials would have had to acknowledge that the system as laid down by the founding emperor was no longer functioning (an acknowledgment many would have considered heretical). Every so often, a well-meaning official would put forth an ambitious proposal for reforms. At the core of almost every plan was the vision of a small, inexpensive, and well-trained army. Rarely, however, could the reform-minded official muster the political will and necessary resources to implement the new policy; never, even if the plan was put into practice, did it achieve its aim of securing the borderlands without help from native soldiers. Over time, as it turned out, not only had the state increasingly depended on the soldiers supplied by native chieftains, it had also found it necessary to recognize in the southern border zone an ever greater number of native domains.

Reliance by the Ming state on native soldiers can be traced to as early as the second half of the fourteenth century. In 1383, it was reported that among those who assisted the government in a military campaign in Guangxi were soldiers from the native domains of Tianzhou Fu and Sicheng Zhou. Such *tu bing* apparently proved so indispensable that when the fighting was over, the Ming commander in charge recommended that two battalions (made up of five thousand native soldiers each) be set up in the local area to help implement "the strategy of the ancients of pitching *man yi* against *man yi*." The two battalions were to be led by the sons of the chieftains of Tianzhou and Sicheng, respectively, and the soldiers assigned there – not unlike those in regular military units – were expected "to engage in both farming and fighting." Although information on the recruitment and organization of native soldiers remains scant, evidence suggests that such soldiers were recruited by chieftains (and their headmen) primarily on an ad hoc basis. In the case of Siming, the proposal by Chen Sui, the "regular" vice prefect we encountered earlier, to implement in as late as the sixteenth century a system to recruit and organize local soldiers actually makes it clear that such a system, at least in the context of the native domain of Siming, was the exception rather than the norm.[40]

Dependence on native soldiers evidently grew in the fifteenth century. Ye Sheng (1420–74), who served as grand coordinator of Guangxi from 1458 to 1462, was among the first senior officials to pay attention. For years, Ye observed, the people of Guangxi had been falling victims to banditry. It was only through the help of native soldiers, he argued, that Ming officials were able to maintain a degree of order in the region. As we will see in Chapter 4, this increased reliance by the state on *tu bing* is most evident in the war against the "Yao" of the Rattan Gorge in 1465–66. Of the estimated 190,000 soldiers reported to have taken part in the military campaign, 160,000 were said to have been native soldiers from Huguang and Guangxi. By the end of the fifteenth century, the decline of the regular military population had apparently made it even more urgent for the centralizing state to rely on *tu bing*. "Whenever there are [military] deployments," observed Deng Tingzan (1430–1500), the supreme commander of Guangdong and Guangxi, in 1496, "[the government now] depends completely on native soldiers."[41]

By the sixteenth century, the Ming state would apparently come to rely on soldiers from native domains to perform duties once reserved for regular troops. Since the 1520s, small contingents of native soldiers had been asked to station at the prefectural seats of Wuzhou (four thousand soldiers), Guilin (three thousand), and Liuzhou (two hundred). According to Wang Shouren (Wang Yangming; 1472–1529), who as supreme commander first recommended the arrangement, the assignments were intended to strengthen the defense of regular administrative areas and to facilitate the deployment of native soldiers. According to this arrangement, major native domains in Guangxi were required to take turn supplying the necessary soldiers. The domain of Tianzhou, for instance, was expected to station eighteen hundred soldiers at Guilin for a year once every four years, whereas the domain of Siming Fu was asked to provide fifteen hundred soldiers for Wuzhou once every five. In addition to posting native soldiers at strategic areas in the eastern half of Guangxi, the Ming state also frequently commissioned them for military services outside the province. In the early fifteenth century, thirty thousand *tu bing* were deployed to assist in the annexation of Annam. In the middle of the

---

[40] For the setting up of two battlions, see *MSL, Taizong shi lu*, 157.2438. For Chen Sui, see Jiang Mian, *Xiang gao ji*, 28:14–17; *YXWZ*, 74:7b–11.

[41] For the observations by Ye Sheng, see his *Ye Wenzhuang gong liang Guang zou cao*, 4:15b. For the Ratten Gorge campaign, see *YJJW*, 2:3. For Deng Tingzan, see *MSL, Xiaozong shi lu*, 116.2105.

sixteenth century, a large number of native soldiers from Tianzhou and other domains were mobilized to fight in the war against the "pirates" off China's southeastern coast. And in the early seventeenth century, some eighteen thousand *tu bing* from Sicheng Zhou and Tianzhou were sent to suppress the rebellions in Guizhou and Yunnan.[42]

But this dependence on native soldiers had its price. If in the early Ming chieftains had agreed to send their troops out of obligations, by the mid-fifteenth century, they did so clearly because they found the deployment to their benefit. Although soldiers from native domains were considered indispensable, they were also seen as trouble-makers. Just as they helped the centralizing state maintain a degree of order, native soldiers were said to have taken part also in pillaging and random killing. Both Ye Sheng and Zhang Xuan (1417–94), a provincial administration commissioner of Guangdong, reported for instance that soldiers from the domain of Sicheng Zhou were notorious for their transgressions. Not only did they seize food and crops wherever they went, they even routinely abducted the very people they were supposed to protect. Jiang Mian, the grand secretary from Quan Zhou we encountered earlier, even equated the deployment of native soldiers by the state with the consumption of a strong but harmful antidote by a patient. Writing with an eye on the case of Cen Meng of Tianzhou of the early sixteenth century, Jiang concluded that "while critical illnesses cannot be cured without using aconite, those who use it would inevitably exhaust their vital force." The dependence on native soldiers thus exposed a fundamental dilemma in the Ming military policy in the border region: to deploy *tu bing* was to run the risk of encouraging disorder; to do otherwise was to give up even the semblance of control.[43]

Over time, not only had the Ming state stepped up its dependence on native soldiers, it had also chosen to recognize an increased number of native domains. Although some officials – such as Yang Shen (1488–1559), a prolific scholar who had spent more than thirty years in the border province of Yunnan – did criticize the institution of chieftaincy as incompatible with the traditional way of government (in which local administrative units were headed by regular officials appointed on a rotational rather than hereditary basis), many did argue for the recognition

---

[42] For the stationing of native soldiers in regular administrative areas, see *GXTZ* (1599), 32:74–76; Gao Xiongzheng, *Siming fu zhi*, 3:17b. For the figure of thirty thousand, see *MSL*, *Taizong shi lu*, 55.814. For the deployment of native soldiers to the coastal region, see Qin Cailuan and Huang Mingbiao, *Washi fu ren lun ji*. For the campaigns in Guizhou and Yunnan, see *MSL*, *Xizong shi lu*, 39.2017–19.

[43] Ye Sheng, *Ye Wenzhuang gong liang Guang zou cao*, 4:1–4a; Zhang Xuan, *Nan zheng lu*, 1b. For Jiang Mian's remarks, see his *Xiang gao ji*, 22:19b.

of more native domains. This was particularly the case for Guangxi from the mid-fifteenth to the end of the sixteenth centuries when frequent disorders prompted officials to recommend repeatedly that more native officials be appointed to help secure the province. Although most of the newly recognized domains were smaller in size than those confirmed at the beginning of the Ming period (a reflection no doubt of the awareness by the imperial court of the troubles associated with large, powerful domains), their proliferation clearly demonstrates the increased need by the Ming state to rely on native agents to organize the borderland population into identifiable and manageable units.[44]

An early example of this increased reliance on native chieftains can be seen in the case of Mo Zheng. In 1439, the chieftain of Nandan Zhou (in Qingyuan prefecture) petitioned the Ming court that he be granted the rank of native prefect and be given the job of supervising all the "non-Chinese" (*man*) in the prefecture. Mo noted in his memorial that whereas people who lived under the rule of chieftains in Qingyuan generally enjoyed peace and tranquility, those who lived under the jurisdiction of regular officials often had to endure attacks by bandits. The reason for this disparity, said Mo Zheng, was the inability of regular officials to establish control beyond the vicinity of the administrative seats. In Mo's scheme, the regular prefect of Qingyuan would continue to handle routine administrative matters, whereas Mo Zheng, the "native prefect," would oversee the *man* population. Mo Zheng's memorial was apparently well received by the Zhengtong emperor: "'Using *yi* to tackle *yi* [*yi yi gong yi*] is of course an established practice from the past," the emperor is reported to have remarked. "If indeed he [Mo] could render us service and save us expenses at the border, why would the court begrudge him an appointment?" Even though the proposed arrangement at the end did not materialize (the records are silent on the reasons), to recognize Mo Zheng's influence, the Ming court did subsequently offer the chieftain of Nandan the title of vice prefect of Qingyuan.[45]

To some officials, what the Ming state needed was not more powerful chieftains but just *more chieftains*. In 1443, Jie Ji (js. 1424), a provincial administration commissioner, repeated what must have been a commonplace observation: The reason Guangxi was plagued by banditry was that many of the regular soldiers posted there were unaccustomed to the region's hostile climate and were thus unable to carry out their duties. To rectify the situation, Jie Ji recommended that a special commissioner be appointed to the southern province, where he would join a number

[44] Yang Shen, *Sheng'an quan ji*, 48.525.
[45] For Mo Zheng, see *MSL*, *Yingzong shi lu*, 57.1101; *GXTZ* (1599), 31:10a.

of provincial officials on an inspection tour, during which they would appoint as many native chieftains as they saw fit. The idea, again, was to rely on native soldiers to combat local bandits. In a few years' time, according to Jie Ji, not only would people in Guangxi "all become law-abiding subjects," the centralizing state could also pull back some of its troops from the region. Even though Jie Ji's proposal was never implemented (the Zhengtong emperor was intrigued enough to order the matter deliberated, however), it clearly shows what some officials thought the state needed to do to maintain order in the southern border zone.[46]

As it turned out, Jie Ji was not alone in his view. The prominent official Qiu Jun (1421–95), in his influential study of the theory and practice of statecraft, *Supplement to the "Extended Meaning of the Great Learning"* (1487), observes also that areas under the rule of native chieftains have generally been immune from the types of disorder that have plagued regular administrative areas. The reason, according to Qiu, is that regular officials – unlike native chieftains – are deemed to possess neither the military expertise nor the long-term interests to genuinely exert control over their jurisdictions. To rectify the situation, Qiu Jun suggests that more native domains be recognized in the border region. In Qiu's scheme, native chieftains who could command more than five hundred people would be given the title of subprefectural magistrate (*zhi zhou*), whereas those who could command fewer would be given lesser titles. An added benefit of this scheme, according to Qiu Jun, is that native people would be more readily assimilated into the Chinese way of life. "Following their acceptance of the court appointment, they [the chieftains] would most certainly develop a sense of gratitude and admiration [for the state]," Qiu Jun claims. "As [this sense of admiration] becomes part of their nature, they would emulate Chinese [*hua*] customs, practice [proper] rituals, and realize that killing and plundering are wrong." To avoid territorial disputes among chieftains, Qiu recommends that stone tablets be erected to indicate the boundaries between domains. In exchange for their appointments, in Qiu Jun's scheme, chieftains would also be each assessed a fixed amount of taxes.[47]

Although the proposal by Qiu Jun was never formally implemented (for reasons that probably had to do with objections by Ming officials who did not want to be seen as conceding territories to native chieftains), the centralizing state did in time come to recognize in Guangxi a variety of additional native domains. A case in point was Xincheng. Located near the prefectural seat of Qingyuan, the area of Xincheng had in fact been

---

[46] For Jie Ji's recommendations, see *MSL*, *Yingzong shi lu*, 108.2192.
[47] Qiu Jun, *Da xue yan yi bu*, 153:11b–13.

under the rule of a native clan (surname Mo) before it was converted into a regular administrative area in the early Ming period. By the mid-fifteenth century, however, unrest in the area had become so rampant that the magistrate Su Kuan (a regular official) was forced to recommend to the court that a member of the Mo clan be appointed as co-magistrate of Xincheng. The purpose of course was to allow the Mo clan, which had been briefly pushed aside by the Ming state, to assume a formal role in keeping order in the area. By the end of the fifteenth century, it was obvious that the position of the regular magistrate had become perfunctory. In 1497, it was decided that the regular official post be abolished and that the area be reverted to chieftain rule.[48]

Other native domains were set up to curb the influence of powerful chieftains. Consider the cases of Yongshun and Yongding. Originally part of Yishan county (Qingyuan), the area of Yongshun and Yongding had apparently long been a target of encroachment by the native domain of Sien. In the 1440s, with the collaboration of the regular magistrate (who was eager to get rid of the troubled area), the territory of Yongshun and Yongding was finally annexed by Cen Ying, the chieftain of Sien. But the annexation did not go unchallenged. Local headmen led a series of rebellions and brought the conflicts to the attention of the imperial court. At the end of the fifteenth century, Ming officials finally put an end to the disorder by establishing in the area two chief's offices (*zhang guan si*), each of which was to be headed by a chief (*zhang guan*; rank 6a) and an assistant chief (*fu zhang guan*; 7b). The Yongshun domain was said to oversee 124 villages, whereas the Yongding domain was responsible for 184. As in the case of other native domains, the chieftaincies of the two offices were hereditary and the chieftains were expected to submit taxes to the state.[49]

Although between the 1430s and the 1530s the centralizing state did convert some seven native domains (one *fu*-level, four *zhou*-level, and two *xian*-level) into regular administrative areas, the overall trend during the Ming was the recognition by the imperial court of an increased number of smaller domains. Consider again the case of Tianzhou. Even though there had been discussions about placing the troubled *tu si* under the jurisdiction of regular officials, efforts to convert Tianzhou clearly gained momentum after the demise of Cen Meng in 1526. Among the

[48] For the history of Xincheng, see *GXTZ* (1531), 51:8b–10a; *GXTZ* (1599), 31:19–20a; *Cangwu*, 17:8; *MS*, 317.8211–12. See also Qin Guiqing, *Guangxi Xincheng tu si shi hua*; Taniguchi Fusao, "Kōsei doshi seido no isshuku."

[49] For the history of Yongshun and Yongding, see the memorial by Yu Qian in *YXWZ*, 5:1–2; *GXTZ* (1531), 51:10a–12; *GXTZ* (1599), 31:23–26; *MS*, 317.8212.

supporters of conversion, Yao Mo, the supreme commander who had led the military campaign against Tianzhou, was especially vocal. Not only had the Cens committed serious transgressions, Yao argued, they had also squandered many opportunities to mend their ways. Although he was aware that a previous attempt to convert the neighboring domain of Sien had not been successful, Yao Mo was convinced that a more serious effort would quickly restore order. In addition to assigning capable regular officials to the converted domain, Yao recommended also that a school be reestablished in Tianzhou so that "the vile customs of the *yi* can be transformed into Chinese [*hua*] ones." Realizing "it is difficult to quickly pacify and control the wild nature of dogs and sheep [i.e., the native population]," Yao Mo concedes that the implementation of direct Ming rule would have to be gradual and that native headmen would have to be allowed to continue to lead their own settlements.[50]

But the case of Tianzhou would turn out to be more complicated. Yao's plan suffered a major setback when Lu Su and Wang Shou, two of Cen Meng's former headmen, decided to rebel. As a result, Yao Mo was forced to retire, and Wang Shouren, perhaps better known by historians as a philosopher than as a military commander, was brought in. Wang's approach to the troubles in Tianzhou was markedly different from his predecessor's. Unlike Yao Mo, Wang Shouren blamed the problems not so much on the native chieftains but on Ming officials themselves. To Wang, it was the incompetence and corruption of regular officials that had led to the disorder in Tianzhou and other native domains in the first instance. But Wang Shouren's major criticism was reserved for the increased dependence on native soldiers by Ming officials. Not only did the frequent deployment of such soldiers place a tremendous pressure on native families, Wang argued, it also created countless opportunities for abuse. To restore order, according to Wang Shouren, it was not sufficient (even if the Ming state had the military might to do so) to convert all native domains into regular administrative areas; the solution, in his view, was to combine the best of both arrangements. "If the installment of regular officials would lead to the submission of the *yi* population, why endure the troubles of not appointing regular officials?" Wang reasoned. "But if as soon as regular officials are appointed the *yi* population begins to rebel, why should men of good will [i.e., Ming officials] . . . insist that regular officials be appointed?"[51]

---

[50] Yao Mo, *Dongquan wen ji*, 4:47–63; quotations are from 4:58b, 52b.

[51] For a contemporary account of the uprising, see *YJJW*, 1:1–9a. For Wang Shouren's views, see *Yangming quan shu*, 14:2b–12b; for the quotation, see 14:14b. For the context of his approach, see Tang Shunzhi, *Guang you zhan gong lu*, 5.

The case of Tianzhou, according to Wang Shouren, required precisely this kind of flexibility. In a departure from his predecessor's policies, Wang not only publicly pardoned the two rebellious headmen but also announced he would seek no further military actions in Tianzhou. More significant, Wang Shouren decided it would be best to reinstate a son of Cen Meng as the chieftain of the embattled domain. Wang defended his decision by appealing for expediency. Just as the diverse conditions in the central plains required different levels of administrative units, Wang argued, the unusual circumstances in the border region demanded different types of arrangements. Besides, Wang Shouren reasoned, to fully convert Tianzhou into a regular administrative area would require a prolonged stationing of regular troops in the region, a burden the people of Guangxi could ill afford. Wang envisioned an administrative structure for Tianzhou that would combine both native and regular elements. Although Tianzhou would retain a chieftain, on Wang Shouren's recommendation, it would also be renamed Tianning ("land of tranquility") and be assigned a regular prefect. The idea was that the son of Cen Meng would continue to be responsible for the day-to-day administration of Tianzhou (now a much diminished area within Tianning prefecture), whereas the regular prefect would serve as a supervisor.[52]

Of Wang Shouren's proposals, the most controversial was perhaps his suggestion that even more native chieftains should be appointed. In particular, Wang proposed that areas that had once been (but were no longer) under the jurisdiction of the chieftain of Tianzhou should be divided into eighteen so-called native police offices (*tu xun jian si*), each of which was to be led by a native chief (*tu mu*), and each of which was to claim control over two or three clusters (*jia*) of settlements. Wang Shouren recommended also that nine such domains be established in the adjacent region of Sien, which in theory had been reverted to regular Ming rule but which had by all accounts remained a troubled area. Wang's rationale was not significantly different from that of Jie Ji or Qiu Jun several decades earlier. By dividing the areas of Tianzhou and Sien into a number of smaller domains, Wang Shouren hoped that while the appointed native chiefs would be able to maintain a degree of order in their domains, they would not be powerful enough to pose serious threats to the state.[53]

As it turned out, other Ming officials would go even further than Wang Shouren. Lin Fu (js. 1502), Wang's successor in Guangxi, argued that there was no need to appoint a regular official to Tianzhou (Wang's

[52] Wang Shouren, *Yangming quan shu*, 14:14a–23a.
[53] For more general discussions of Wang Shouren's actions in Guangxi, see Taniguchi Fusao, "Ō Shujin to shōsū minzoku"; Shin, "Last Campaigns of Wang Yangming."

suggestion to rename the region was never followed through). "The nature of the *yi* is different from that of Han people," Lin claimed. Not only did *yi* people plunder for a living, they were also given to debauchery and brutality. "As a measure of control and defense," according to Lin Fu, "it was the practice of the past not to station Han officials [in the border region] for fear that when Han and *yi* lived together, they would easily become suspicious of one another." Moreover, if native domains were to be replaced by regular administrations as a matter of policy, said Lin Fu, "the defense of the border would have to be borne by us [the Ming state] alone." Were this to take place, Lin cautioned, the state would have to choose between committing more resources for its military, which it could not afford, and retreating its line of defense, which would result in chaos. But Lin Fu did put forth one recommendation of change: given its much diminished state, Tianzhou should be designated a *zhou*-level (rather than *fu*-level) domain.[54]

Even in eastern Guangxi where the Ming state had established direct rule, it had become common by the second half of the sixteenth century for officials to suggest setting up additional native domains. For instance, following the military campaign against Gutian of 1570–71 (see the discussion in Chapter 4), it was recommended by the officials involved that while some villages should be put under direct Ming rule, others that had proven to be troublesome should be placed under the control of three newly established native police offices. Similarly, following a military campaign in the Fu River region in 1573, it was suggested by the grand coordinator Guo Yingpin (1500–86) that six native *xun jian si* be set up. Although very little is known about these newly created domains, some sixty-six hundred soldiers were said to have been recruited to station there. Finally, following a military campaign in the area of Bazhai ("eight stockades," which overlapped part of southern Liuzhou) in 1580, it was recommended that three native police offices be established there. Each provided by the Ming state with a supply of seeds and oxen, the three native *xun jian si* in Bazhai were meant to function not only as policing forces but also as self-sufficient economic units – descriptions that would have applied to the regular guards and battalions in the early half of the Ming period.[55]

[54] For Lin Fu's memorial, see *Cangwu*, 24:31b–42; quotations are from 24:32.
[55] For Gutian, see *GXTZ* (1599), 33:10–13. For the Fu River region, see 33:53b–55. For Bazhai, see 33:47. For discussion, see Zhang Yigui and Xu Shiru, *Ming dai Guangxi nong min qi yi shi gao*, Chaps. 2, 3, and 5. For the spread of native domains, see Taniguchi Fusao, "Mindai Kōsei no dojunkenshi"; Su Jianling, "Lun Ming dai Guangxi dong bu de tu si."

By the late Ming, although some would continue to reject the creation of native domains as a major step back in the project of transforming or "civilizing" the border region, most officials seemed to have accepted the practice of relying on native chieftains. Su Jun (1541–99), a provincial vice administration commissioner and compiler of the 1599 edition of the *General Gazetteer of Guangxi*, was one strong supporter. Having had a chance to survey the history of conflicts in the southern province, Su was no doubt more knowledgeable about the issues than many of his contemporary commentators. In his view, to use force to replace native chieftains with regular officials would be "unnecessary, unwise, and unfeasible." It would be unnecessary (*bu bi*), according to Su Jun, because for most chieftains who had become unruly, the threat by the Ming court to rescind their titles or ranks would be sufficient to force a change in behavior. It would be unwise (*bu ke*) to do so because so long as the centralizing state continued to rely on native soldiers to fight its wars, any attacks on native domains would only undermine its border defense. Finally, it would be unfeasible (*bu neng*) to do so because the climate and terrain in the border region were such that it was impossible for most regular soldiers to stay long. To maintain order in the border zone, Su reckoned, the centralizing state would have to be practical.[56]

Boundaries of power

In May 1637, Xu Hongzu (Xu Xiake; 1586–1641), the indefatigable explorer, set out to travel across Guangxi en route to the southwest. His year-long journey through the province would bring him to not only many of its popular sites but also some of its less-trodden paths. Xu's detailed diaries describe not only the typical perils of travel – occasional illnesses, unpredictable weather, unreliable escorts, and so on – but also the unusual obstacles placed by the region's native chieftains. He reports he had to repeatedly revise his itinerary – to the extent that he had to travel first to Guizhou instead of to Yunnan, his original destination – in order to avoid the frequent warfare in native domains. Xu's depictions of native chieftains are not entirely negative – the *tu guan* of Dujie Zhou, for example, comes across as a fairly learned man – but the overall impression Xu Hongzu gives of the *tu si* region is clearly one of impoverishment and lawlessness. Xu's observations, although they are necessarily personal and

[56] For Su Jun's arguments, see YXWZ, 56:34–37a. For alternative views, see Su Jianling, "Lun Ming dai Guangxi dong bu de tu si," 123–24.

episodic, nevertheless afford us one last glimpse of the politics of chieftaincy in Ming-dynasty Guangxi. The episodes chosen below do not yield a unified image of a "chieftain system." Together, these stories do illustrate how the ambiguities and tensions inherent in the institution of native chieftaincy had come to manifest themselves by the late Ming as well as how the resulting "system" had departed from the model envisioned by the Hongwu emperor in 1368.[57]

The first episode from Xu Hongzu's diaries we will focus on clearly reminds us of the convoluted politics in the southern borderland. Internecine warfare among the Cens of the Right River region, as we have seen, was not a new phenomenon in the late Ming. In the decade leading up to Xu's visit, however, internal strife had evidently worsened. The latest power struggle apparently had to do with the right to succeed to the chieftaincy of Zhen'an Fu, a strategically located tu si that shared borders with Yunnan, Annam, as well as the powerful native domains of Tianzhou and Guishun Zhou. Following the death of the chieftain Cen Jixiang (who had left behind no heirs), the chieftains of Tianzhou and Guishun both sought to expand their domains. But as neither side had a clear advantage over the other, both appealed for outside help. But instead of seeking assistance from the Ming court, as other chieftains in similar situations had done, both sides sought military support from Mac Kinh Khoan of Cao Bang just across the border in Annam. Although the Mac surname group was only a shadow of its former self – for a period in the sixteenth century (1527–1592) it had replaced the Lê clan as the ruler of Annam – Mac Kinh Khoan still retained a formidable fighting force. The result, according to Xu Hongzu, was a chaotic stalemate: neither Tianzhou nor Guishun had a winning strategy, but neither side was willing to back down.[58]

What is remarkable about this latest power struggle is not so much how little control the Ming court had over chieftains or how fluid political boundaries were in the southern border region – although both are evident and relevant – but how wide the gap had become between the theory and reality of the so-called chieftain system. To Xu Hongzu, what the Ming court should have done in the case of Zhen'an was to take advantage of the succession crisis to convert the domain into a regular administration. Short of that, the court should have intervened early on

---

[57] For his travels in Guangxi, see Xu Hongzu, Xu Xiake you ji, juan 3A–4A; for the chieftain of Dujie Zhou, see 4A.518–19. For a recent study of Xu's travel writings, see Ward, Xu Xiake.

[58] Xu Hongzu, Xu Xiake you ji, 4A.478–79, 496–97. For background on the Macs of Cao Bang, see John K. Whitmore, "Mac Dang-dung," in DMB, 1029–35; Wang Gungwu, "Ming Foreign Relations," 330.

and settled the fight between Tianzhou and Guishun before it became serious. To his dismay, Xu found that Ming officials were reluctant even to admit that there was a problem, let alone solve it. When local administrators were finally sent to investigate the turmoil in Zhen'an, such officials would simply dismiss them as mere "disputes among chieftains" and argue that such clashes should be "of no concern to the centralizing state." And because local officials were reluctant to initiate major military campaigns (because wars were both costly and risky), according to Xu, they were quite willing to ignore the fact that the Annamese chief, through his collaboration with Tianzhou and Guishun, was able to intrude on the Ming territory. Native domains, even in the late-Ming period, no doubt still functioned as buffers between China and its neighbors, but their ability to deter intrusion and demarcate political boundaries was clearly much more compromised than what their supporters had hoped it to be.[59]

The second episode from Xu's diaries we will pay attention to further illustrates this gap between fact and fancy in the Ming border region. As we have seen, one of the developments in sixteenth-century Guangxi was the recognition by the Ming state of a large number of native police offices. The primary task of such offices was to maintain order in areas where the centralizing state had claimed control but had otherwise deemed it unwise to set up regular administrative offices. In the late Ming, one such area was Bazhai (also known as Shizhai, "ten stockades"). As we have seen earlier, following a successful military campaign in 1580, it was suggested by officials that the area of Bazhai be reorganized into three relatively small native domains – (Siji Zhen, Gupeng Zhen, and Zhouan Zhen) – and that each domain would be placed under the supervision of a native police office. In time, it was hoped that not only would order be restored in the Bazhai area but a degree of self-sufficiency would also be developed in the newly reorganized towns.[60]

But not all worked out according to plans. Not only had bandits reappeared in Bazhai, according to Xu Hongzu, by the time of his visit the three domains (or towns) that had been established in 1580 had also fallen into disarray. Of the three, Xu reports, only Siji remained intact. Gupeng was in ruins, and Zhouan was merely "a hamlet of few households." Nor had the chieftains of the native *xun jian si* been of much help.

[59] Xu Hongzu, *Xu Xiake you ji*, 4A.479–80.
[60] For the establishment of *xun jian si*, see *MHD*, 131.672; Su Jianling, "Lun Ming dai Guangxi dong bu de tu si," 146–47. For Bazhai (Shizhai), see the memorial by Zhang Ren (js. 1547) in *YXWZ*, 9:24–33a; Zhang Yigui and Xu Shiru, *Ming dai Guangxi nong min qi yi shi gao*, 74–77.

In the case of Zhouan, the chieftain family (surname Wu) had actually abandoned its post and moved to the nearby regular administrative seat, where it seemed to have successfully blended in by intermarrying with a prominent local family. It was not until 1636 when Bazhai had once again become a troublesome spot that Ming officials demanded that the Wu family heir return to his post in Zhouan. Even then, Xu notes, the eleven-year-old boy who was the lone descendant of the Wu clan was not about to actually assume the chieftaincy of Zhouan. Instead, the young man, named Wu Chengzuo, took up residence in the town of Siji to the north and continued his study there. To Xu Hongzu, Bazhai might appear as just another treacherous area he had to travel through to get to Guizhou, but to Ming officials who had once hoped that the creation of native police offices would help bring order to the southern border region, the examples of Zhouan and Gupeng were clearly even more unsettling.[61]

Our final story from Xu Hongzu's diaries reveals not so much a gap between theory and reality but an inherent tension in the institution of native chieftaincy. On his way to Guizhou, Xu was apparently advised by an assistant regional commander named Lu Wanli that he should avoid passing through the domain of Sicheng Zhou. This suggestion came about, as it turned out, because Commander Lu had had a serious clash with the chieftain of Sicheng just two years earlier. At that time, according to Xu's notes, the chieftain Cen Yunhan had just been granted by the imperial court the title of regional vice commander and had begun to demand local Ming officials to pay him proper respect. All seemed fine until a guard commander named Feng Run decided not to follow the protocol during a visit to Sicheng. Outraged, Cen Yunhan promptly had Feng and his men incarcerated. Lu Wanli, who had nominal jurisdiction over the Right River region in general, did at the end come to Feng's rescue. But it was not until the rescuing party had sustained some casualties that it was able to extract the men to safe ground.[62]

What is ironic about this episode is that Cen Yunhan was by most other measures of his time an exemplary chieftain. His father, Cen Shaoxun, chieftain of Sicheng from 1574 to 1612, had commanded native armies to fight in the Ming campaigns against Bazhai in Guangxi and Bozhou in Sichuan. Yunhan himself was both a scholar and a warrior, according to a family genealogy he most likely commissioned. Not only was

---

[61] Xu Hongzu, *Xu Xiake you ji*, 4A.559. In his diaries, Xu mistakenly refers to Siji as Suji and uses a different character for Gupeng.
[62] Xu Hongzu, *Xu Xiake you ji*, 4A.563.

Yunhan well versed in the *Book of Poetry* (*Shi jing*) and the *Zuo's Tradition* (*Zuo zhuan*), two major Confucian classics, he was said to be also an accomplished calligrapher and painter (a more recent source claims that he had once enrolled as a government student). His poetry, as his family genealogy, could in fact be found inscribed on rocks located in present-day Lingyun county in northwest Guangxi. Most important to the Ming state, Yunhan was a willing and capable commander, who became indispensable in the military campaign against the native domain of Shuixi in Guizhou in the early 1620s. It was for his contributions to this and other Ming military campaigns that he was given the title of regional military commissioner (rank 3a) and, in time, the even more prestigious designation of regional vice commander. Why the chieftain of Sicheng chose to clash with the local Ming commanders we may never be sure (Xu's brief note does not allow us to probe the interpersonal dynamics at work). What seems clear is that even when the institution of native chieftaincy functioned as it meant to (as it did more or less in the case of Sicheng), the underlying tension of the arrangement had made conflicts almost unavoidable.[63]

Together, these stories thus offer us a glimpse of how the institution of native chieftaincy had come to function by the end of the Ming dynasty. To an extent, the *tu si* arrangement did operate the way it was intended by the Hongwu emperor. Cen Yunhan, the chieftain of Sicheng, not only participated in the government military campaigns but had also acquired, judging from his poetry, a degree of cultural literacy, just as the Ming founder had hoped for. Wu Chengzuo, chieftain of Zhouan, might have neglected his policing duty, but he, too, seems to have been touched by the "rituals and institutions" (*wen jiao*) of the Ming. Even in the case of Zhen'an Fu, the Ming court did at one point intervene successfully on behalf of one of the warring domains. More to the point, however, the episodes considered here show that the *tu si* "system" had become by the late Ming a highly flexible arrangement. Military alliances between the Macs of Cao Bang and the Cens of Guishun or Tianzhou were tolerated because Ming officials wanted to and could explain them away as matters not concerning the state. The domain of Zhouan was allowed to become defunct because the area seemed to have been able to make do without a *tu si*. And Cen Yunhan of Sicheng was given great latitude to exercise power so long as he also performed his military duties. The institution

---

[63] For the Cen family and the stone inscriptions, see Dang Dingwen, *Guangxi li dai ming ren ming sheng lu*, 135–36; Taniguchi Fusao and Bai Yaotian, *Zhuang zu tu guan zu pu ji cheng*, 195. For Cen Yunhan's service, see MSL, *Xizong shi lu*, 29.1446.

of native chieftaincy might have stemmed in part from the Ming rulers' romantic notion of tributary relations, but by the end of the dynasty, the *tu si* arrangement had become more clearly so than before an instrument not for transformation but for status quo.

The institution of native chieftaincy, in form if not necessarily in spirit, survived the Ming and beyond because it allowed both the court and native chieftains to claim to have greater control than they actually possessed. During the Ming dynasty, officials from almost all parts of the political spectrum supported the *tu si* "system" because they saw it as a vehicle to "civilize" the borderland population as well as a buffer to separate the central plains from the "non-Chinese from beyond" (*wai yi*). For native chieftains, the conferment of titles and ranks by the Ming court not only provided added legitimacy to their rule but also at times enabled them to expand their domains. To create a semblance of order, Ming rulers had over time made up a variety of rules, but chieftains were far from passive participants in this symbolic universe. As the episode of Sicheng demonstrates, native chieftains were fully capable of turning the *tu si* arrangement on its head for their benefit. Similarly, as we have noted, some chieftains had come to use the opportunities to compile family genealogies (as required by the court) not only to affirm their right to succeed to the chieftaincies but also to bolster their images by claiming lineage ties with some of the more illustrious surname groups from China proper. The Ming court from time to time was able to command native soldiers to fight on its behalf, but such military operations were almost always just as beneficial to the chieftains in charge. The institution of native chieftaincy was no doubt a state supported apparatus, but it could not have functioned if the chieftains themselves had not also found it to be a useful construct.

The Ming founder probably had not anticipated such outcomes when he issued his proclamation to the chieftains of Guangxi in the autumn of 1368. To the Hongwu emperor, who had ascended the throne after defeating the Mongols and other rivals, "to pacify all-under-heaven through military achievements [and] to transform people from afar through rituals and institutions" were not unjustified ambitions. Whether through force or moral suasion, the ruler believed, the centralizing state would in time establish order not only in its core area but also in all four corners of its territory. In retrospect, what the Hongwu emperor had underestimated were the monumental task of maintaining control in the border region and the remarkable fluidity of political boundaries. What the emperor had not expected as well was how the institution of native chieftaincy would outlast the dynasty itself. Not only did the *tu si* arrangement survive the Qing and the early Republican periods, the theory and practice of indirect rule have also manifested themselves in different guises in post-1949 China. Although the creation of the so-called autonomous administrative areas (*zi zhi qu*) in contemporary China has its distinct historical roots, the presence of such nominally self-ruling polities demonstrates that even to this day the centralizing state has had to recognize the fluidity of its borders as well as the boundaries of its power.[64]

[64] For the quotation, see *MSL, Taizu shi lu*, 36A.667–68.

4   Mapping of settlement

> Also appearing and disappearing [in Guangxi] are Yao, Zhuang, and
> myriad stocks of *yi*, whose contiguous settlements are [patterned] much
> the same as the design of an embroidery. When content they are humans;
> when discontent [they behave as if] they are beasts. [It is for these reasons
> that] defense [against them] cannot but be resolute.
>
> *Essential Information for Governing Guangxi* (1602)

In the spring of 1372, Wu Liang (d. 1381), Marquis of Jiangyin, was
ordered by the Ming founding emperor to conduct a major military campaign in the southern border zone. There, near the intersection of present-
day Guangxi, Guizhou, and Hunan provinces, where the "non-Chinese"
(*man yi*) population was said to have long been troublesome, the operation was reportedly a success. Not only did Wu and his troops manage to
pacify more than two hundred native settlements (*dong*; *zhai*), according
to the records, they were also able to register some eighty thousand people. Following the campaign, not only did the *man yi* in the area "rectify
[their] hearts" and "come to be transformed" (*xiang hua*) according to
an (over-optimistic) account, they also began to submit taxes and follow
the laws of the centralizing state, "just as [the people of] the interior [*nei
di*]." To extend the reach of the state, Ming officials also reestablished
in the area the county of Huaiyuan ("cherishing afar"). In doing so, they
were hopeful that what had been an area "outside the pale" would in time
become an integral part of the "central dominion."[1]

Despite such early efforts, the area of Huaiyuan would remain for
much of the Ming period beyond the control of the centralizing state.
In 1437, a certain *man* leader Wei Chaozhen was said to have ter-
rorized the local population by engaging a band of nearly two thousand "bandits" in a series of raids. In the second half of the fifteenth
century, unrest apparently spread to the nearby Rong county where

---

[1] For the campaign and its aftermath, see *MSL*, *Taizu shi lu*, 71.1322; *GXTZ* (1531),
55:2b–3a. Quotations are from 55.3a.

"bandits" from Huaiyuan were reported to have seized a number of villages. Conditions seem to have continued to deteriorate in the latter half of the Ming period. In the 1531 edition of the *General Gazetteer of Guangxi*, it is noted that the county of Huaiyuan – which comprised only nine *li*[2] of registered households – "is falling day by day into [the hands of] the Yao and Zhuang." Unrest in the area evidently reached a climax in the mid-sixteenth century. In 1547, groups of "Yao bandits" were said to have managed to chase away the magistrate of Huaiyuan and seize control of the administrative seat. Although the county would remain in name – for a period, officials who had been appointed to Huaiyuan were forced to reside in the capital of Liuzhou prefecture – it was not until 1574 that the Ming forces were able to subdue some of the "Yao" groups and reestablish a degree of order in the area. And it was not until 1589, according to the records, that a new county seat of Huaiyuan was finally built and that a semblance of tranquility was restored.[3]

To Ming authorities, the history of Huaiyuan was far from exceptional. From the perspective of the centralizing state, the region of Guangxi – of which the area of Huaiyuan formed only a small part – remained a perilous frontier where a minority of registered, civilized subjects (referred to as *min* or *bian min* in the records) settled precariously among a majority of unregistered, uncivilized population (identified generically as *man*, *yi*, or *man yi*). To many an observer, *min* lived primarily in or near scattered administrative towns, whereas *man yi* populated the surrounding terrain; the former engaged in sedentary agriculture, while many of the latter practiced "slash-and-burn" farming; *min* owed taxes and corvée to the state, whereas most *man yi* bore no obligations. Relations between *min* and *man yi* were far from cordial; reports accusing the latter of pillaging villages and attacking travelers appear regularly in the Ming records. In the name of peace, officials often had to wage wars – some of which were among the most violent in the military history of the Ming – against "bandits." The war of Huaiyuan of 1573–74 was only one of many such examples: over 160,000 soldiers were said to have been mobilized, more than 140 "haunts" (*chao*) were reported to have been destroyed, and at least 3,500 people were recorded to have been killed. Although the war of Huaiyuan might have restored a degree of order to the area, to Ming

---

[2] For the population unit *li* ("hundred"), see the corresponding note in Table 2.1.
[3] For Wei Chaozhen, see *MSL, Yingzong shi lu*, 30.599. For the troubles in Huaiyuan, see Guo Yingpin, *Xi nan ji shi*, 3:17–26a; *GXTZ* (1599), 33:20–23. For the number of *li* and the quotation, see *GXTZ* (1531), 1:9b. For a discussion, see Zhang Yigui and Xu Shiru, *Ming dai Guangxi nong min qi yi shi gao*, 156–70.

rulers and officials – not to mention the *man yi* who perished – it was a clear reminder of the violent ways of the border zone.[4]

The history of Huaiyuan is however more than a story of confrontation. Unlike in native domains (see Chapter 3), where the Ming state was in general little interested in differentiating among the population, in Huaiyuan and other regular administrative areas, officials were increasingly involved – if only to determine on whom they could levy taxes and corvée duties – in distinguishing between settlements that were relatively orderly and those that were particularly rebellious. To Ming officials, what this often meant was to differentiate between areas that were populated by *min* and those that were occupied by *man yi*. Although Ming rulers and officials did continue to subscribe to the rhetoric of "civilizing" the "non-Chinese," in practice, given the limited resources of the state, it is evident that they often had to *perpetuate* – rather than eliminate – the perceived distinctions between *min* and *man yi*. The history of Huaiyuan, as that of the southern border zone during the Ming, is thus not simply a story of expansion and incorporation; it is also a story of identification and demarcation.

The *min* minority

Although the population in Guangxi might have in fact expanded over the course of the Ming, the story the official records tell, as we have seen in Chapter 2, is a rather different one. From the point of view of Ming observers, the *min* in the southern border province was constantly under siege: not only were the lives of many a registered, tax-paying subject routinely threatened by warfare and banditry, over time a significant portion of their land had also been taken over by the *man yi* population. In such observers' views, the world the *min* lived in was far from an expanding one; instead, it was a world the boundaries of which the *min* population had to constantly define and defend, a world in which the primary challenge was not growth, but survival.

Whether fact or fancy, this image of the *min* under siege had been projected by officials since almost the start of the Ming dynasty. Not only did travelers from beyond Guangxi comment frequently on the scarcity of *min* in the southern borderland, even people who were from the province also remarked routinely on the proliferation of the region's *man yi* population. Although such observations are often no more than stock testimonies – the chance to demonstrate one's indignation over the perceived absence

---

[4] For the war of 1573–74, see Guo Yingpin, *Xi nan ji shi*, 3:17–26a; Qu Jiusi, *Wanli wu gong lu*, 4:7–13.

of civilization in the border region was perhaps too tempting for most officials to pass up – they do reflect, if not the actual decline of the population in specific areas, the challenges the centralizing state faced in asserting control over the southern border zone.

Over the course of the Ming, images of a besieged *min* population had appeared in various contexts. Among such depictions, the most common were observations by officials of the *disappearance* of tax-paying households. For example, in a memorial dated 1443, it is reported by the commissioner Jie Ji and others that despite efforts by officials to establish control, the *man yi* in Guangxi had continued to be a serious menace. As a result, the numbers of soldiers and registered subjects (*min*) in the province "have diminished day by day." Likewise, in a memorial submitted in 1460 by the grand coordinator Ye Sheng, it is noted that as a result of rampant banditry, the size of the *min* population in Guangxi had dwindled to only 40–50 percent of that during the Hongwu reign. Similarly, in a memorial submitted in 1492 by the administration commissioner Li Mengyang (1432–1509), it is observed that in the southern province "the actual number of [registered] households is no more than six hundred some *li*." In what would become a commonplace remark, Li surmised that the registered population in Guangxi was probably "equivalent to that of only a major county in the lower Yangzi region."[5]

Not surprising, this image of a dwindling *min* population can be found also in reports concerning the fiscal conditions of Guangxi. In 1453, Shen Yi (js. 1448), a regional inspector, observed that as a result of frequent banditry, people in the southern border province had been fleeing their land in droves. To lessen the impact of the exodus, Shen recommended that the tax quota for Guangxi be reduced so that people who remained would not have to bear the extra tax burden. The decline in tax receipts is reported also in a 1521 memorial submitted by Wang Qi (d. 1534) and Huang Zhong. In it, the administration commissioners note that while the grain tax quota for Guangxi had been set at 420,000 piculs, the actual annual collection had by their time amounted to only slightly more than 230,000 (they place the blame in part on the disappearance of *min* households and in part on the decline of tax submission by native chieftains). The fall in tax revenues had apparently become even more serious by the second half of the

---

[5] For the memorial by Jie Ji and others, see *MSL*, *Yingzong shi lu*, 108.2192. For Ye Sheng's, see his *Ye Wenzhuang gong liang Guang zou cao*, 4:12b. For Li Mengyang, see *MSL*, *Xiaozong shi lu*, 60.1152. If we assume the total number of *li* in Guangxi during the Hongwu reign was just over eleven hundred (see Table 2.1), Li Mengyang would seem to agree with Ye Sheng that the registered population in the province had by the middle of the Ming period shrunk by about 50 percent.

sixteenth century. In 1574, Tang Lian (js. 1562), also a regional inspector, reported that by his time only less than one third of the annual tax quota for the province was being fulfilled. Likewise, Wu Wenhua (1521–98), a grand coordinator of Guangxi in the early Wanli reign (1573–1620), estimated that nearly half of the land in the province was either occupied by *man yi* or left uncultivated. To encourage settlement, Wu recommended that taxes in the southern border region be reduced.[6]

More dramatic than the provincial-level observations are testimonies concerning the depletion of *min* population in specific areas. In the case of Bobai county (Wuzhou), it is reported in a 1469 memorial – which seeks to eliminate the local posts of vice magistrate and assistant magistrate – that the size of the registered population there had shrunk from 33 *li* during the Hongwu reign to only 7 *li*. Similarly, in the case of Maping county, home of the prefectural seat of Liuzhou, it is noted in a memorial dated to the early sixteenth century that the size of the *min* population had decreased from 17 *li* in the early Ming period to only 1.5 *li*. But perhaps most striking of all is the report concerning Xiuren county (Pingle). There, if our source is to be trusted, by the turn of the seventeenth century, only two or three Han households had remained.[7]

Over the course of the Ming, testimonies concerning the proliferation of *man yi* in the southern border province also appear regularly in the records. In 1465, Feng Jun (js. 1460), a secretary in the Ministry of Justice and a native son of Yishan county (Qingyuan), was noted to have observed that in Guangxi while "Yao and Zhuang are many, [registered] residents are few in number." In a 1546 memorial prepared by the Ministry of War, it is asserted also that whereas only two tenths of the population in Guangxi were *min*, the rest was made up of Yao, Zhuang, and Lang. Echoing such impressions, in the late sixteenth century, Wang Shixing observed that while in many parts of Guangxi, such as Pingle, Wuzhou, and Nanning prefectures, one could find *min* and *yi* living among each other – "as chess pieces in play" – in Liuzhou, Qingyuan, and Sien prefectures, one would find *min* people living exclusively inside walled towns. "Areas outside the walls," according to the one-time assistant administration commissioner of the southern province, "are occupied entirely by Yao and Zhuang."[8]

[6] For the memorial by Shen Yi, see *MSL, Yingzong shi lu*, 229.5015. For that by Wang Qi and Huang Zhong, see *MSL, Shizong shi lu*, 8.298. For Tang Lian, see *MSL, Shenzong shi lu*, 32:751. For Wu Wenhua, see his *Yue xi shu gao*, 2:1–9, 3:5a.

[7] For Bobai county, see *MSL, Xianzong shi lu*, 70.1380. For Maping, see *GXTZ* (1531), 19:13b; in another part of the 1531 provincial gazetteer (1:9a) and in the 1461 *Da Ming yi tong zhi* (83:19a), the number of *li* for Maping in the early Ming period is said to be 7 rather than 17. For Xiuren, see *DYYZ*, 2:19a.

[8] For the observations by Feng Jun, see *MSL, Xianzong shi lu*, 13.289; for his biography, see *GXTZ* (1531), 44:22b–24a. For the 1546 memorial, see *MSL, Shizong shi lu*, 312.5844.

Even in parts of Guangxi (such as Guilin prefecture) where the number of registered households was relatively large, the *min* population was still frequently deemed to be outnumbered by that of the *man yi*. In the early sixteenth century, Zhang Ji, an official with special responsibility for Guilin and Pingle (and whom we encountered briefly in Chapter 2), observed that the *min* population in the two prefectures probably amounted to no more than 20–30 percent of the area's population. In the case of Guilin alone, it is reported also in a military handbook dated to the second half of the sixteenth century that of all the counties and subprefectures within the prefecture, only Lingui, home of the prefectural and provincial seats, and Quan Zhou, located at the northeastern edge, were free of troubles brought by Yao and Zhuang bandits. In the case of Yangshuo county (about 60 kilometers southeast of Lingui), it is noted that the *min* population there had by the mid-sixteenth century settled in only 30–40 percent of the land in the area. "The rest," according to the handbook, "is occupied by Zhuang people."[9]

What should one make of this plethora of testimonies concerning the dwindling of the *min* population in the southern border region? On the one hand, such reports no doubt reflect the difficulties the Ming state faced in keeping an accurate count of its subjects. Given the links between censuses and tax collection, it is not surprising that officials, especially those in the borderlands, would be tempted to under-report the population under their jurisdiction. On the other hand, although most of the reports – the one for Xiuren county, for example – should not be taken at face value, not all should be dismissed casually. As a result of wars and nature-induced disasters, parts of Guangxi probably did experience, if only temporarily, a significant decline in population.

At the same time, the increased identification and demarcation of *man yi* in the officials records were clearly linked to the reach of the centralizing state. As Ming authorities sought to establish a greater degree of control in the southern border zone, not only did officials distinguish between people who were "civilized" and those who had not been "transformed," they also found it important to differentiate between settlements that paid taxes to the state and those that did not. Seen from this perspective, the purported depletion of *min* and proliferation of *man yi* in Guangxi might in fact reflect *not* a decline of population in the southern border province but, rather, an increased awareness by officials of people who managed

For Wang Shixing, see his *Guang zhi yi*, 5.381. For a discussion of the various *man yi* labels, see Chapter 5.

[9] For the observations by Zhang Ji, see *YXWZ*, 5:43a. For Guilin, see *Cangwu*, 4:2b–3a; for Yangshuo, see *Cangwu*, 4:3b.

to continue to lie outside the administrative-cum-fiscal structure of the centralizing state.

Economics of violence

By all accounts, the southern border zone remained during the Ming a violent place. Although representatives and agents of the state would attribute the disorder in the borderland in part to the overzealousness of local officials and officers, the opportunism of various types of scoundrels and outlaws, as well as the duplicity of individual *min* landlords and middlemen, most would put the blame squarely on the alleged propensity for violence of the *man yi* population. And although Ming officials would in time find it useful to distinguish among the "non-Chinese" (see Chapter 5), most would continue to regard the demarcation of *min* and *man yi* as an essential organizing principle.

According to the records, Ming officials had long been aware that the violence in the southern border zone was attributable in part to the representatives and agents of the centralizing state. One important factor contributing to the disorder was the fact that many who actually served in the southern border region were either unqualified or otherwise incompetent. Shi Wanxiang, an investigating censor, observed for instance in the 1490s that most of the administrative posts in the southern border provinces were routinely staffed by elderly *jian sheng* (by then a title available for purchase), who had by the time of their appointments probably given up hopes for more desirable positions. Echoing Shi's observation, Tian Rucheng, in the mid-sixteenth century, also noted that most of the administrators in the southern borderland were either dejected officials who had been demoted or bookish scholars who lacked practical experiences. As a result, according to Tian, some of the violence that could have been quelled at its root was allowed instead to turn into much more serious problems.[10]

Another contributing factor, Ming observers reckoned, had to do with the overzealousness and corruption of some of the military officers and soldiers in the southern border zone. Although it was a common practice in the Ming period for individual soldiers to be given awards on the basis of the number of enemies killed in combat, the problems inherent in such incentive schemes were particularly apparent in the military confrontations in the southern borderland. According to Qiu Jun, a native

---

[10] For the observations by Shi Wanxiang, see *MSL, Xiaozong shi lu*, 93.1715. For the place of *jian sheng* in the examination system, see Ho, *Ladder of Success*, 32–33. For Tian Rucheng, see *YJJW*, preface:1b.

son of present-day Hainan Island (just off the coast of Guangdong) we met briefly in Chapter 3, the dramatic increase in the number of bandits in the southern provinces in the second half of the fifteenth century was in fact largely the result of indiscriminate killings by government forces. As Ming soldiers, in search of rewards, went about terrorizing the region in their military campaigns, Qiu Jun observed, formerly innocent people were given no choice but to engage in banditry. But overzealousness on the part of Ming officers and soldiers was only part of the problem. In time, it appears, representatives and agents of the centralizing state would also become interested in encroaching on the land of individual settlers. As early as 1438, for instance, it was reported that several officers from the Central Guard of Guilin had conspired to seize possession of the properties of a certain well-to-do "Yao" household. Although the officers in question were eventually caught and punished, for every case of encroachment recorded, there were probably many more that had been left unrecognized.[11]

In addition to the problems brought by local officials and military officers, Ming observers would in time also come to recognize the troubles caused by people who were deemed beyond the reach of the law. Although little is known about such "outlaws," it seems that people who were so labeled were either locals or migrants who had for one reason or another managed to disappear from the government registers. For many a Ming commentator, the disorder in Guangxi was in fact attributable not so much to the alleged propensity for violence on the part of the *man yi* but to the instigation by such troublemakers. "The Yao and Zhuang are by nature naive and straightforward," wrote Wang Shangxue (js. 1538) of Maping county (Liuzhou) in a memorial probably dated to the mid-sixteenth century. "Those who are crafty and greedy account for not even one in a hundred." Su Jun, in the 1599 edition of the provincial gazetteer, would echo this view: "Nowadays those who devise policies for Guangxi speak often of attacks by the *yi di* [another generic reference for "non-Chinese"] against the central dominion but do not realize that the troubles were not [brought by] the *yi*." In Su's judgment, it was the outlaws (*wang ming zhi peng*) who had migrated from the central plains and the loafers (*you shou ba min*) from within Guangxi who were the source of much problems in the province.[12]

---

[11] For the award schemes of the Ming, see *MHD*, 123.631–35; for the practices in Guang-dong and Guangxi, see *Cangwu*, juan 16. For the observations by Qiu Jun, see his *Qiongtai wen hui gao*, 21:42. For encroachments, see, for example, *MSL*, *Yingzong shi lu*, 47.917.
[12] For the memorial by Wang Shangxue, see Fang Yu, *Nanning fu zhi*, 9:11–12a. For Su Jun, see *GXTZ* (1599), 33:4b.

But the troubles in the southern border zone were not limited to the presence of unscrupulous officials and parasitic crooks. According to Ming observers, in time, registered *min* households would also become a major source of problems for the centralizing state as they increasingly interacted with the local *man yi* population. Of the many troubles noted in the records, a particularly vexing one for the Ming authorities was the formation of a variety of landlord-tenant relationships between *min* households and the *man yi* population. Ji Zongdao (js. 1499) of Maping observes for instance in an early-sixteenth-century memorial that "unlike in the central plains where people engage in their own farming, in Guangxi, people generally employ Yao and Zhuang to cultivate their fields." Su Jun, likewise, reported that "farmers [in Guangxi] do not engage in their own farming but delegate [their work] to the Zhuang." Although the particular arrangements of such landlord–tenant relationships would vary widely – whereas some *min* landlords, especially those in Guilin prefecture, were said to have recruited *man yi* tenants from as far as the province of Huguang, others were reported to have simply purchased land deeds (*quan*) from the local *man yi* population – by the second half of the Ming period, the practice of tenancy had apparently become such a source of troubles (especially with regard to tax evasion and related violence) that many officials would demand that it be prohibited. Following a military campaign in Maping county in the early 1580s, for instance, it was recommended by the officials in charge that landlords who profited from dealing with Yao and Zhuang tenants should have their possessions confiscated. The situation apparently had not improved much by the turn of the seventeenth century. In the case of Guilin, according to a military handbook compiled around that time, given their continual dependence on "Yao" and "Zhuang" tenants, *min* households were nothing but "meat on a stool," waiting to be devoured.[13]

The second set of problems brought by registered *min* households had to do with tax collection. Although the details are not clear, it seems to be the case that not a few *man yi* settlements in the regular administrative areas of Guangxi would in time come to be expected to pay taxes to the centralizing state. Just how individual "Yao," "Zhuang," and other

---

[13] For the memorial by Ji Zongdao, see *GXTZ* (1531), 19:13a. For Su Jun, see *GXTZ* (1599), 3:47b. For the recruitment of *man yi* tenants, see, for example, Gu Yanwu, *Tian xia jun guo li bing shu*, 30:1, quoting the 1549(?) edition of the *Gazetteer of Quan Zhou* (*Quan zhou zhi*); Guo Yingpin, *Xi nan ji shi*, 1:1a. For the purchase of land deeds, see Wang Shixing, *Guang zhi yi*, 5.381. For the problems with tenancy, see Guo Yingpin, *Xi nan ji shi*, 4:39b–40a; *GXTZ* (1599), 33:4b–5. For reactions against the practice, see, for example, *GXTZ* (1599), 25:56b; *MSL, Shenzong shi lu*, 32.758. For Maping, see Qu Jiusi, *Wanli wu gong lu*, 4:27b. For Guilin, see *DYYZ*, 1:10b–11a.

man yi settlements ended up having to deliver taxes is not obvious from the records. What seems to have happened, however, was that following some military campaigns in the more "troublesome" areas in the southern border zone, Ming officials were sometimes able to induce individual *man yi* populations to agree to pay taxes (at half the rate for the regular *min*, for example) in exchange for a measure of peace. Even though the arrangement was meant to allow the centralizing state to extend its reach, officials would find out in time that what was intended as a way to impose order would in fact engender its own set of disorder. For Ming observers, one of the most vexing problems of the arrangement had to do with the fact that, rather than deliver their taxes directly to the local administrative seats, many of the *man yi* would rely on *min* middlemen to perform the service. As a result, according to Ming officials, whereas some devious *min* middlemen would routinely conceal more than half of what the *man yi* had submitted to them (and blame the latter for underpayment), others would demand their clients to pay several times more than it was officially required. To minimize opportunities for exploitation (and violence), officials did encourage *man yi* people to deliver their taxes themselves. But because such *man yi* were evidently afraid of dealing with Ming officials, how successful such efforts were is not clear.[14]

Despite their recognition of the troubles brought by local officials and *min* middlemen, most Ming observers would continue to regard the presence of a large *man yi* population in the southern border zone as the major source of problems for the centralizing state. "Since the times of the Qin and Han [dynasties]," remarked Qiu Jun in the second half of the fifteenth century, "those who have brought [the most] harm to the central dominion have been the *hu* in the north and the *yue* in the south." Compared with the threats posed by the *hu* (such as the Mongols) in the north, Qiu argued, the problems caused by the *yue* (used here as another generic label for the "non-Chinese" in the south) were actually much more difficult to deal with. Whereas the *hu* could be kept out of the central dominion by a strong border defense, Qiu Jun observed, the *yue* had so blended in with the *min* that they could not be easily isolated. In a memorial dated to 1493, Zhou Qi (js. 1481) of Maping notes also that the conditions in Guangxi had become so deteriorated that people would "rather spend a day without food than a day without troops." He cautions that "if [the province] is not under control in ten years, the *min* would

---

[14] For *min* middlemen and the tax rate for *man yi*, see Wang Shixing, *Guang zhi yi*, 5.381; Wei Jun, *Xi shi er*, 3:11a. For efforts to encourage direct payment, see *YXCZ*, 18:17–18a, quoting a late-Ming edition of the *Gazetteer of Pingle Prefecture* (*Pingle fu zhi*).

have no land [to farm]; if it is not under control in twenty years, the land would have no *min* [to occupy it]." Similarly, Jiang Mian observes in his preface to the 1531 edition of the provincial gazetteer that in Guangxi, "there has not been one year in which *yi* bandits did not come around for attacks."[15]

For Ming observers, the problems with the *man yi* had to at least at some level do with the latter's unruly nature. It is not uncommon to find in Ming-dynasty records references such as "when dispersed [the *man yi*] behave as *min*; when assembled they become bandits" (*san ze wei min; ju ze wei dao*) or that "when content [the *man yi* act like] they are humans; when discontent [they behave as if] they are beasts" (*hao ren nu shou*). (Although such remarks were meant to underscore the flickery nature of the "non-Chinese," they also hint at the fluid boundaries between *min* and *man yi*.) The alleged unruly nature of the *man yi* was thought to extend also to their handling of internal disputes. "When a Yao kills a Yao, the imperial court would not be disturbed [by the Yao]" (*Yao sha Yao, bu dong chao*), according to a popular rhyme from the Ming period. "When a Zhuang kills a Zhuang, an official complaint would not be filed [by the Zhuang]" (*Zhuang sha Zhuang, bu gao zhuang*). Just as Ming observers found it noteworthy that the *man yi* population would often use violence to resolve disputes, they were also struck by how tenacious the *man yi* could be. It was not unusual, according to reports from the Ming period, for individual "Yao" and "Zhuang" families to be locked in the same feuds even after nine generations had passed.[16]

But even Ming observers recognized that the troubles with the *man yi* must be understood in broader economic terms. According to reports, not only did people who engaged primarily in hunting, gathering, slash-and-burn farming, and trading find it necessary to supplement their food supplies by periodically attacking itinerant merchants and raiding *min* settlements, even those who practiced sedentary agriculture also sometimes deemed it desirable to encroach on the land of registered *min* households. In one case concerning a certain part of Yining county (Guilin), for example, it was noted that a group of "Zhuang" troublemakers – who had apparently been recruited to defend the area in the first place – had gathered together from time to time to cut off the water supply for the

---

[15] For the comments by Qiu Jun, see his *Da xue yan yi bu*, 153:6–7a. For the memorial by Zhou Qi, see *YXWZ*, 5:38; *MSL, Xiaozong shi lu*, 76.1463. For Zhou's biography, see *GXTZ* (1531), 47:3b–5a. For Jiang Mian, see *GXTZ* (1531), preface:4b.

[16] For observations of the nature of *man yi*, see *MSL, Taizu shi lu*, 34.613; *DYYZ*, 1:1b. For their tenacity, see, for example, Wang Shixing, *Guang zhi yi*, 5.382.

min households there. As a result, many of those who were affected had to abandon their land and move elsewhere. Although it is difficult to determine from official accounts alone the full context of the violence in the southern border zone, on the evidence available, it is clear that the disorder in the borderland was less the result of the unruly nature of those identified as *man yi* but more the outcome of their desires for food, land, and other resources.[17]

The "Yao" of the Rattan Gorge

From the point of view of the centralizing state, the propensity for violence on the part of the *man yi* population in southern border zone was probably best illustrated by the case of the "Yao" of the Rattan Gorge. Extending some 60 kilometers along the Qian River between the county seat of Wuxuan and the prefectural capital of Xunzhou, the Rattan Gorge area (see Map 4.1), whose geography was (and is) distinguished by soaring cliffs and meandering waterways, was by all accounts a strategic transportation node in the southern province. Boats carrying grain, salt, and other supplies from the capital of Wuzhou prefecture, according to the records, often had to sail along the Qian River through the Gorge to reach the central and northern sections of Guangxi. Although there were reportedly different types of *man yi* active in the area, it was the "Yao" who were said to be the source of much troubles. Not only did they emerge frequently from their dwellings on both sides of the Gorge to terrorize the hapless travelers, according to reports, they also routinely banded together to attack the villages and towns of nearby regular administrative areas.[18]

Reports on the disorder of the so-called Yao people in the Rattan Gorge area can be traced to almost the beginning of the Ming dynasty. As early as 1375, for reasons unclear, soldiers from the newly established Liuzhou Guard were said to have had to launch an attack against the "Yao bandits" from the Gorge area. Likewise, in 1425, apparently in response to the continual obstruction of traffic by *man* bandits, a major military campaign was conducted in the area under the direction of the regional commander Gu Xingzu (ca. 1390–1460). But allegations against the "Yao" would persist. In 1437, it was reported by Shan Yun (who had succeeded Gu) that, in reponse to the increased encroachment by *man* bandits, *min*

---

[17] For the desire of the *man yi* to gain access to goods, see, for example, Tang Shunzhi, *Guang you zhan gong lu*, 7b. For an account of the violence in Yining, see *YXWZ*, 44:20–22a.

[18] For a Ming-period description of the Rattan Gorge, see *YJJW*, 2:1–2a.

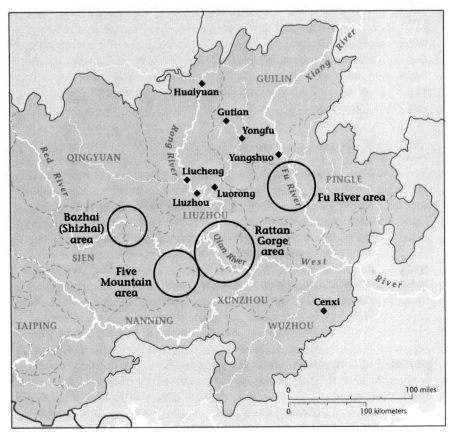

Map 4.1. Areas of Major Violence. *Source: GXTZ* (1599), juan 33.

people from the greater Gorge area had demanded that efforts be made by the government to confine the "Yao" to the mountains.[19]

In time, disorder attributed to the Yao would also be reported in areas beyond the vicinity of the Rattan Gorge. In around 1440, bandits from the Gorge area were said to have looted dozens of *min* households in the counties of Guiping (home of the prefectural seat of Xunzhou), Pingnan (Xunzhou), Teng (Wuzhou), and Rong (Wuzhou). In 1464, bandits from the Rattan Gorge were reported to have broken into the prefectural seat of Wuzhou, ransacked the treasury, and released the

[19] For the attack of 1375, see *MSL, Taizu shi lu*, 98.1673. For the campaign of 1425, see *Xuanzong shi lu*, 4.112. For the report by Shan Yun, see *Yingzong shi lu*, 35.673.

prisoners found. And in 1465, *man* bandits from the Gorge area were said to have forced their way into the administrative seat of Teng county, looted the treasury, and seized the official seal of the magistrate. By the second half of the fifteenth century, disorder attributed to or inspired by the "Yao" of the Rattan Gorge was reported to have even spread to the province of Guangdong. In 1465, Qiu Jun would go so far to claim that "there were originally no bandits in Guangdong; where there are bandits, they came from Guangxi."[20]

By the time Han Yong – who had served as a vice minister of war and a grand coordinator in the northern border region – was appointed as the *de facto* commander-in-chief of Guangdong and Guangxi in 1465, the Yao of the Rattan Gorge had clearly become a major concern of the centralizing state. Although Qiu Jun, who was no doubt looking out for the interest of Guangdong, had suggested in a memorial that the government should aim to *contain* the bandits inside Guangxi, Han Yong concluded that a direct assault against the Yao of the Rattan Gorge would best fulfill the objectives of the state. Altogether, 190,000 soldiers (the majority of whom was apparently from native domains) were reported to have been mobilized for the war of 1465–66. As part of his strategy, Han Yong first ordered his troops to the counties of Xiuren and Lipu (located northeast of the Gorge), where they were directed to suppress "bandits" who were thought to have long abetted the Yao. Han then divided his forces into several units and ordered them to approach the Gorge from different directions. Following a series of intense battles, some of which were evidently fought all the way at the top of the mountains in the Gorge area (see Figure 4.1), Hou Dagou (Hou the Big Dog), the alleged Yao leader, was finally captured along with many followers. As a result of the campaign, according to the official report, 324 "haunts" and "stockades" were destroyed, 3,207 "bandits" were decapitated, 2,718 women were captured, and countless people were injured or drowned to death. For primarily symbolic reasons, Han Yong ordered the rattan vines that grew across the Qian River be removed. What had until then been known as the Big Rattan Gorge (Dateng Xia), according to Han would hence be referred to as the Chopped Rattan Gorge (Duanteng Xia).[21]

(margin note: concern for centralizing state)

[20] For the disorder of 1440, see *MSL, Yingzong shi lu*, 81.1624. For Wuzhou, see *MSL, Xianzong shi lu*, 1.27. For Teng county, see *MSL, Xianzong shi lu*, 22.430. For Qiu Jun, see *MSL, Xianzong shi lu*, 13.294.
[21] For Qiu Jun, see *MSL, Xianzong shi lu*, 13.294. For the war of the Rattan Gorge, see *MSL, Xianzong shi lu*, 27.541; *GXTZ* (1531), 56:1–3a; *YJJW* 2:3–4; Yin Geng, *Teng xia ji lüe*, 1–4a. For a discussion, see Mote, "Ch'eng-hua and Hung-chih Reigns," 377–80.

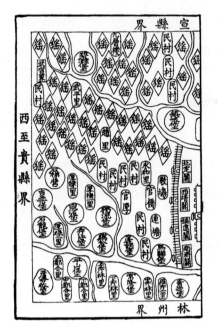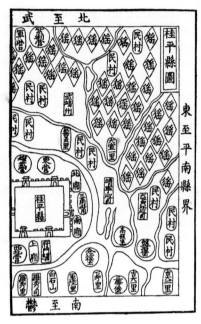

Figure 4.1. The Rattan Gorge Area. *Source: DYYZ*, juan 3, before ye 3. The mountain Jiucenglou (Nine-Story Edifice), found in the top left portion of the map, was where many "Yao bandits" were said to have congregated. The administrative seat identified (by the city wall) was the capital of Xunzhou prefecture.

establishing order

To establish a semblance of order in the area following the military campaign, Han Yong offered, among others, the following recommendations. First, because of the dwindling size of the regular military population in Guangxi (see Chapter 2), Han proposed that an additional ten thousand soldiers from Huguang (on top of the existing allotment of ten thousand) be assigned to the province. For the same reason, he suggested that an earlier arrangement of allocating five thousand native soldiers from Guizhou to Guangxi be reinstated. Second, given the hazardous geography of the Rattan Gorge and the continuous threats posed by bandits, Han Yong proposed that a native domain – one that would be led by a member of the Cen clan of Tianzhou – be established in the middle of the troubled area. To help set up the *tu si*, Han suggested that a portion of the land that had been left vacant as a result of the war be granted to the newly recognized chieftain. Third, in addition to the native domain, Han Yong also recommended that a new battalion and a number of police offices be set up around the Gorge. Although these new military units would in theory be led by regular officials, they would in practice be run by native headmen.[22]

Despite such measures, reports on disorder in the Gorge area would again appear regularly in the records in the early sixteenth century. Although Ming officials would, as it was customary, attribute the violence to the unruly nature of the *man yi* population, at least one, the supreme commander Chen Jin, seemed to understand that the underlying tensions might have to do with the desire of the so-called Yao bandits for basic provisions. In 1508, in exchange for peace, Chen Jin was said to have ordered all commercial boats to carry a supply of salt and other foodstuff to the people of the Rattan Gorge every time they carried goods up the Qian River. How, and whether, this policy – for which Chen would be criticized by his fellow officials – was implemented, we cannot be sure. But even if it was carried out, the arrangement would prove inadequate. By 1528, following his actions in Tianzhou (see Chapter 3), Wang Shouren would apparently find it necessary to launch another attack in the Rattan Gorge area. As a result, more than eleven hundred "bandits" were reported to have been decapitated, and nearly six hundred of their family members were said to have been captured.[23]

But problems associated with the Rattan Gorge would persist. According to Tian Rucheng, who had firsthand experience in the area, the immediate cause of the troubles in the 1530s was the desire by two native headmen – who had been assigned to the Gorge by the centralizing state to help maintain order – to take over the land of Hou Shenghai, reputedly a descendant of Hou Dagou. To seize land from Hou, the two headmen were reported to have first accused the former of engaging in disorder and then had him murdered in 1537. Following Hou Shenghai's death, a military fort under the command of one of the native headmen was established at Hou's estate. Vowing to avenge his brother's death, Hou Gongding soon launched an attack against the fort and killed more than two hundred soldiers. In part because of this open rebellion, by 1538, Ming officials had decided that another major assault was needed to restore order in the Gorge area. Over fifty thousand soldiers were reported to have taken part in the war. As a result, Hou Gongding was quickly put to death, some fifteen hundred "bandits" were either killed or captured, and nearly three thousand men and women were said to have been "pacified."[24]

---

[22] For the recommendations by Han Yong, see *Cangwu*, 1–12a.

[23] For Chen Jin's policy, see *YJJW*, 2:6. For the war of 1528, see Wang Shouren, *Yangming quan shu*, 15:6b–14a; *GXTZ* (1531), 56:16b–17a. For a discussion, see Shin, "Last Campaigns of Wang Yangming."

[24] For the war of 1538, see *MSL, Shizong shi lu*, 227.4717; *YJJW*, 2:7b–11a; Yin Geng, *Teng xia ji lüe*, 4b–5b. For discussions, see Gao Yanhong and Yao Shun'an, *Ming dai*

The wars against the so-called Yao bandits of the Rattan Gorge would loom large in the historical horizon of many a Ming-dynasty observer. To be sure, the military campaigns, especially the one led by Han Yong in 1465–66, were themselves major undertakings. But it was also because of reports such as those by Tian Rucheng that images of a violent frontier would find their way into the conciousness of many Ming officials and travelers. We may never know what actually prompted the disorder in the Rattan Gorge area or whether people there would find the label "Yao" meaningful. For all we know, when Shan Yun reported that the *min* in the Gorge area had demanded the government to confine the "Yao" to the mountains, it might have been the case that it was the *min* who wanted to take over the land of people who had not yet been registered by the centralizing state. In any case, what is evident from the records is that the century-long wars, and the reports they engendered, did serve to reinforce the perceptions among Ming observers that the southern border zone was indeed a violent place and that it was important for local officials to identify areas and settlements that were particularly troublesome.

The "Zhuang" of Gutian

From the perspectives of Ming officials, the alleged propensity for violence on the part of the *man yi* in Guangxi could also be observed readily in the case of the "Zhuang" of Gutian. In contrast to the area of the Rattan Gorge, the county of Gutian was by all accounts relatively isolated. Located about 50 kilometers west of the provincial capital and surrounded by "high mountains and towering peaks," the area of Gutian was apparently accessible only through a limited number of strategic passes. Despite its isolation, Gutian was said to have a registered population of ten *li* (about fifteen hundred households) in the early Ming period. The composition of the local population, according to officials, began to change in the mid–fifteenth century when *min* residents started to recruit "Zhuang" people to the area to be their tenants. In time, not only would such so-called Zhuang tenants succeed in chasing away the local *min* population, according to the records, they would also become a serious threat to the residents in the surrounding region.[25]

Guangxi nong min qi yi shi, 19–51; Zhang Yigui and Xu Shiru, *Ming dai Guangxi nong min qi yi shi gao*, 78–100.

[25] For a general description of Gutian, see Guo Yingpin, *Xi nan ji shi*, 1:1. For efforts to reconstruct the history of the "Zhuang" in the late imperial period, see Su Jianling, *Ming Qing shi qi Zhuang zu li shi yan jiu*; Tsukada Shigeyuki, *Chiwan-zoku shakaishi kenkyū*; idem, *Chiwan-zoku bunkashi kenkyū*.

Whatever the sources of the conflicts in the area might be, by the late fifteenth century, disorder associated with such "Zhuang bandits" would come to symbolize for many the challenges the state had to face in the southern border region. Although troubles had been simmering for some time, it was in the early 1490s, according to the records, that so-called Zhuang rebels, led by leaders Qin Wanxian and Wei Chaowei, finally forced out the local magistrate and seized control of the county seat of Gutian. Although local authorities, under the leadership of the supreme commander Min Gui (1430–1511), would respond by launching a full-scale attack against the troublemakers, the military campaign would turn out to be a disaster. Two of the Ming commanders, Ma Jun and Ma Xuan, were killed in an ambush, and the government troops, whose movement was apparently severely hindered by the area's particular terrain, were at the end forced to retreat. As a result, for over half a century, the county of Gutian was said to have become a Zhuang territory. Not only did magistrates who had been officially assigned to Gutian have to take up residence in the provincal capital instead, regular *min* households – or what had been left of them – were also said to have fled the area in droves.[26]

In time, disorder attributed to the so-called Zhuang bandits of Gutian would be reported in areas throughout northeastern Guangxi. In 1520, in response to another failed attack by the government forces, the rebels of Gutian were said to have spread to nearby counties and taken control of a number of villages there. No doubt more disturbing for Ming officials, in 1553, a band of "bandits" from Gutian was reported to have forced its way into the county seat of Lingquan (about 70 kilometers northeast of Gutian) and looted the government treasury. Even more alarming, in early 1565, a group led by Wei Yinbao (son of Wei Chaowei) was said to have managed to break into the provincial capital, seize more than 40,000 taels of silver from the treasury, and murder the administration vice commissioner. Later that year, the same group was apparently able to force its way into the provincial capital again, this time reaching as far as the gates of the princely estate before it was beaten back.[27]

In time, a number of proposals would be put forth to deal with the problems. Not long after the deaths of the commanders Ma Jun and Ma Xuan in 1492, Zhou Qi of Maping (located about 100 kilometers

---

[26] For the Ming military campaign, see *MSL, Xiaozong shi lu*, 61.1188; *Cangwu*, 18:6a. For its aftermath, see Guo Yingpin, *Xi nan ji shi*, 1:1b; according to Guo, following the failed campaign, only thirty some *min* households were left in Gutian.

[27] For an overview of the disorder, see Guo Yingpin, *Xi nan ji shi*, 1:1b–2a; *GXTZ* (1599), 33:10–11.

southwest of Gutian) proposed in a memorial that a major attack – two hundred thousand soldiers in his recommendation – be launched against the Zhuang bandits. For reasons that no doubt had to do with the costs and logistics involved, Zhou's proposal was never adopted. In 1499, it was suggested by the supreme commander Deng Tingzan that a smaller but still potent force of ninety thousand soldiers be assembled to combat the rebels. But even Deng's relatively modest recommendation did not result in action. Although officials did launch two smaller-scale attacks against the so-called Zhuang bandits in 1519 and 1526, respectively, neither could be declared a success. In light of such failed efforts, in 1530, it was proposed by the regional commander Zhang Jing (d. 1555) that, rather than attempt to annihilate the troublemakers, officials should focus on preventing them from spreading to other parts of the province by setting up a dozen or so military forts at the strategic mountain passes that surrounded Gutian. But for a variety of reasons, even this plan seems to have not been followed through.[28]

In part because of the inaction of the centralizing state, by the late 1560s, the troubles associated with the so-called Zhuang bandits of Gutian were reported to have reached a boiling point. Even in the provincial capital, where there was a sizable army stationed, local residents were said to have become increasingly fearful for their lives. Not only had more and more soldiers been placed around the city of Guilin, according to the regional commander Yu Dayou (1503–79), those who were responsible for defending the provincial seat had also become more and more vigilant, "as if powerful enemies are constantly at the gate." To put an end to this torment, Yu observed in 1567, people in Guilin "all desire to have a show-down with the bandits at the earliest opportunity." In part as a result of Yu's prompting, in 1570, a major attack against the troublemakers of Gutian was finally launched.[29]

What is interesting about the war of 1570–71 is that, from the start, Ming officials were interested in distinguishing between Zhuang people who were "tractable" (*shan*) and those who were "intractable" (*e*). Before the formal commencement of the military campaign, efforts were apparently made to classify the ten *li* of settlements in Gutian into *shan* (of which there were four) and *e* (the remaining six). Whereas Zhuang people who were identified as "tractable" would be spared, those who were labeled "intractable" would be targeted for attacks. The war, which

---

[28] For the proposal by Zhou Qi, see *MSL, Xiaozong shi lu*, 76.1463. For Deng Tingzan, see *MSL, Xiaozong shi lu*, 149.2623. For other efforts, see Guo Yingpin, *Xi nan ji shi*, 1:1b.

[29] For his observations, see Yu Dayou, *Zheng qi tang ji*, 16B:1b, 7a.

lasted nearly three months and might have involved some 140,000 regular and native soldiers, was apparently a success. According to official reports, Wei Yinbao, the Zhuang leader most wanted by the government, was eventually caught and executed, more than seventy-three hundred "bandits" were either captured or slaughtered, and close to thirty-two hundred *mu* (18 square kilometers) of land were confiscated.[30]

What is signficant about the case of Gutian is not so much the extent of disorder attributed to the so-called Zhuang bandits or the scale of the military response of the centralizing state. What is noteworthy about the episode is how Ming officials, even after their seemingly successful campaign of 1570–71, had to continue to distinguish between people who remained outside their direct control and those who had come to accept a certain level of state supervision. Following the war, the county of Gutian – which would, for symbolic purposes, be renamed Yongning ("perpetual tranquility") and elevated to the level of a subprefecture – was apparently divided into two halfs. Whereas people who had earlier been identified as *e* would be placed under the rule of newly recruited native chieftains, those who had been labeled *shan* would be incorporated into the regular administration of the state. But even in the case of the "tractable" Zhuang, according to Ming officials, special accommodations would have to be made. Even though the people in question would be organized into units of *li* and be expected to pay taxes to the government (just as in the case of registered *min*), it would be up to the elders of individual "Zhuang" villages to decide how much tax would be delivered.[31]

Mapping *min* and *man*

Over time, as we have seen, the extension of the centralizing state, as reflected in part in the increased frequency of major military campaigns in the southern border zone, had reinforced – rather than erased – the distinction between *min* and *man yi*. Not only did Ming officials find it important to differentiate between people who were ready to provide taxes and corvée duties and those who were not, they also obviously had

---

[30] For the classification of settlements in Gutian into "tractable" and "intractable," see Yu Dayou, *Zheng qi tang ji*, 16B: 25–28a. For accounts of the campaign and its aftermath, see Guo Yingpin, *Xi nan ji shi*, 1:2b–7; *GXTZ* (1599), 33:11–13.

[31] For the post-war arrangements, see *MSL*, *Muzong shi lu*, 57.1408; the memorial is quoted and discussed in Tsukada Shigeyuki, "Min Shin jidai ni okeru Chiwan-zoku tōchi taisei," 164. For discussions of the wars of Gutian, see Gao Yanhong and Yao Shun'an, *Ming dai Guangxi nong min qi yi shi*, 69–81; Zhang Yigui and Xu Shiru, *Ming dai Guangxi nong min qi yi shi gao*, 49–63.

a strong interest in distinguishing between settlements that were orderly and those that were rebellious. In the case of Guangxi, efforts to demarcate *min* and *man yi* were perhaps most noticeable in areas where the state had extended its administrative and military apparatuses; in areas where native chieftains were dominant (namely, the Left and Right river regions), Ming officials apparently had neither the capacity nor interest to make similar distinctions.

Examples of such efforts by Ming officials to distinguish between *min* and *man yi* can be found in a variety of government records. Among them one of the more remarkable is no doubt the *Record of the Office of the Supreme Commander at Cangwu* (*Cangwu zong du jun men zhi*), a military handbook first compiled in 1552 by the supreme commander Ying Jia (1494–1554) and supplemented in the 1570s by his successors Ling Yunyi and Liu Yaohui (1522–85). To Ying Jia, who had been a grand coordinator in the northern border province of Shanxi, the compilation of a comprehensive military handbook for the southern provinces was clearly long overdue. In a memorial dated to 1552, Ying Jia observes that "even though the problem of banditry can be found everywhere, nowhere does its scale surpass that of the Guang regions." In Guangdong and Guangxi, he reports, "there has not been a year without banditry, and there has not been a year in which troops need not be deployed." In Ying Jia's view, a useful handbook should include information not only on the types and organization of the local government forces but also on the size and distribution of the *man yi* population. A staunch supporter of military actions, Ying Jia had in time come to favor the tactic of "surgical strikes" (*diao jiao*) over the alternative strategy of large-scale expeditions (*da zheng*). Unlike the latter approach, which sought to eliminate all the rebels in a given area in a sustained military campaign, "surgical strikes" aimed at attaining quick victories by striking hard at strategically selected targets. More so than in the case of large-scale expeditions, officials who carried out *diao jiao* would have to determine in advance the precise locations of the purported offenders. It was no doubt in part for this reason that Ying Jia would take it as his task as the supreme commander for Guangdong and Guangxi to compile a detailed military handbook for the region.[32]

---

[32] For the memorial by Ying Jia, see *Cangwu*, 24:42b–48a; for the quotations, see 24:42b. For a biography of Ying Jia, see He Linxia, "*Cangwu zong du jun men zhi* yan jiu," 486–90. For an explanation of *diao jiao*, see Mao Kun, *Mao Lumen xian sheng wen ji*, 29:10b–16a. The need to strike quickly and often unexpectedly apparently had to do with the fact that many of the so-called bandits were able to learn in advance through their spies the planned movements of government troops. See, for example, the account in Tang Shunzhi, *Guang you zhan gong lu*, 7–11.

To a major extent, the *Record of the Office of the Supreme Commander* was (and is) a reminder of how much a military concern the *man yi* population must have been even (or especially) in the sixteenth century. Compared with the standard officially compiled local gazetteers, the *Record* is at once more limited in scope and more in-depth in treatment. Included in the handbook are a selection of official documents related to the establishment in the prefectural capital of Wuzhou in 1470 of the office of the supreme commander, descriptions of the organization of the regional military apparatus, information on the size and distribution of guards and battalions, and details concerning the funding, training, and management of local military officers and soldiers. To better prepare themselves and other officials to handle the disorder in the southern provinces, Ying Jia and his fellow compilers also found it useful to include in the *Record* a chronology of the major disorders in the region as well as a selection of official writings (memorials, essays, etc.) that they deemed particularly useful for future policy formulation. Also important is the inclusion in the handbook of a long section on Annam, which the Ming state had briefly occupied in the early fifteenth century and which had, even into the latter half of the Ming period, remained a concern for officials in the southern border zone.[33]

But what is perhaps most interesting about the *Record* is its section on administrative geography (*yu tu*). Here the compilers not only found it useful to include a map for each of the prefectural units in the two southern provinces but also considered it important to compile a profile for each of the counties and subprefectures in the region. Included in each profile are a description of the location of the administrative area in question (often complete with figures of distance from its neighboring units), information on major waterways, a brief history of the area (with particular emphasis on adminstrative changes), a list of local government positions, and details concerning the area's police offices and courier stations (*yi*). The reason for the incorporation of such information is obvious: from the perspectives of Ying Jia and his successors, not only was it important for officials in charge to have at their disposal a guide to the geography of the southern region, it was necessary also for them to understand the extent of the reach of the government. More significant, in putting together the profiles, the compilers of the handbook apparently also found it useful to include information on the distribution of the local *man yi* population. Not only were Ying Jia and others interested in distinguishing between *min* and *man yi* settlements, they were also keen

---

[33] For a discussion of the *Record* as a source, see He Linxia, "*Cangwu zong du jun men zhi yan jiu.*"

on differentiating between those *man yi* settlements that seemed relatively orderly and those that appeared troublesome.[34]

Perhaps not surprising, such observations on the distribution of *man yi* settlements are most readily offered in the *Record* for areas in Guangxi where the centralizing state had established a relatively strong presence. For instance, in Guilin prefecture, where the provincial capital was located and where officials had registered a comparatively large *min* population, the compilers of the handbook were evidently particularly interested in distinguishing between areas occupied by *min* and those dominated by *man yi*. In Quan Zhou, where "*min* villages are numerous," there were, according to the *Record*, a total of only fourteen "Yao haunts," all of which could be found 100 *li* (50 kilometers) south of the adminstrative seat. Likewise, in Guanyang county (located south of Quan Zhou), despite the area's mountainous terrain, according to the *Record*, only five of the mountains were occupied by the so-called Yao and Zhuang; the rest of the county, apparently, was populated by *min*. In the handbook, not only do the compilers sometimes identify by names the specific locations of the *man yi* settlements, they also often try to distinguish between them based on their perceived level of orderliness. In the case of Yining county (located about 25 kilometers northwest of the provincial capital), for example, of the 103 *yi* "stockades" identified in its profile, 82 are said to have become submissive (*ting fu*) whereas the other 21 are reported to have remained obstructive (*geng hua*). Similarly, in Lingquan county (located about 30 kilometers northeast of Yining), of the 35 "Zhuang stockades" in the area, 27 are said to have become "tame" (*liang*) whereas 8 are reported to have continued to cause troubles.[35]

In addition to the *Record of the Office of the Supreme Commander*, examples of efforts by Ming officials to distinguish between *min* and *man yi* can also be found in the early-seventeenth-century military handbook *Essential Information for Governing Guangxi (Dian Yue yao zuan)*. For Yang Fang, who as the grand coordinator ordered the compilation of the new work, the presence of a large *man yi* population in Guangxi had obviously continued to be a major source of troubles. To maintain order in the southern border region, according to Yang, what local officials needed was a handbook that gathered together information not only on the size of the government forces and the number of weapons available but also on the geography and distribution of the *man yi* population in the province. Although earlier efforts to compile such information had produced some results, Yang Fang argued, previous handbooks were

---

[34] *Cangwu*, juan 4–6.
[35] For descriptions of the distribution of *man yi* settlements in Guilin, see *Cangwu*, 4:1–6.

ultimately unsatisfactory because the information gathered was either inadequate or not presented in a consistent format. By adopting a more systematic approach, Yang observed, the compilers of the new work were able to produce a set of illustrated profiles that not only took into account the latest changes in the configuration of *man yi* settlements but also proved to be more convenient for officials to use.[36]

Compared to the *Record*, the *Essential Information* was clearly meant to serve a more specific function. Divided into four sections (*juan*) and organized according to the administrative structure of the province, the new handbook is composed of a series of illustrations (*tu*) and profiles (*tu shuo*) that is no doubt aimed at providing local officials a quick introduction to the military problems of each administrative area in Guangxi. Included in each profile are a short description of the administrative area in question, the types and numbers of soldiers available, the amounts of grain and silver necessary to support them, as well as an inventory of the weapons on hand. In the short description included in each profile, it is not uncommon for the compilers to mention some of the more important geographic features of the area, the size and distribution of the local *man yi* population, the origins and extent of the military problems in the jurisdiction, and the arrangements that have been put in place to resolve them. As in the case for the *Record*, information in *Essential Information* is most detailed for areas in the eastern half of Guangxi where the centralizing state had established a relatively strong presence. In the profile for Quan Zhou, for example, it is reported that while there were periodic disorders in the northern and eastern sections of the subprefecture, it was in the general area of Xiyan in the west that the "Yao" were particularly troublesome. It was for this reason, according to the compilers, that the number of soldiers assigned to the Xiyan police office was far greater than those for the police offices elsewhere in Quan Zhou. As well, in the case of Guanyang county, it is noted that although the administrative area was in general a "joyful land" (*le tu*) – where nine out of every ten so-called Yao people had been transformed into law-abiding subjects – troubles still remain in the western part of the county. Descriptions such as those of Quan Zhou and Guanyang were obviously not meant to be comprehensive; what they convey is a particular set of concerns local officials shared as they sought to maintain a semblance of order in the southern border region.[37]

But what makes the *Essential Information* particularly noteworthy is not so much its texts but its maps. Especially when compared with the

---

[36] For the rationale of the new compilation, see *DYYZ*, preface:1–5, 1:1–2.
[37] For Quan Zhou, see *DYYZ*, 1:27–28a; for Guanyang, see *DYYZ*, 1:29–30a.

schematic drawings found in the *Record* and in most local gazetteers of the time, the illustrations in the new handbook are exceptional for their level of details if not necessarily for their accuracy. At least two points should be made about these visual representations. First, the compilation of the maps was evidently undertaken with great seriousness. According to the compilers of the *Essential Information*, the project was conducted in two stages. First, draft versions were collected from local officials for each of the counties and subprefectures in the province. Then, to standardize the format, senior provincial officials were convened to discuss and revise each of the submissions. The maps resulted thus not only reflect a level of firsthand observations by local officials but also exhibit a high degree of coherence. The second point one should make about the illustrations has to do with the techniques adopted. In contrast with the authors of most local gazetteers of the Ming period, the compilers of the *Essential Information* were clearly conscious of their use of cartographic symbols. As explained in the notes on conventions (*tu li*) included in the handbook, a set of rules has been applied uniformly to the composition of the maps: government offices are represented by standing rectangles, military forts (*bao*) by circles, strategic passes (*ai*) by horizontal rectangles, *min* villages by long ovals, and the "haunts" of the so-called Yao and Zhuang by a shape "neither square nor round." Although the illustrations in the new handbook may not be considered accurate by present-day standards, it is evident that the compilers did make an effort to map out in considerable details the distribution of *min* and *man yi* settlements in the southern border region.[38]

To appreciate the significance of the maps included in the new handbook, it is useful to draw some comparisons. Consider, again, the case of Quan Zhou. Figure 4.2 shows a map of the subprefecture found in the 1599 edition of the provincial gazetteer. Although the map does indicate the relative locations of various important administrative and geographic features – the walled city, the sub-administrative units of cantons (*xiang*; in circles), rivers and mountains, military forts, police offices, and so on – it is not difficult to understand why Yang Fang and others would prefer producing an updated version of the map. In the illustration of Quan Zhou found in the *Essential Information* (Figure 4.3), not only do the compilers consider it worthwhile to indicate – in addition to the features included in the 1599 map – the locations of the local courier (*yi*) and postal relay (*pu*) stations, they obviously also find it important to identify (by diamonds) the distribution of the so-called Yao people in the area.

---

[38] For the process of compilation, see *DYYZ*, 1:1b–2. For explanations of the symbols used, see *DYYZ*, 1:4. For a discussion of the use of legends in Ming-dynasty maps, see Brook, "Gazetteer Cartography of Ye Chunji."

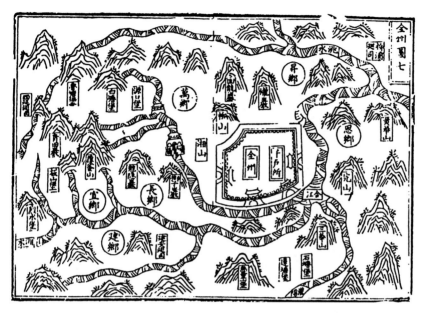

Figure 4.2. Quan Zhou (1599). *Source: GXTZ* (1599), following the prefaces.

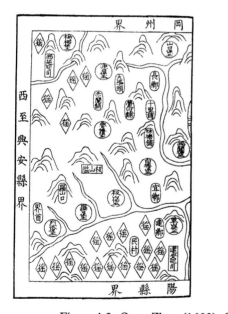
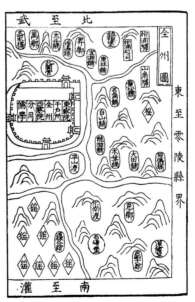

Figure 4.3. Quan Zhou (1602). *Source: DYYZ*, juan 1, before ye 27.

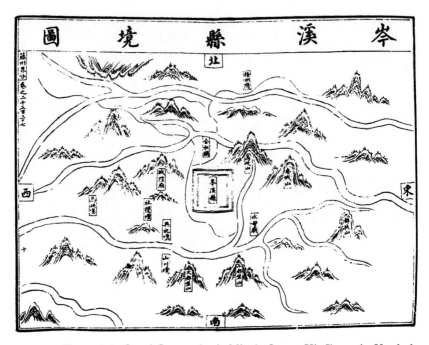

Figure 4.4. Cenxi County (early Ming). *Source:* Xie Jin et al., *Yongle da dian,* 2337:10.

Consider also the case of Cenxi county in Wuzhou prefecture. Again, as can be seen in Figures 4.4 through 4.6, neither the map preserved in the *Yongle Encyclopedia* (*Yongle da dian;* 1408) nor the one included in the 1599 edition of the provincial gazetteer of Guangxi comes close to offering the level of detail found in the map of Cenxi in the *Essential Information.* The last of the three illustrations is noteworthy also because it corresponds quite closely to the geographical descriptions found not only in the 1602 handbook but also in the 1599 provincial gazetteer. Although the maps in the *Essential Information* are in many ways unique, the practice of identifying the distribution of *man yi* settlements would apparently be taken up by the compilers of later gazetteers. In the case of Cenxi county, even though the illustration included in the 1631 edition of the *Gazetteer of Wuzhou Prefecture* (see Figure 4.7) is not as visually complex as the map in the 1602 handbook, it does indicate (by small circles) the relative locations of the "Yao" and "Zhuang" peoples in the area.[39]

---

[39] For the profile of Cenxi, see *DYYZ,* 2:48–49a. For the descriptions in the provincial gazetteer, see *GXTZ* (1599), 33:56–61.

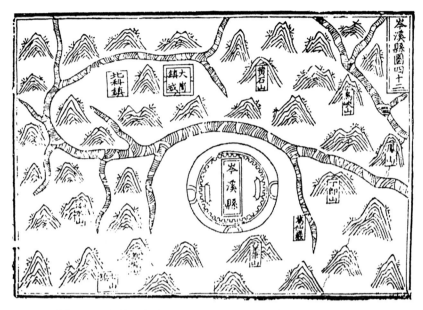

Figure 4.5. Cenxi County (1599). *Source: GXTZ* (1599), following the prefaces.

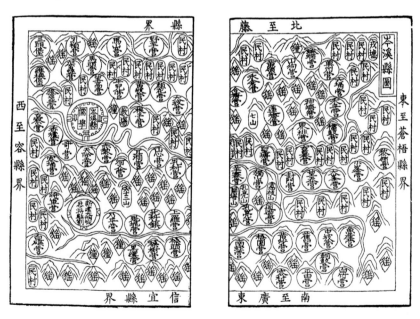

Figure 4.6. Cenxi County (1602). *Source: DYYZ* (1602), juan 2, before ye 48.

Figure 4.7. Cenxi County (1631). *Source:* Xie Junwei et al., *Wu zhou fu zhi*, 1:6b–7a.

Even though it is not always easy to determine how accurate the maps found in our sources were (or were meant to be), it is evident that, by the seventeenth century, officials in the southern border region were able in some cases to indicate fairly precisely the locations of individual *man yi* settlements. For example, in the 1631 edition of the gazetteer of Wuzhou prefecture noted earlier, the compilers actually include in a section titled "Yao Settlements" (*yao dong*) a detailed list of place names where peoples identified as Yao, Zhuang, and Lang were said to reside. The list is note-worthy for several reasons. First, the place names are arranged accord-ing to the administrative structure of the prefecture. It was no doubt the intention of the compilers that interested officials should be able to find out easily from the list where individual *man yi* populations were located in any given administrative area in the prefecture. Second, not only were the compilers able to point out quite specifically the locations of individual *man yi* populations (sometimes to the point of identifying the cantons and wards [*du*] in which the "Yao," "Zhuang," or "Lang" groups in question could be found), they were sometimes able also to provide an estimate of the population of individual *man yi* settlements. Third, although some of the groups identified are reported to have been "pacified" and have begun delivering taxes to the government, they were obviously still considered by Ming officials as distinct from the registered *min* of the state.[40]

Boundaries of order

To understand how the extension of the centralizing state during the Ming period managed to reinforce – rather than erase – the perceived distinctions between *min* and *man yi*, let us consider as our last example the case of Zhaoping.

For Ming officials, the creation in 1576 of a new county seat at Zhaoping ("glory and peace") along the Fu River was clearly something of a triumph. As in the case of the Rattan Gorge region, the Fu River area, which lay between Guilin and Wuzhou prefectures, had long been regarded by officials as strategic but highly troublesome. In his 1465–66 campaign against the "Yao" of the Rattan Gorge discussed earlier, for instance, as part of his plan to restore order in Guangxi, Han Yong apparently found it necessary to first lead his troops to the Fu River region to suppress the bandits there. Likewise, in 1517, in response to the continual unrest along the River, Chen Jin, the supreme commander, concluded that a major campaign was once again necessary. As a result of the military operation, according to the records, more than seventy-five hundred "bandits" from the area were either slaughtered or captured. To extend its administrative reach in the Fu River region, the Ming state did create, in 1477, a subprefectural seat at Yongan ("perpetual peace"; about 50 kilometers south of the prefectural capital of Pingle). But it was not until almost a century later, following a series of military campaigns led first by the grand coordinator Guo Yingpin and later by his successor Wu Wenhua, that a county seat was established at Zhaoping (to the east of Yongan on the west bank of the River) and that peace and order in the area were declared by the state.[41]

For the officials in charge, the creation of the county of Zhaoping was part of a broader strategy to establish a new order in the Fu River region. Following the 1572–73 campaign led by Guo Yingpin, in which some sixty thousand regular and native soldiers were said to have taken part and close to ten thousand "bandits" were reported to have been killed or captured, it was decided that a two-prong approach was necessary.

---

[40] Xie Junwei et al., *Wuzhou fu zhi*, 2:5–8.
[41] For a general account of the Fu River area, see *GXTZ* (1599), 33:50–53. For Chen Jin, see *Cangwu*, 18:11–12a. For the establishment of Yongan Zhou, see the commemorative essay by Shang Luo (1414–86) in *YXWZ*, 23:20–23. For campaign accounts, see Guo Yingpin, *Xi nan ji shi*, 2:8–15; Wu Wenhua, *Yue xi shu gao*, 1:30–45.

Not only was it important for the state to create a new administrative seat and to appoint an assistant regional commander to coordinate the military affairs in the Fu River region, according to Guo Yingpin and others involved, it was critical also to recruit native chieftains to the area to help restore a degree of order. Native soldiers who agreed to settle in designated locations were each promised ten *mu* (or more than 5,000 square meters) of land and to be exempted, at least for the first two years, from taxation. The objective of such measures was no doubt to encourage settlement in the newly "pacified" area. What is noteworthy is that even as officials sought to extend the administrative and military apparatuses of the centralizing state, they also found it necessary to continue to recognize the special roles of native chiefs and soldiers.[42]

As far as Ming officials were concerned, the military campaigns of the 1570s had produced welcome changes. According to the compilers of the 1617 edition of the *Gazetteer of Zhaoping County*, ever since the end of the wars and the creation of the administrative seat in 1576, the area of Zhaoping had indeed attained a level of peace. Although most of the Yao and Zhuang people in the area had been eradicated as a result of the military operations, according to the compilers, those who had remained had been recruited by well-to-do *min* households to serve as their tenants. As part of the efforts by officials to extend the reach of the state, not only had a "yellow register" (*huang ce*) been compiled for the local population not long after the county had been established, a careful survey of the land – during which "the land of the *min* was returned to the *min* [and] the hills of the Zhuang were returned to the Zhuang" – had also been conducted by the end of the sixteenth century. As a result, not only did Ming officials now have a record of the registered households in the area, they were also able to determine the amount of taxes owed the state.[43]

But the creation of the county of Zhaoping did not bring an end to the troubles in the area. Over time, some of the so-called Zhuang people would decide – for reasons not clearly explained in the records – that they were no longer willing to serve as tenants of *min* landlords. For instance, in a case first noted in the 1617 county gazetteer, a certain Zhuang "scoundrel" (*jian*) Wei Gongxin was accused of inciting others to claim ownership of the land under their cultivation and to withhold rents from their landlords. As a result, according to a petition submitted in 1637 by a local county student, *min* landlords who had been deprived

---

[42] For the campaign of 1572–73 and its aftermath, see Guo Yingpin, *Xi nan ji shi*, 2:8–15.
[43] Excerpts of the *Gazetteer of Zhaoping County* can be found in Li Shunan et al., *Zhaoping xian zhi*, 7:23. A preface to the 1617 gazetteer is preserved in Chen Xiangyin and Qin Yongjiang, *Guangxi fang zhi yi shu kao lu*, 330–31.

of their incomes (but who were still responsible for the taxes owed to the state) had been living in dire straits: "Those who were once rich are now poor, those who are poor but abled have fled, and those who are old and weak are left to die." The troubles brought by Wei Gongxin, according to the petition, were compounded by the corruption of individual officials, who were all too willing to exploit the false claims for their own gains. If the encroachments by Wei Gongxin and others were left unchecked, the county student warned in his petition, no *min* households in the area would have any hope for survival. Although the case of Zhaoping would in time be resolved in favor of the *min* landlords, it seems clear that just as Ming officials sought to create a new order in the area as they extended the reach of the centralizing state, they also inadvertently engendered a new set of disorder.[44]

Over time, as we have seen, Ming officials had found it increasingly important, especially in areas where the government had extended its regular administrative apparatus, to distinguish between people who were registered, tax-paying subjects and those remained outside the state's formal administrative structure. But although officials would at times trace the disorder and violence in Guangxi to corrupt administrators and unscrupulous *min*, most officials would readily argue that the presence of a large *man yi* population in the southern border region was itself a major source of problems for the centralizing state. Indeed, for many late-Ming observers who followed with interests the goings-on in Zhaoping, the troubles brought by Wei Gongxin must have served to confirm their perception of the inherent unruliness of the *man yi*. But the demarcation of *min* and *man yi* must not be understood simply in the context of administrative control. As we will see in the following chapter, over time, representatives and agents of the centralizing state would find it increasingly important not only to reinforce the perceived boundaries between "Chinese" and "non-Chinese" but also to identify and categorize the "non-Chinese" populations.

---

[44] For the case of Wei Gongxin, see Li Shunan et al., *Zhaoping xian zhi*, 7:23–5; for the quotation, see 7:24a.

5 Culture of demarcation

> Unlike the *wo* in the south, the *lu* in the north, and the *fan* in the west, each of whom has primarily one set of customs, the various *yi* in the southwest are not only numerous in type but are also distinct in their customs and practices.
>
> Wang Shixing, *Record of Extensive Travels* (pref. 1593)

In the winter of 1452–53, a memorial was submitted to the Jingtai emperor by the supreme commander of Guangdong and Guangxi concerning the southern border region. According to Wang Ao (1384–1467), who had been appointed to the newly created post in part as a response to the uprising of Huang Xiaoyang in 1449–50, the trouble with the region was that local officials were ill-prepared for the task of pacifying the native people (*tu ren*). Wang Ao observed that even though the natives there were "not of the same variety" (*zhong lei fei yi*) – among the different *zhong lei* he identified were *sheng* Yao, *shu* Yao, Zhuang, Kuan, Ling, and Lao – and that their languages and clothing were distinct from those common in the central dominion, their temperament was not dissimilar to that of the registered subjects (*min*) of the state. The primary concern of the *tu ren*, according to Wang Ao, was their own livelihood. It was not the disposition (*ben xin*) of the natives to rebel; only when they were pushed (by unscrupulous officials, in particular), Wang observed, would they band together to cause troubles.[1]

What is interesting about Wang Ao's memorial is in part his position as the highest-ranking official in the southern provinces and in part his diagnosis of the problem. As some of his contemporaries, Wang attributed the disorder in the southern border region not to the allegedly rebellious nature of the native population but to the incompetence and corruption of local officials. Born into a family of relatively modest means from northern China, Wang Ao had demonstrated throughout his career

---

[1] For Wang Ao's memorial, see *Cangwu*, 29:1–4a; *GXTZ* (1599), 38:8–9; *YXWZ*, 5:6a–9a. For the uprising of Huang Xiaoyang (Huang Hsiao-yang), see *DMB*, 659–61.

that he was just as concerned about the lapses of fellow officials as he was about the unruliness of the people. In early 1440, for instance, as an assistant censor-in-chief, Wang was assigned to assist in a military campaign against a group of native rebels in northwest Sichuan. On arrival, Wang Ao concluded immediately that it was the local military commissioner and his accomplices who were responsible for inciting the rebellion. Not only did Wang manage to have the officials in question punished, according to the records, he was able also to quickly pacify the rebels. Although Wang Ao's relatively benevolent attitude toward the "non-Chinese" natives might not be universally shared, when court officials went searching for "a minister of high standing" to take charge of the military affairs in the southern border region after the devastating rebellion of Huang Xiaoyang, Wang appeared to be the right person at the right time.[2]

But what is just as noteworthy about Wang Ao's memorial is his demarcation and categorization of the peoples in the southern border region. To be sure, Wang's classification of the "Yao" into *sheng* and *shu* (in the sense of "wild" versus "tame," or "savage" versus "civilized") was neither original nor particularly informative. The formulation had evidently been used by the Khitans with regard to the Jurchens in as early as the tenth century, and it had been adopted, in reference to the "Yao" of Guangxi, by the Yuan-dynasty official Yu Ji (1272–1348) in a military campaign account written a century before Wang Ao's time. But even though Wang shared neither the assumptions nor analytical tools associated with modern-day ethnographers, his demarcation and categorization of the native population is a clear reminder that Ming officials were increasingly interested in distinguishing among the "non-Chinese" population. As the centralizing state sought to extend its reach in the south, more and more officials and travelers from the central plains also took to the roads and recorded their observations of the peoples of the southern border zone. The increasingly detailed categorization of the *man yi* population of course does not necessarily indicate an advancement of knowledge on the part of Ming observers. What it does demonstrate is the growing desire by the representatives and agents of the state to reinforce a system of differences through not only textual studies or fanciful imaginations but also – more and more importantly – firsthand observations.[3]

---

[2] For Wang Ao's biography, see *MS*, 177.4699–702; *DMB*, 1340–43. For the rebellion in Sichuan, see *MSL, Yingzong shi lu*, 62.1174–75, 1179–80; *MS*, 311.8027. For Wang's appointment as supreme commander, see the memorial by Yu Qian in *YXWZ*, 5:3–6a; *GXTZ* (1531), 55:10–11; *Cangwu*, 17:11.

[3] For the early uses of the categories *sheng* and *shu*, see Mote, *Imperial China*, 211 ff. For Yu Ji's account, see his *Daoyuan xue gu lu*, 38.336–39; *YXWZ*, 35:1–9a. The term *shu yao*

Demarcating *hua* and *yi*

As we have seen, in addition to generic labels such as *man* and *yi*, Ming officials would also identify the so-called non-Chinese in the southern borderland by more specific appellations. But before we examine this phenomenon, let us consider one obvious but hugely difficult question: how did people who are identified in the records as *man yi* refer to themselves? Unfortunately, evidence is scant. In the 1599 edition of the *General Gazetteer of Guangxi*, it is reported that people known by officials as Gelao and Donglao "would falsely call themselves 'Yao' whenever they venture out to plunder." This relatively cryptic reference raises a number of interesting questions. Did members of the so-called Gelao and Donglao decide to misrepresent themselves because they wanted people identified as Yao to be blamed for their plundering? Or did they choose to pass themselves off as Yao because they believed they would then be perceived as more fearsome? And what, after all, were the actual words spoken by such Gelao and Donglao when they referred to themselves as Yao? We do not know the answers to these and many other equally intriguing questions. But what is clear is that the categorization of "non-Chinese" was not solely the work of the representatives and agents of the centralizing state; even people who were so identified would come to take advantage of the proliferation of *man yi* labels.[4]

To understand how Ming officials went about demarcating and categorizing the population in the southern border zone, let us consider the highly interesting work *Record of Things Heard on the Torrid Frontier* by Tian Rucheng. Although as a native son of Hangzhou in the lower Yangzi region Tian might seem an unlikely candidate to be our guide to the southern borderland, he did serve for a relatively long time in the provinces of Guangdong and Guangxi. As an assistant administration commissioner of Guangxi from 1538 to 1541, Tian Rucheng in fact helped coordinate two major military campaigns in the region, one against some native chieftains near the border with Annam, the other against the so-called Yao bandits in the Rattan Gorge area. In compiling the *Record of Things Heard*, Tian was clear what he wanted to accomplish. Because most of the troubles in the southern border zone could be traced to the *man yi*, according to Tian Rucheng, it would be helpful for local officials to have as a reference an account of previous efforts to bring order to the region. And because different groups of *man yi* would be "civilized" at different paces,

was also used in the Ming period to refer generically to those *man yi* who functioned as intermediaries between local officials and the area's *sheng* population; see, for example, Tang Shunzhi, *Guang you zhan gong lu*.
[4] For the claims by Gelao and Donglao, see *GXTZ* (1599), 33:3.

Tian explained, it would be useful also for him to offer an overview of the variety of *man yi* in the region. In his work, not only does Tian recount at length fourteen episodes of borderland confrontations – among which are the military campaigns against the native domain of Tianzhou (see Chapter 3) and the "Yao" of the Rattan Gorge (Chapter 4) – he also includes detailed descriptions of nineteen major categories of *man yi*: Miao, Luoluo, Gelao, Mulao, Yanghuang, Zhongjia, Songjia, Caijia, Mangjia, Longjia, Ranjia, Bo, Dòng, Yao, Zhuang, Lao, Li, Dan, and Ma. Of the "peoples" so identified, according to Tian Rucheng, many could be further differentiated on the basis of specific customs or physical appearance. It is unclear how Tian came up with his cataloging scheme. Although Tian Rucheng obviously drew from writings of earlier periods, as we will see, he seems to have also included information derived from firsthand observations.[5]

Even though the catalog compiled by Tian Rucheng is in many ways noteworthy, the increased demarcation and categorization of the population in the southern border zone is probably best observed by comparing and contrasting a wide range of official and unofficial sources. For the case of Guangxi, consider the findings in Table 5.1. Among the texts cited are the memorial by Wang Ao discussed earlier, the three editions of the provincial gazetteer, the 1602 military handbook *Essential Information for Governing Guangxi*, and three "miscellaneous" writings by officials who once served in the province. To be sure, the majority of the sources included are by nature anecdotal. Neither Wang Ao nor even Tian Rucheng, for instance, set out to compile a comprehensive list of *man yi* active in Guangxi. (In the case of Tian, I have included in the table only those groups of *man yi* he explicitly identified as present in the southern province.) Even in the cases of Wang Shixing and Wei Jun (js. 1604), the cataloging schemes adopted are probably best understood as mental tools rather than as reflections of reality. But despite the limitations of the sources, it seems clear from the pattern observed in the table that there was indeed a growing tendency among Ming officials to identify and categorize the native population in the southern border zone.

To observe this trend, let us examine more closely the relevant sections in the three provincial gazetteers. Consider first the 1493 edition. Although the full text of this first-ever provincial gazetteer of Guangxi is no longer extant, in a preface to the work that has survived,

---

[5] For Tian Rucheng (T'ian Ju-ch'eng), see *MS*, 287.7372; *DMB*, 1286–88. For his rationale, see *YJJW*, preface:1–2a, 4:22–23a. For Tian's cataloging scheme, see *YJJW*, 4:11–22a. For a discussion of some of the *man yi* groups, see Hostetler, *Qing Colonial Enterprise*, 136–37, 141–46.

Table 5.1. *Categories of "non-Chinese" in Guangxi, 1452–1612*

		1452	1493	1531	1558	1593	1599	1602	1612
Yao	猺	•	•	•	•	•	•	•	•
Zhuang	獞	•	•	•	•	•	•	•	•
Lao	獠	•	•	•	•		•[a]		•
Ling	狑	•	•		•	•	•	•	•
Kuan	欵	•							
Man of Guangyuan	廣源蠻			•[b]			•		•
Man of Xiyuan	西原蠻			•			•		•
Dan	蜑/蜒				•		•		•
Dong	狪					•	•	•	•
Yin	狋					•	•		
Lang	狼					•		•	
Yang	羘					•			
Banyizhongnü	斑衣種女						•		•
Daliang	大良						•		•
Shanzi	山子						•		•
Dàn	狚							•	•
Di	狄							•	
Miao	苗							•	
Bing	狝								•
Ge	仡								•

Sources:
1452: *Cangwu*, 29:1–4.
1493: *GXTZ* (1531), "Guangxi jiu zhi xu," 3–4.
1531: *GXTZ* (1531), 53:1–2.
1558: *YJJW*, 2:1b-2a, 4:18b–22a.
1593: Wang Shixing, *Guang you zhi*, shang.216–18.
1599: *GXTZ* (1599), 33:1–4a
1602: *DYYZ*
1612: Wei Jun, *Xi shi er*, 8:9–13.
[a] The text distinguishes between two types of *lao*: Gelao and Donglao.
[b] The text identifies also other *man* groups (e.g. *Man* of Fushui) that were apparently active during the Song dynasty.

Cheng Tinggong (js. 1475), an administration vice commissioner, notes that in Guangxi just as there are four types of *min* (i.e., scholars, farmers, artisans, and merchants), there are also four categories of *yi*: Yao, Zhuang, Lao, and Ling. Among the "non-Chinese," Cheng distinguishes between those who are *shu*, or who "offer taxes and fulfill corvée duties," and those who are *sheng*, who "practice pillaging and looting." Although it is unclear from this preface alone how much firsthand knowledge Cheng Tinggong had about the "non-Chinese" in the southern province, together with

Wang Ao's memorial a few decades earlier, his remarks do suggest that the categorization of the native population in Guangxi into "Yao," "Zhuang," "Lao," and "Ling" had by the fifteenth century become a fairly common practice.[6]

The categorization of the native population in Guangxi evidently underwent only minor changes in the 1531 provincial gazetteer. As in the case of Cheng Tinggong, the compilers of the new edition also divided the "non-Chinese" population in the province into four major categories. But rather than recognize "Ling" as a discrete type, the compilers of the 1531 gazetteer opted to identify *Man* (as in *Man* of Guangyuan, *Man* of Xiyuan, etc.) as a distinct category. What is noteworthy about this edition of the provincial gazetteer is that even though the compilers clearly made an effort to bring up to date the history of borderland conflicts, their descriptions of the four major *yi* groups are almost all quotations from sources dated before the Ming. For the compilers of the gazetteer, although it was important to acknowledge the differences among the native population and to learn to deal with its threats, precise description and categorization were apparently not high priorities.[7]

By contrast, the categorization of the native population in Guangxi clearly underwent significant changes in the 1599 edition of the provincial gazetteer. In contrast to his predecessors, Su Jun, the compiler of the new edition, divided the "non-Chinese" in Guangxi into not four but eleven major categories. In addition to Yao (whom Su Jun further classified into *sheng* and *shu*, as well as "white" and "black"), Zhuang, Lao (Gelao and Donglao), Ling, and *Man* (*Man* of Xiyuan, *Man* of Guangyuan, etc.), the compiler of the 1599 gazetteer also identified as major *yi* groups Yin, Dong, Dan, Shanzi, Banyizhongnü, and Daliang. Although some of these categories had appeared in Tang- and Song-dynasty records, others were evidently relatively recent inventions. More significant, the descriptions of the *yi* in the 1599 edition of the provincial gazetteer are not simply recycled from earlier sources; even in the cases of the so-called Yao and Zhuang, one could find nuggets of information that seem to have been derived from observations.[8]

To observe this firsthand pattern of increased demarcation and categorization, let us examine more closely also the early-seventeenth-century military handbook *Essential Information for Governing Guangxi*. As can be seen from the maps included in the work, not only were the compilers

---

[6] For the preface by Cheng Tinggong, see *GXTZ* (1531), "Guangxi jiu zhi xu," 3–4.
[7] *GXTZ* (1531), 53:1–3a.
[8] *GXTZ* (1599), 33:1–4.

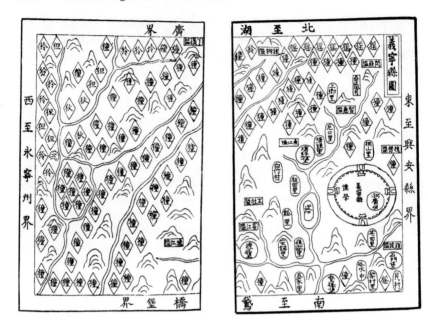

Figure 5.1. Yining County (1602). *Source: DYYZ*, juan 1, before ye 23.

interested in distinguishing between *min* and *man yi* settlements (see Chapter 4), they were also keen on differentiating among the native population. In the map of Yining county of Guilin (see Figure 5.1), not only do the compilers identify a large number of Yao and Zhuang settlements, they also recognize the presence of those of Ling, Dàn, and Di (the appearance of the label "Di" is curious because it is almost always used in Ming-dynasty records to refer to the "non-Chinese" in the northern border zone). Similarly, in the map of Huaiyuan county of Liuzhou (see Figure 5.2), in addition to Yao and Zhuang settlements, the compilers also recognize the presence of those of Miao and Dong. In all, eight categories of *man yi* are identified in the handbook. Although in general the contents of these illustrations should not be interpreted literally – for instance, the proliferation of "Yao" settlements in the map of Yongning Zhou (see Figure 5.3) is clearly something of an anomaly, especially given the fact that almost all other sources of the time testify to the domination of the area by the "Zhuang" – these maps do provide a glimpse of how late-Ming officials visualize the southern border zone.[9]

---

[9] For descriptions of Yining, Huaiyuan, and Yongning, see *DYYZ*, 1:23–24a, 41, 21–22a, respectively.

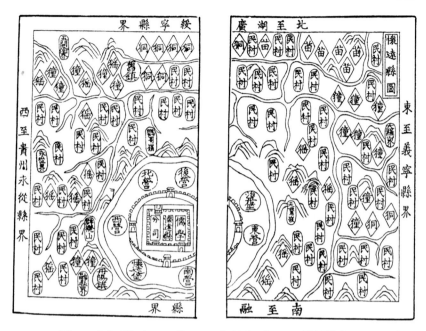

Figure 5.2. Huaiyuan County (1602). *Source: DYYZ*, juan 1, before ye 40.

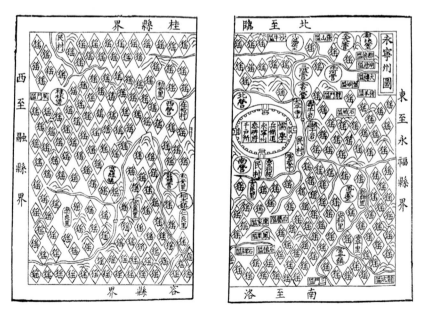

Figure 5.3. Yongning Zhou (1602). *Source: DYYZ*, juan 1, before ye 21.

But what is noteworthy about Table 5.1 is not simply the pattern of increased demarcation and categorization. What is interesting is also the fact that not a few of the categories identified have appeared in Chinese records only since the Ming period. Consider, for example, the case of "Ling." Although as a label "Ling" has appeared in the compound forms "Geling" and "Linglao" since at least the Song dynasty, its usage as a stand-alone appellation seems to have originated in the Ming. In one of the earliest references to the category (dated 1443), Jie Ji, an administration commissioner of Guangxi, was quick to liken the Ling with the Yao and the Zhuang. Not only did the Ling live deep in the mountains, far away from the direct control of local authorities, according to Jie Ji, they also dedicated themselves to plundering and killing. Although the Ling are recognized in the 1493 provincial gazetteer as one of the four major *yi* groups in Guangxi, information about them is limited and at times contradictory. For example, in Tian Rucheng's *Record of Things Heard*, not only are the Ling described as being accustomed to living in the open in the remote mountain valleys in central Guangxi, they are also said to resemble chimpanzees in appearance, speak an incomprehensible language, and practice food-gathering and hunting for their living. "Even the Yao nearby cannot understand them." By contrast, in a gazetteer of Qingyuan prefecture dated to the late Ming or early Qing, the Ling in the area are described as a variant (*bie zhong*) of the Zhuang – "their temperament, customs, diets, dwellings, clothing, tools, weddings, funerals, ceremonies, and sacrifices are all the same as those of the Zhuang" – and are said to have been offering taxes to the state. Although it is tempting to dismiss the different depictions as the works of confused observers, it might be more useful to think of "Ling" a relatively flexible category that acquired different meanings in different contexts.[10]

Consider also the case of "Shanzi." Unlike people identified as the Ling, who were ostensibly present in many parts of Guangxi, those who were referred to as Shanzi ("mountain people") were apparently active primarily in the area of Nanning prefecture. In the early 1520s, Wang Ji, who was an assistant magistrate of Heng Zhou, reported that there lived in the mountains near the administrative seat a population called Shanzi, who not only spoke a language different from Chinese (*hua*) but

[10] For Jie Ji's report, see *MSL, Yingzong shi lu*, 108.2192. For Tian Rucheng's depiction, see *YJJW*, 2:1b–2a; the quotation is from 2:2a. The descriptions attributed to *Qingyuan fu zhi* (now lost) are found in *YXCZ*, 24:11a. To add to the confusion, elsewhere in the gazetteer, the Ling are apparently said to be a *bie zhong* of the Yao (see *YXCZ*, 24:11b). In the 1733 edition of the *General Gazetteer of Guangxi*, it is suggested that the Ling were so named because they constituted a distinct (*ling wai*) group of *yi* (see *GXTZ* [1733], 92:7b). For a discussion, see Fan Honggui, "Tan tan Ling ren."

also dressed and wore their hair in styles that set them apart from the regular population. Purportedly first brought into submission (in the official parlance, "summoned and soothed" [*zhao fu*]) by a guard commander earlier in the Ming dynasty, the Shanzi, according to Wang Ji, had since lived in relative peace. They engaged in farming, weaving, and logging, and they entered periodically into town to trade. Men and women of the Shanzi type were said to enjoy mating in the open – in the 1564 edition of the *Gazetteer of Nanning Prefecture*, the mating practices of the Shanzi are reported to "resemble those of beasts" – but unlike other *man yi* populations, according to Wang Ji, Shanzi families did employ go-betweens to arrange for marriages.[11]

Other categories of *man yi* that appeared for the first time in the Chinese records include "Dong" and "Bing." As in the case of the Ling, information on the so-called Dong and Bing peoples is limited and at times contradictory. In the gazetteer of Qingyuan prefecture mentioned earlier, it is noted that the Dong and the Bing are simply *bie zhong* of the Yao. Not only are they "by nature ruthless and violent," according to the gazetteer, "when they pay visits to officials, they know nothing of kneeling and bowing but instead sit with their legs crossed as a gesture of respect." By contrast, according to a gazetteer of Huaiyuan county dated most likely to 1592, the customs of the Dong were not that different from that of the Yao or the Zhuang (or, for that matter, the Ling, the Dàn, or the Miao), who were also present in the area. It was the custom of the *yi* peoples in Huaiyuan "to esteem the young and despise the old," according to the gazetteer, and it was their practice "to not rely on go-betweens [to arrange] for their marriages." To add to the confusion, whereas Wang Shixing would claim in his *Record of Extensive Travels* that "the Ling and the Dong are the same," Wei Jun, in his *Miscellanea of Guangxi* (pref. 1612), would insist that the Dong and the Bing "belong to the same stock [*lei*] as the Lao."[12]

But perhaps the most interesting category of *man yi* that first appeared during the Ming are the so-called Lang people. While some historians have traced the label "Lang" to the term *lang huo* that had evidently been used in the Song dynasty to indicate native headmen, the earliest

[11] For descriptions of the Shanzi, see Wang Ji, *Jun ji tang ri xun shou jing*, 1b–2; Fang Yu, *Nanning fu zhi*, 11:10b–11a.

[12] For the gazetteer of Qingyuan, see *YXCZ*, 24:11b. For the gazetteer of Huaiyuan, see *YXCZ*, 18:18b. For other Ming-period descriptions, see Wang Shixing, *Guang you zhi*, shang.216–18; Wei Jun, *Xi shi er*, 8:9a; *GXTZ* (1599), 33:3b. In the 1733 edition of the *General Gazetteer of Guangxi*, it is suggested that the label "Dong" might have come from the term *dong* that has been used for native settlements in the southern region (*GXTZ* [1733], 92:10a).

extant references to "Lang" (dated to the early fifteenth century) seem to indicate that the appellation was originally adopted by Ming officials to refer specifically to those who constituted the fighting forces of the native chieftains in Guangxi. Although the reasons for this choice of label remain unclear – the remark in the 1733 edition of the provincial gazetteer that the Lang (literally, "wolf") were so named in part because of their disorderliness (*lang ji*) is not particularly enlightening – it seems possible that by the fifteenth century native soldiers had become so dominant and fearsome that they would come to be associated in the mind of Ming officials with the perceived cunning and ferocity of wolves. This affirmation of the prowess of native soldiers can be found, for example, in a 1437 memorial in which the regional commander Shan Yun reports to the court that the residents from the area of Xunzhou have come before him and requested that "wolf soldiers" (*lang bing*), "who are feared by bandits," be recruited to their area to help combat banditry. This recognition of native soldiers as an indispensable – albeit beastly – force can be found also in a 1458 memorial in which the grand coordinator Ye Sheng concludes that "the only ones *man* bandits in Guangxi fear are the native Lang-family soldiers."[13]

By the sixteenth century, the label "Lang" appears to have become a designation of a "people" rather than of just a military population. In a memorial prepared by the Ministry of War in 1546, for instance, it is noted that in Guangxi "half [the population] are Lang people, three-tenths are Yao and Zhuang, and two-tenths are *min*." In this context, "Lang people" (*Lang ren*) was evidently a reference not just to native soldiers but to the entire population under the rule of native chieftains. In the 1577 edition of the *Gazetteer of Taiping Prefecture*, a reference is also made to the Lang *min* of the Left and Right river regions. In this case, the Lang *min* are said to be descendants of "the *yi lao* of the Western Plains," who were apparently active in the area in as early as the Jin period in the third and fourth centuries. In the late sixteenth century, Wang Shixing, in his *Record of Extensive Travels*, reports also that "the folks [*bai xing*] in native prefectures and counties are all Lang *min*." In contrast to other *yi* peoples in Guangxi, Wang Shixing observes,

---

[13] For *lang huo*, see Fan Chengda, *Gui hai yu heng zhi*, 145. On the origins of the label "Lang," see Luo Xianglin, "Lang bing Lang tian kao"; Mo Junqing and Lei Guangzheng, "Lang ren Lang min Lang bing"; Bai Yaotian, "'Lang' kao." I remain unconvinced, however, by the linguistic evidence presented in these otherwise learned studies that seeks to link the label "Lang" to a culturally identifiable population. For association with the term *lang ji*, see *GXTZ* (1733), 92:7. For Shan Yun's memorial, see *MSL, Yingzong shi lu*, 35.673. For Ye Sheng's comment, see his *Ye Wenzhuang gong liang Guang zou cao*, 4:14b. For a more recent discussion, see Su Jianling, "Ming Qing shi qi Zhuang Han min zu," 20–30.

"[in the areas of] clothing, food, and language, [the Lang] are rather similar to the Chinese [*hua*]."[14]

By the late Ming and early Qing, the term *Lang ren* or *Lang min* had apparently come to refer to people who lived in regular administrative areas but who had originally come from the domains of native chieftains. In the 1631 edition of the *Gazetteer of Wuzhou Prefecture*, for instance, it is reported that the Lang *ren* in Wuzhou had initially been recruited to the region in the early sixteenth century to combat banditry. As the area became depopulated, however, the Lang were asked by officials to stay in Wuzhou to take up farming. Similarly, in his *News from Guangdong* (1700), Qu Dajun (1630–96), a poet and well-known Ming loyalist, notes also that the Lang *ren* in Guangdong had originally come from Guangxi to assist in the suppression of local disturbances. Numbering tens of thousands, Qu observes, the Lang "are by nature rather submissive and fearful of the law." Concentrated in the administrative areas of Luoding, Dongan, and Xining (all located in the western part of Guangdong), the Lang are said to have to pay an individual "sword tax" (*dao shui*) to the local authorities. As part of their services, according to Qu Dajun, the Lang "keep watch at the city walls, wash and sweep yamen offices, [and] supply coal and firewood."[15]

As it should be evident, the increased demarcation and categorization of the borderland population in Guangxi was far from a coordinated act. To be sure, the project of demarcation had its own logic: Ming officials interested in differentiating among the *man yi* often did so using place of abode (e.g., Shanzi or "mountain people"), physical appearance (e.g., Banyizhongnü or "women of variegated clothes"), or perceived level of orderliness (e.g., Daliang or "very tame") as their criteria. But as we have seen in the cases of the categories "Ling" and "Dong," when it came to actually defining the distinctions, officials were not always in agreement. But if the demarcation and categorization of the borderland population seems at times arbitrary, it is important to remember that such classifications did have significant ramifications. In the case of the Lang, even though one cannot be certain whether people who are referred to in the records as Lang did identify themselves as such, in time, the so-called Lang people would come to be seen as a collective. And even though "Lang" as a category has not survived the modern period, it was apparently recognized by the Qing state well into the nineteenth century.

---

[14] For the 1546 memorial, see *MSL, Shizong shi lu*, 312.5844. For the Lang *min* of the Left and Right river regions, see Cai Ying'en and Gan Dongyang, *Taiping fu zhi*, 1:1b. For Wang Shixing, see his *Guang you zhi*, shang.218.

[15] For Wuzhou, see Xie Junwei et al., *Wuzhou fu zhi*, 2:8b. For Guangdong, see Qu Dajun, *Guangdong xin yu*, 7.244.

Customs of their own

Just as there was a growing desire or perceived need among officials to identify and categorize the borderland population, there was also an increased interest among them for firsthand observations. Although Ming officials would continue to cite Tang- and Song-dynasty sources in writing about the "non-Chinese" in the southern border region – that the *man yi* were fond of variegated clothing, that they practiced slash-and-burn farming, that they were by nature licentious, that they lacked proper rituals, and so on – in time, many would supplement such stock descriptions with their own observations. Although such writings by Ming officials should not be seen as necessarily more objective or accurate than those from earlier times, together, they do reflect the changing concerns and sensibilities of the cultural elites from the central plains.

Consider, for instance, the evolution of the depiction of the Yao. Even though some historians have traced the so-called Yao people of the Ming period to the Moyao (literally, "without corvée") identified in the seventh-century texts *History of the Liang* (*Liang shu*) and *History of the Sui* (*Sui shu*), it was during the latter half of the Tang dynasty that "Yao" as a stand-alone appellation seems to have first appeared in the records. In one of the earliest references to the Yao as a population, found in the administrative gazetteer *Illustrated Descriptions of the Administrative Regions in the Yuanhe Period* compiled by Li Jifu (758–814), it is reported that in the circuit of Jiangnan (present-day Zhejiang, Jiangxi, Hunan, and Guizhou provinces), there "live a group of *man* named Yao [written with the 'people' radical] who claim that as a result of some worthy acts of their ancestors they are exempted from corvée duties." Whether the people identified as Moyao or Yao in these early works were related to those referred to as Yao (written with the "dog" radical) in the Ming records we cannot say. What is evident is that officials in the Tang period, many of whom would no doubt consider an appointment to the southern region a death sentence, were not especially interested in distinguishing among the *man yi* population; to them, "Moyao" and "Yao" were simply categories of people who did not have to pay taxes or provide corvée duties to the state.[16]

By contrast, by the Song dynasty, especially after 1127 when the imperial court was forced to retreat to south of the Yangzi River and when the region corresponding to present-day Guangxi was increasingly integrated

---

[16] Li Jifu, *Yuanhe jun xian tu zhi*, 29: 1b-2a. For a summary of evidence linking Yao to Moyao, see Okada Koji, *Chūgoku Kanan minzoku*, 64–74. For a dissenting view, see Cushman, "Rebel Haunts and Lotus Huts," 55–59, esp. n. 12. For a discussion of Moyao, see Schafer, *Vermilion Bird*, 51–52.

into the centralizing state, officials would apparently come to associate the label "Yao" with a more specific set of attributes. According to the *Essential Documents of the Song*, which in its present form was principally collated by the Qing-dynasty scholar Xu Song (1781–1848), and the *Comprehensive Study of Important Documents* (1324) by Ma Duanlin (ca. 1254–ca. 1325), people identified as Yao were especially active in areas corresponding to present-day southern Hunan and northern Guangxi. Not only did they not have to pay taxes or provide corvée, the so-called Yao people were also said to have frequently conspired with local *min* landholders to conceal the latter's actual landholdings.[17]

Even more noteworthy no doubt are the depictions of the Yao by Fan Chengda. According to Fan's *Descriptions of Forests and Marshes of the Gui Region* (1175), of which a significant portion has fortunately been preserved in Ma Duanlin's *Comprehensive Study*, the Yao were in fact descendants of Panhu, the legendary dog of the mythical Emperor Ku, which had since the early imperial period been frequently attributed as the progenitor of the *man yi* in the southern region.[18] According to Fan Chengda, the Yao clearly had their own way of life:

They live high and deep in mountains that spread across thousands of *li* in the midst of Ba, Shu, Hu, and Guang [i.e. present-day Sichuan, Guizhou, Hunan, and Guangxi]. Their hair is bundled in the style of a mallet, their feet are bare, and their clothing is variegated and coarse. Even though they are named Yao [a pun on the term for corvée], they in fact do not provide any corvée.... They use *mu ye* [clay] to cover their huts, and they grow a combination of rice, *shu*-millet, *su*-millet, beans, and taro for food. They break apart bamboo tubes for cooking. In their spare time, they hunt for wild animals to supplement their diet.[19]

The Yao, apparently, also had an unusual temperament:

It is the custom [of the Yao] to kill for revenge. They are suspicious by nature and are not afraid to die. They can also endure hunger when they are away fighting. [When at war it is the practice of the Yao] to wear at the waist a long sword on the left and a big cross-bow on the right and to hold in the hands a long spear. They run up and down the mountains as if they could fly. As soon as a child can walk, [the Yao] heat up a piece of metal to sear the heels to benumb them so that the child can step on thorny bushes without getting hurt. When a son is born, his weight is measured, and the same weight of metal is soaked in poison. Once the

---

[17] Xu Song et al., *Song hui yao ji gao*, 198.68–72; Ma Duanlin, *Wen xian tong kao*, 328.2574–75.

[18] For the myth of Panhu, see Fan Ye et al, *Hou Han shu*, 86.2829–30.

[19] Ma Duanlin, *Wen xian tong gao*, 328.2575; Fan Chengda, *Gui hai yu heng zhi*, 141.

son grows up, the metal [that has been set aside] would be wrought into a sword for him to use for the rest of his life.[20]

What were particularly vile about the Yao, in Fan's view, were their social customs:

At the start of each year, they would offer sacrifices to Panhu by mixing fish, meat, wine, and rice in a wooden bucket. As part of their ritual they would cover the bucket and shout. On the first day of the tenth month, individual settlements would offer sacrifices to the Great King of Dubei [a mythical figure]. Young men and women would form separate rows and dance hand-in-hand in a custom called "the Stepping of Yao." When both [a man and a woman] are willing, the man will break into laughter and run to the women's side and take his beloved away to become husband and wife. [Marriage] is not left to the [discretion] of the parents. Those who cannot find a mate would have to wait for the following year. If a woman has no direction [i.e., remains unmatched] in two years, her parents might want to kill her for not being wanted.[21]

According to Fan Chengda, the Yao would emerge frequently from their settlements to pillage and loot. Although initially such attacks would take place only when famines struck, in time the Yao would apparently attack even when they enjoyed good harvests. In Fan's view, the suppression of Yao bandits was made all the more difficult not only because they were often assisted by *min* collaborators but also because after their lootings the Yao could often elude the government forces by quickly dispersing into the mountains.[22]

The depiction of the Yao by Fan Chengda is especially interesting not only because it helped establish "Yao" as a clearly identifiable category of *man yi* but also because it would form the basis of much of the portrayal of the Yao in later Chinese accounts. For example, in the 1531 edition of the *General Gazetteer of Guangxi*, the descriptions of the Yao are explicitly stated as taken from Fan's *Descriptions of Forests and Marshes*:

Originally found in the areas of Xing'an, Yining, and Gutian of Jingjiang as well as Rongshui and Huaiyuan of Rong Zhou [in present-day northeast Guangxi], [the Yao] are born deep in the mountains and up the rivers. Many are surnamed Pan. Their hair is bundled in the style of a mallet and their feet are bare. They pay no taxes and provide no corvée. They grow a mixture of rice, beans, and taro

---

[20] *Ma Duanlin, Wen xian tong kao*, 328.2575; Fan Chengda, *Gui hai yu heng zhi*, 141–42.

[21] Ma Duanlin, *Wen xian tong gao*, 328.2575; Fan Chengda, *Gui hai yu heng zhi*, 142.

[22] Ma Duanlin, *Wen xian tong gao*, 328.2575; Fan Chengda, *Gui hai yu heng zhi*, 143. For Fan Chengda's tenure in Guangxi (1173–75), see Yu Beishan, *Fan Chengda nian pu*, 167–214. For his travel writings, see Hargett, *On the Road in Twelfth Century China*. For his informal jottings, see *Fan Chengda bi ji liu zhong*. For another song-dynasty perspective on the Yao, see Zhou Qufei, *Ling wai dai da jiao zhu*, 118–20.

for food . . . and in their spare time hunt for wild animals to supplement their diet. It is their custom to kill for revenge. They are suspicious by nature and are not afraid to die. . . . They can travel through dangerous terrain as if they could fly. As soon as a child can walk, they heat up a piece of metal to sear the heels to benumb them so that the child can step on thorny bushes without getting hurt.[23]

Although it is unclear whether the compilers of the 1531 gazetteer actually found the descriptions accurate, what is evident is Fan Chengda's continual influence on the collective imagination of Ming officials and travelers.

Despite Fan's influence, by the second half of the sixteenth century, as more and more travelers to the south left behind records of their visits, not a few would venture to supplement Fan Chengda's observations with their own. Consider Tian Rucheng's depiction of the Yao in his *Record of Things Heard on the Torrid Frontier*. Although Tian would repeat many stock descriptions – that the Yao would sear their heels so that they could travel easily up and down the mountains, that they used swords that were poisonous, that it was customary for young men and women to pair off by themselves rather than by employing go-betweens, that the Yao engaged in pillaging and plundering whenever they could not find enough to eat, and so on – he would also include details that are not mentioned in earlier sources. For example, according to Tian Rucheng, it was customary for a newly-wedded Yao woman to bring with her only "a pair of straw-sandals" to her husband's home ("as a sign of her readiness to leave"), and it was not unusual to find Yao people getting drunk to amuse themselves. What is interesting also is the claim by Tian that the Yao could trace their ancestry to the so-called Eight *Man* (Baman) mentioned in various ancient texts. By dissociating the Yao from the myth of Panhu the dog and by associating them more squarely with some of the *man* groups documented in the historical records, Tang Rucheng, it seems, was hoping to make a strong case that the Yao had indeed long been an identifiable population in the southern border zone.[24]

Even more detailed are the descriptions by Wang Shixing in his *Record of Extensive Travels*. Although in his depiction of the so-called Yao people Wang was as culpable as Tian Rucheng in recycling some of the stock images (especially the impression that Yao men and women were especially predisposed to illicit intercourse), most of Wang's writings on the subject are in fact devoted to describing in detail the physical appearance of the Yao and their particular customs. Not only did Wang Shixing seem intrigued by the styles of dress of the Yao – women wore the so-called

[23] *GXTZ* (1531), 53:1; cf. Fan Chengda, *Gui hai yu heng zhi*, 141–42.
[24] *YJJW*, 4:18b–19.

dog's tail blouse (*gou wei shan*), "as a gesture of not having forgotten their ancestry," while men wore short shirts and earrings – he also found it noteworthy that it was customary for Yao men to marry the daughters of their own sisters or the widows of their own brothers. In his depiction Wang appears to be struck also by the seemingly uncouth way of life of the Yao. "All through their lives men and women do not sleep on beds and do not know how to make blankets." Instead, observed Wang Shixing, members of each family would simply build a fire pit on the ground inside their dwelling and sleep on the floor around it. According to Wang, it was not the practice of the Yao to take medicine. When people fell sick, they would resort to performing divination and offering sacrifices to local gods.[25]

In addition to providing more detailed descriptions, Ming visitors to the south would apparently also come to distinguish between different types of Yao. As we have seen, in the 1599 edition of the *General Gazetteer of Guangxi*, Su Jun, the compiler, would identify four categories of Yao. Whereas "black" Yao and *sheng* Yao (the differences between the two are not clear from the gazetteer) are reported to reside in relatively remote areas, "white" Yao and *shu* Yao are said to enjoy close ties – to the extent of intermarriage – with the *min* population. In the 1631 edition of the *Gazetteer of Wuzhou Prefecture*, the compilers, likewise, would identify three main categories of Yao. Although not much information is provided for the so-called Coil-piling (Panlong) Yao, Plank-wearing (Daiban) Yao, and Plain-dwelling (Pingdi) Yao, it is evident from the labels that the distinctions are made at least in part on the basis of the physical appearance or the place of abode of the people in question. Last but not least, in a seventeenth-century gazetteer of Lingui county (home of the provincial capital), the compilers would observe the presence of at least three categories of Yao. Whereas the Plain-dwelling Yao and the Very Tame (Daliang) Yao are said to share some similar customs with the *min*, the Mountain-dwelling (Gaoshan) Yao are reported to need to lead a more nomadic life, having to move from one mountain to another every few years.[26]

To understand this pattern of increased demarcation and categorization, consider also the evolution of the depiction of the so-called Zhuang people. Although the origins of the category remain unclear, historians have traced its appearance to a mid-thirteenth-century memorial submitted by Li Zengbo, in which the one-time military commissioner

---

[25] Wang Shixing, *Guang you zhi*, shang.216–17.
[26] *GXTZ* (1599), 33:2a. For Wuzhou, see Xie Junwei et al., *Wuzhou fu zhi*, 2:8b. For Lingui, see *YXCZ*, 24:4–5.

of the Western Circuit of Guangnan (i.e., Guangxi) suggests, somewhat cryptically, that the government could consider deploying the *zhuang ding* of Yi Zhou (in central Guangxi) in its military operations. Whether the *zhuang ding* (literally, "men who collide") mentioned by Li Zengbo were in fact related to the Zhuang (written with the "dog" radical) referred to in later sources we cannot say. What is evident is that references to Zhuang "people" (*ren*) began to proliferate in the fourteenth century. In his account of the 1334 military campaign in Guangxi, for example, the Yuan-dynasty official Yu Ji clearly identifies Zhuang *ren* as one of the four main categories of *man yi* in the southern border region.[27]

Despite such early references, it was not until the Ming dynasty that one begins to find extended descriptions of the so-called Zhuang people. Consider, for example, the following passage from the 1531 edition of the *General Gazetteer of Guangxi*:

People who live in the *xi dong* settlements in Nandan, of Qingyuan, are called Zhuang. At first the people never ventured into the regular administrative territory. During the Zhiyuan period [1264–1294] of the Yuan [dynasty], Mo Guoqi [a Zhuang elder?] presented a map and submitted his land [to the imperial court]. [As a result, he was] appointed the military commissioner of the greater Qingyuan area. It was from that time on that Zhuang people began to be incorporated into the regular administrative territory. Nowadays, they are most populous in [the counties of] Lipu, Xiuren, and Yongfu of Guilin. [Among the Zhuang in Qingyuan prefecture,] those who live in the fringe areas of Yishan and Sien as well as those who have of late come to be registered, are called *shu* Zhuang; they are relatively tame. Those who have kept their distance are called *sheng* Zhuang; they are obstinate and cannot be easily subdued. [Among the latter,] those who live in Xincheng, Libo . . . are particularly ruthless.[28]

Although this passage is unlikely to have been written by the compilers of the 1531 gazetteer, it is evident that by the sixteenth century "Zhuang" as a population would be identified and defined not only by a geographical boundary (found in Guilin and Qingyuan prefectures) but also by a (albeit abbreviated) historical narrative.

As in the case of the Yao, by the second half of the sixteenth century, not a few Ming observers would apparently find it desirable to offer more detailed descriptions of the so-called Zhuang people. Consider again Tian Rucheng's *Record of Things Heard*. In his entry on the Zhuang, not only does Tian make a point of associating them with certain seemingly uncouth practices – the Zhuang are said to like to eat and

---

[27] For the memorial by Li Zengbo, see his *Ke zhai za gao*, 17:40. For Yu Ji's account, see note 3 of this chapter. For a discussion of the origins of the category, see Zhang Shengzhen, *Zhuang zu tong shi*, 575–77.
[28] *GXTZ* (1531), 53:1b–2a.

drink with their hands as well as to live in two-story thatched dwellings called *ma lan* in which the ground floor is usually reserved for housing animals such as oxen, goats, pigs, and dogs – he also reports that Zhuang people are good at using poisons ("even the Yao are afraid of them"), especially the kind known as *gu*. On the fifth day of the fifth month of each year, Tian notes, individual *gu* practitioners would gather into a container all kinds of poisonous insects and let them swallow one another. At the end, the sole surviving insect would be put aside for future use. No one who is unfortunate enough to be bitten by such most-poisonous insects, according to Tian Rucheng, shall harbor any hope to survive.[29]

In time, other observers would come to associate the use of *gu* poisons more closely with Zhuang women. In a gazetteer of Yongfu county (dated most likely to the late sixteenth or early seventeenth century), it is noted that "*gu* poisons are not found among common folks but are kept by Zhuang women only." On the fifth day of the fifth month of each year, according to the legends, the compilers of the gazetteer report, Zhuang women would travel to the rivers in their local areas where they would lay out on the ground sets of new clothes and basins filled with water. There they would sing and dance naked to summon "the kings of poisons" (*yao wang*). After a sufficient number of poisonous insects have been collected in the basins, the women would pour the water onto ground that is both shady and humid. In time, the women would harvest the fungi grown in the chosen areas, grind them into powder, and place the powder on the tips of pieces of goose feather, which they would then insert into their hair. After some time, small silkworm-like *gu* creatures would emerge from their hair. Such *gu* worms would apparently not be poisonous at first. Zhuang women who would place such *gu* worms in their own food initially use them simply as a love potion. In time, according to the legends, the *gu* worms would become poisonous, and the bodies of the Zhuang women who keep them would become so itchy that the women would have no choice but to relieve their sufferings by feeding the poisonous worms even to their own sons.[30]

For Ming observers, the purpose of drawing attention to the practice of *gu* poisoning was not simply to reinforce the impression that the southern region was a perilous frontier. Rather, it was to reaffirm the

---

[29] *YJJW*, 4:19b–20; cf. Fan Chengda, *Gui hai yu heng zhi*, 137–38.

[30] For the association of the Zhuang with *gu* poisons, see *Yongfu xian zhi*, quoted in *YXCZ*, 18:9–10a; Xie Zhaozhe, *Baiyue feng tu ji*, quoted in *YXCZ*, 18:8b; Kuang Lu, *Chi ya*, shang.8–9. For discussions, see Diamond, "Miao and the Poison," esp. 9–10; Schafer, *Vermilion Bird*, 102–103.

boundaries between "civilized" and "uncivilized" or between "Chinese" and "non-Chinese." After all, the unstated assumption was that it was inconceivable for women from the central plains to commit such improprieties. Other accounts from the late Ming would point to other alleged misconducts of Zhuang women. For example, in his *Record of Extensive Travels*, Wang Shixing notes that, as in the case of the Yao, it is customary for Zhuang women not to move in with their husbands immediately after the wedding. A young wife, according to Wang, would travel to her husband's home in times of harvests and festivals. But even on such occasions she would neither speak with him nor stay overnight but would instead spend the night in a friend's house. It is only after one or two years, either after the husband has built a new dwelling or after the wife has become pregnant with another man's child, Wang Shixing reports, that she would finally agree to move in with her husband.[31]

In addition to drawing attention to the perceived improprieties of Zhuang women, in time, Ming observers would also come to distinguish between different categories of Zhuang. In the gazetteer of Yongfu county mentioned earlier, for instance, it is noted that there were in the area of Yongfu (Guilin) at least two types of Zhuang people: the Southern Zhuang originally from the southern region of Guizhou and the Zhuang of Hubei. Whereas the Southern Zhuang are said to have arrived in Yongfu during the Zhengtong period in the first half of the fifteenth century, the Zhuang of Hubei are reported to have arrived half a century later during the Hongzhi reign (1488–1505). And whereas the Southern Zhuang are said to have dwindled in number, the Zhuang of Hubei are reported to have over time extended their reach. Not only did the two groups come from different areas, according to the gazetteer, they also differed in their practices. Compared with the Zhuang of Hubei, the Southern Zhuang were apparently more "civilized." The latter did not live in *ma lan*, did not eat dogs, and, most important from the perspective of Ming officials, did not leave their parents uncared for. In addition, Ming observers also distinguished between the so-called Zhuang of the Fu River (Fujiang Zhuang), who were active in eastern Guangxi, and the Zhuang of the Right River (Youjiang Zhuang), who were found in the central part of the province. Not much, however, is known about either of these groups.[32]

---

[31] Wang Shixing, *Guang you zhi*, shang.217–18.
[32] For Southern and Hubei Zhuang, see *GXTZ* (1599), 33:10a; *Yongfu xian zhi*, quoted in *YXCZ*, 24:6b–7. For Fujiang Zhuang and Youjiang Zhuang, see Qu Jiusi, *Wanli wu gong lu*, 4.347.

Discourse on distinction

To understand this growing desire or perceived need among Ming observers to identify and categorize the borderland population, let us consider the broader context of political and cultural change. Early Ming emperors, flush with their victories over the Mongols, were apparently eager to proclaim the universal appeal of their rule. As early as 1368, the Hongwu emperor was already sufficiently versed in the imperial rhetoric to declare his goal to be first to "pacify all under heaven through military achievements [wu gong]" and then to "transform people from afar through rituals and institutions [wen jiao]" Likewise, the Yongle emperor, who had ascended the throne by overthrowing his nephew, was understandably keen on asserting his legitimacy. In a message sent to a Mongol chief in 1403, the self-appointed successor to the dynastic founder was not hesitant to invoke the notion of the mandate of heaven: "After the fortune of the Yuan had declined, my father received the mandate of heaven and [proceeded to] tame all-under-heaven. My father first installed me as the Prince of Yan, and as the successor to my father's rule, I respectfully continue to receive blessings from heaven." Even the Xuande emperor, who in 1427 would end the Ming occupation of Annam, had at first tried to promote education in the protectorate by appointing to the schools there instructors from the central plains. "In using Chinese [xia] ways to change yi ways," the emperor decreed, "nothing should come before this [effort to promote education]."[33]

Such political confidence, however, began to recede in the second quarter of the fifteenth century. Despite the fact that the Yongle emperor, in an effort to emulate the Mongol khans of the Yuan dynasty, had led five military campaigns deep inside the territory of present-day Mongolia and that the Xuande emperor had maintained a degree of order on the northern border zone in part by taking part in minor skirmishes himself, no Ming rulers since seemed to possess both the political vision and the military expertise necessary to lay claims again on the steppe region. Over time, Ming officials would in turn argue for an aggressive stance and a conciliatory position toward the Mongols, but neither policy was consistently implemented and neither was able to bring about long-term peace. At least twice in its history (in 1449 and 1550), the Ming capital in Beijing would actually come under direct attack by Mongolian forces. To be sure, the rhetoric of universal rule continued, but as the early assertiveness of the centralizing state gave way to an increased awareness

---

[33] For the Hongwu emperor, see *MSL, Taizu shi lu*, 36.667. For the Yongle emperor, see *MSL, Taizong shi lu*, 17.306; quotation (with modifications) is from Tsai, *Perpetual Happiness*, 165. For the Xuande emperor, see *MSL, Xuanzong shi lu*, 3.90–91.

of its vulnerability, Ming rulers and officials also had to adjust their political lenses. Whereas the Hongwu emperor and his immediate successors
would emphasize the unifying power of the centralizing state, later rulers,
especially after the mid-fifteenth century, would prefer to reinforce the
boundaries between "Chinese" and "non-Chinese."[34]

This sense of vulnerability no doubt had its earlier origins, but its man-
ifestation can be traced directly to the Tumu debacle of 1449. Although
historians have faulted the Zhengtong emperor, son of Xuande, for following the advice of the eunuch Wang Zhen, as Morris Rossabi has
argued, given the context, it was not unreasonable for the young emperor
to want to lead a military campaign against the Mongols. What set apart
the expedition of the Zhengtong emperor, however, was not how eagerly
he undertook it but how seriously he and his advisors bungled it. Orches-
trated by Wang Zhen as a preemptive strike against the Oyirods (Western
Mongols) led by Esen (d. 1455) – who had repeatedly demanded more
trading opportunities with the Ming – the plan was to have the emperor
lead an army of half a million men (the actual number was probably
smaller) to the Datong defense area in northern Shanxi, where the mere
show of force of the Ming was thought to be sufficient to deter the Mongols. The scheme failed. Even before the ill-prepared Ming army was able
to reach Datong, Wang Zhen had concluded that the threats posed by
Esen were real and that it would be wise to retreat. As the Ming army
withdrew to Tumu, a small military station just beyond the inner Great
Wall, Esen's forces struck. The Ming army was obliterated, Wang Zhen
was killed, and the young emperor was captured.[35]

Not only did the Ming state suddenly find itself without an emperor,
the foundation of its dynastic rule was also shaken as a result. Not since
the capture by the Jurchens of the Song emperors Qinzong (r. 1126)
and his father, Huizong (r. 1102–25), in 1126 had the centralizing state
been subjected to a similar threat. To Ming officials, the memory of
that episode, in which the Song court was forced to give up its capital in Kaifeng and set up anew in Hangzhou, was no doubt a source of
great anxiety. After the Tumu debacle, while some officials did suggest
retreating to the south, under the leadership of Yu Qian (1398–1457),
the minister of war, the Ming court decided that not only would it stay
in Beijing, it would also reject Esen's demand for ransom. To show its

---

[34] For the continual threats posed by the Mongols, see Rossabi, "Ming and Inner Asia,"
224–41.
[35] For recent accounts of the Tumu debacle, see de Heer, *Caretaker Emperor*; Waldron,
Great Wall of China, 88–90; Rossabi, "Ming and Inner Asia," 233–34; Mote, *Imperial
China*, 627–28. For Wang Zhen (Wang Chen), see *DMB*, 1347–49. For Esen, see *DMB*,
416–20.

resolve, the Ming court promptly installed Prince of Cheng, half-brother of Zhengtong, as the Jingtai emperor. Although the Ming managed to fend off Esen – who would be killed in an internal revolt in part for his perceived ineffectiveness in dealing with the Ming – and limit the immediate damage brought by the misguided expedition, the seeds of political instability had been sown. Just as it had unexpectedly found itself without a ruler after the debacle, following the release by the Mongols of the captured emperor in 1450, the Ming court suddenly had to cope with having two "sons of heaven." When the Zhengtong – now Tianshun – emperor finally emerged victorious from a power struggle in 1457, a period of terror followed. Officials who had strongly supported the Jingtai emperor were purged from the government. Yu Qian was no exception; he was charged with treason and was promptly executed.[36]

More significant, haunted by the Tumu experience, the Ming court seemed genuinely unable to come up again with a unified border strategy. Although some leading officials, such as Bai Gui (1419–75) and Xia Yan (1482–1548), would push for the recovery of the Ordos – the territory of the great bend of the Yellow River, which had been lost to the Mongols – others, such as Yu Zijun (1429–89) and Yan Song (1480–1565), would argue for a more defensive strategy, citing often the lessons of Tumu and the perils of over-extension. And whereas early Ming emperors such as Hongwu and Yongle, as shown by their rise to power, had been accustomed to making bold decisions, later Ming rulers had largely led sheltered lives and were much less capable of forming independent judgments. In part because of its inability to formulate a consistent border strategy, the Ming court had since the mid-fifteenth century become much more concerned with defining its boundaries and in reaffirming the distinctions between "Chinese" and "non-Chinese." In the northern region, as Arthur Waldron has shown, this effort to reassert the physical and cultural boundaries between *hua* and *yi* would result in the building of a long, costly, and ultimately ineffective wall along the border. In the south, as we will see, where the *man yi* did not seem to pose as great a threat to the centralizing state as the Mongols in the north, boundaries between "Chinese" and "non-Chinese" were apparently drawn by differentiating and categorizing the border population.[37]

[36] For the political fallout of the Tumu debacle, see de Heer, *Caretaker Emperor*; Twitchett and Grimm, "The Cheng-t'ung, Ching-t'ai, and T'ien-shun Reigns."

[37] Waldron, *Great Wall of China*, esp. Chaps. 6–8. With regard to the south, Waldron observes that by the turn of the sixteenth century "[p]rosperity and intellectual revival there [had] led to the reassertion of ways of thought that stressed the differences between the 'civilized' and the 'barbarian'" (109). For an alternative perspective, see Johnston, *Cultural Realism*.

The need for this "defense of the boundaries between *hua* and *yi*" (*hua yi zhi fang*) – a phrase often found in the Ming records – was articulated perhaps most clearly in the second half of the fifteenth century by the influential scholar-official Qiu Jun. A native of Qiongshan at the southern tip of the Ming realm, Qiu was probably one of very few highly placed officials at the time who had come from an area with a large *man yi* population. A student at the Imperial Academy in Beijing during the Tumu debacle, Qiu Jun was clearly influenced by what he had seen during the upheaval. Despite the turbulent time he lived in, Qiu in many ways had a model career. Awarded the highest (*jin shi*) examination degree in 1454, Qiu Jun was immediately assigned to the prestigious Hanlin Academy, where he served almost continuously for nearly a quarter of a century. He took part in many major editorial projects, including the compilation of the official records of the Zhengtong (later Tianshun) emperor as well as that of the Chenghua emperor (r. 1465–87). Through these projects, Qiu Jun was able to not only access a vast quantity of government documents but also shape the official records according to his view of history. Throughout his career, Qiu was not shy in making his opinions known. In addition to his memorials and official compilations, Qiu Jun was the author or editor of numerous works, on subjects ranging from philosophy and rituals to history and statecraft.[38]

Among Qiu Jun's writings, the best known and most influential is no doubt his *Supplement to the "Extended Meaning of the Great Learning."* Although it is billed as a supplement to the Song-dynasty work *Extended Meaning of the Great Learning* by Zhen Dexiu (1178–1235), Qiu's composition has in fact a much different aim and character, focusing not on personal ethics but on government administration. Presented in 1487 to the newly enthroned Hongzhi emperor (r. 1488–1505), the *Supplement*, which runs to 160 juan or chapters (more than fifteen hundred pages in reduced-size reprints), the work is at once a masterly display of scholarship and a comprehensive blueprint for government actions. Divided into 12 sections and 119 subsections, Qiu's text sets out to cover almost every aspect of government, from protocols at court to the appointment of officials, from military defense to the control of "non-Chinese." Other topics covered include state finance, rituals and music, schools and education, as well as law and order. Each subsection in the text would include a précis of past approaches to the problem under discussion, often accompanied by extensive quotations, and each would feature Qiu Jun's own suggestions for the Ming ruler. Although Qiu's ideas were at

---

[38] For Qiu Jun (Ch'iu Chün), see *DMB*, 249–52; Wang Wanfu, *Ming Qiu Wenzhuang gong Jun nian pu*.

times controversial, that his work was ordered to be disseminated first by the Hongzhi emperor and later by the Wanli emperor (r. 1573–1620) clearly testifies to its political relevance and influence.[39]

In Qiu Jun's view, it is part of what he considers "the coherence of all-under-heaven" (*tian xia zhi li*) that there exist boundaries between Chinese and non-Chinese. In the section on "subordinating the non-Chinese" (*yu yi di*), Qiu emphasizes at the outset that to govern successfully it is important for the centralizing state to ensure that "from within bandits would dare not to harm its law-abiding subjects" and "from beyond the *man yi* would dare not to invade our Chinese [*huaxia*] territory." The age of the sage-kings was a time of peace for the central dominion, Qiu Jun argues, because a clear distinction was made between the inner zones, where the rituals and institutions from the center were spread, and the outer zones, against which military defense was organized. The border problems of earlier dynasties, especially the Han and the Tang, according to Qiu, stemmed precisely from the rulers' "failure to defend attentively the boundary between inside [*nei*] and outside [*wai*]" and to prevent "the amalgamation of the customs of *hua* and *yi*." Mindful of the continual threats posed by the Mongols, Qiu Jun cautions against the rush to allow non-Chinese people to submit to and settle inside the Ming. Given their inherent aversion to rigid control, Qiu argues, those *yi di* who have reluctantly come forward to submit are not unlike "birds in cages and tigers in traps," eagerly awaiting for the first chance to set themselves free. To Qiu Jun, that there should be clear boundaries between Chinese and non-Chinese is evidenced by the mountains and rivers that have separated the two; it would be a mistake, according to him, if the centralizing state were to try – whether through alliances or through force – to breach such natural barriers.[40]

Of the strategies to preserve such boundaries, the most important, in Qiu Jun's view, is effective border defense. Although the centralizing state would at times need to attack or negotiate with the non-Chinese, such actions, writes Qiu, should be carried out with the knowledge that the state is neither in need of their possessions nor in awe of their power. Commenting on the analysis by the Tang scholar-official Lu Zhi (754–805), Qiu Jun argues that although the centralizing state might have to pursue different strategies under different circumstances, it is not an inferior choice to adopt a defensive policy and to aim primarily at keeping

---

[39] For Qiu Jun and his *magnum opus*, see Chu, "Ch'iu Chün (1421–1495) and the 'Ta-Hsüeh Yen-I Pu.'"

[40] Qiu Jun, *Da xue yan yi bu, juan* 143–44. For quotations, see 143:1b, 2b–3a, 6, 8b. For Qiu Jun's views on border defense, see Lee Cheuk Yin, "Qiu Jun 'Da xue yan yi bu.'"

the *yi di* out of the central dominion. And in his comments on the proposals offered by the Song-dynasty reformer Fan Zhongyan (989–1052), Qiu particularly praises Fan's emphasis on defense (*bei*). Even though he does not agree with all of Fan's recommendations, Qiu Jun finds some of the proposed measures – such as the strengthening of the city-wall of the imperial capital – still highly relevant for the Ming period. Qiu's focus on defense no doubt reflects his experience during the Tumu debacle, but it also underscores his broader philosophical view on the distinctions between "Chinese" and "non-Chinese." "That between heaven and earth there exist *hua* and *yi* is similar to that in heaven there exist *yin* and *yang* [forces]," Qiu Jun asserts. "To have one is to have the other, and [as a result] there is absolutely no reason to annihilate [the *yi* and] their kinds."[41]

To strengthen the Ming border defense, Qiu Jun proposes not only to reinforce individual garrisons but also to fortify the border with an extended wall. Qiu argues that even though mountains and rivers provide the necessary physical barriers, in areas where natural markers are insufficient to deter the *yi di*, it is reasonable to supplement them with artificial ones. Qiu concedes that wall-building is expensive but contends that as long as such extensions are built gradually and strategically – in his estimates, one hundred thousand people would labor for sixty days every year for three years – the benefits would far outweigh the costs. Qiu Jun recognizes that the challenges faced by the Ming are complicated by the fact that after the collapse of the Yuan dynasty, many Mongol soldiers have decided to stay and pledge allegiance to the Ming. Although some of such Mongols settlers have blended into local societies, others have been relocated to the capital region and summoned from time to time to participate in various military campaigns. The problem with such arrangements, according to Qiu Jun, is that the Mongols are at heart unreformed. They might agree to take part in military campaigns, but some would just as soon "remove their uniforms and loot the people." To Qiu, there is no greater challenge for the Ming than to isolate such Mongol settlers and to neutralize their threats.[42]

In the south, where he came from, Qiu Jun realizes that the Ming faces different problems. Unlike in the north, where the non-Chinese are separated from the Chinese by natural barriers, in the southern region,

---

[41] Qiu Jun, *Da xue yan yi bu*, 147:15–16. On Lu Zhi, see 148:14b–16a. On Fan Zhongyan, see 149:3b–8b. For the quotation, see 147:7a.

[42] For wall-building, see Qiu Jun, *Da xue yan yi bu*, 150:6–7a; 151:6–7. For Qiu's views on the Mongols inside the Ming, see 144:16b–17; for the quotation, see 144:17a. For a recent discussion; see Robinson, "Images of Subject Mongols."

Qiu observes, the non-Chinese (*yue*) have long lived alongside the registered subjects (*min*) of the state. Although some of the early *yue* groups, such as Ouyue, Minyue, Dongyue, and Yuyue, have long been integrated into the central dominion, Qiu Jun notes, the descendants of Nanyue, who have remained active in Huguang, Guangdong, and Guangxi during the Ming, "have still not come to be completely transformed by the kingly rule [of the centralizing state]." Qiu laments that even though members of Nanyue have constantly preyed on the people around them, the state has had great difficulties defending against such unruly bands because of the lack of clear physical boundaries.[43]

To fortify the Ming defense in the south and to reinforce the boundaries between Chinese and non-Chinese, Qiu Jun supports a two-prong solution. In his proposal, Qiu argues that not only should the centralizing state recognize an even greater number of native chieftains in the southern border region (see Chapter 3), it should also clearly establish the boundaries of individual domains. To avoid conflicts, Qiu suggests, it might be necessary for some *min* to give up their land in exchange for land outside of native domains. Not only could such chieftains assist the Ming in its military operations, Qiu Jun reckons, they could also check each other's power. In areas where chieftains are deemed undesirable, Qiu recommends that interactions between Chinese and non-Chinese be limited. Merchants who wish to travel to the mountains to trade with the Yao or the Zhuang should be restricted to bartering. No money should change hands, and no non-native goods should be purchased from the non-Chinese. With these restrictions in place, Qiu Jun argues, "the money they [i.e., the non-Chinese] acquired [through banditry] would be of no use; and even if they want to use it, there would be nothing for sale." In the absence of natural barriers, Qiu believes, artificial ones would suffice.[44]

Underlying Qiu Jun's ideas is his conviction that "Chinese" and "non-Chinese" are fundamentally different. To Qiu, while the Chinese have long dominated the center, the non-Chinese have occupied the margins. Over time, the *hua* have "mixed with and assimilated to one another" (*hun er tong*), whereas the *yi* have developed a wide range of temperaments and customs. And while *yi* people who live close to the Chinese have come to share some of the latter's practices, those who are far away have remained unruly and rebellious. In maintaining peace, Qiu observes, the earliest rulers of the centralizing state were concerned less with transforming the

---

[43] Qiu Jun, *Da xue yan yi bu*, 153:6–7a; for the quotation, see 153:6b.
[44] Qiu Jun, *Da xue yan yi bu*, 153:11b–13, 14b–17a; for the quotation, see 153:15b.

customs of the non-Chinese than with confining the *yi* to their own places. Qiu Jun even appeals to the authority of the Ming founder and argues that in his "Ancestral Instructions" (*Zu xun*) the emperor has wisely forbidden unprovoked use of force against "the *yi* of the four quarters." To strengthen the Ming border defense, Qiu contends, it is imperative that this injunction be taken seriously and that clear boundaries between Chinese and non-Chinese be restored.[45]

Over time, in addition to the writings by Qiu Jun, the growing desire or need by Ming observers to reinforce the boundaries between "Chinese" and "non-Chinese" can also be observed through a wide range of published and unpublished titles. Consider, for example, the body of works concerned with the "non-Chinese of the four quarters" (*si yi*). In these texts – among them are Zheng Xiao's (1499–1566) *Notes on the non-Chinese of the Four Quarters of the Ming Imperium* (*Huang Ming si yi kao*; pref. 1564), Yan Congjian's (js. 1559) *Exhaustive Inquiries on the Strange Lands* (*Shu yu zhou zi lu*; pref. 1574), Luo Yuejiong's (jr. 1585) *Record of Tribute Guests* (*Xian bin lu*; pref. 1591), Ye Xianggao's (1559–1627) *Notes on the non-Chinese of the Four Quarters* (*Si yi kao*; 1606), and Mao Ruizheng's (js. 1601) *Record of the Interpreters of the Ming Imperium* (*Huang Ming xiang xu lu*; pref. 1609) – the term *si yi* is used to refer to a wide range of peoples, from those who lived in faraway countries to those who populated the border regions of the centralizing state. In general, the objective of these works is not to advance a policy position but to provide a record of the "non-Chinese" peoples who had real or imagined ties to the central dominion. In Luo Yuejiong's *Record of Tribute Guests*, for example, more than a hundred foreign and borderland places and peoples with alleged tributary ties to the Ming are cataloged: in the north are the Tatars (Eastern Mongols) and the Uriyangkhad; in the east are Korea, the Jurchens, Japan, and Liuqiu (Ryūkyū); in the west are Hami, Gaochang, Turfan, among others; and in the south are Annam, Cham, among other countries in "the southern seas," as well as various "non-Chinese" peoples in Sichuan, Yunnan, Guizhou, and Guangxi. The proliferation of such works on *si yi*, particularly in the last century of the Ming, no doubt reflects the authors' increased awareness of the wider world, but just as important, it also demonstrates the growing desire of scholar-officials to help project a degree of order through identifying and categorizing the various "non-Chinese."[46]

---

[45] Qiu Jun, *Da xue yan yi bu*, 153:1b–2a; 155:15b–16a.
[46] For a list of Ming-period works on *si yi*, see Franke, *Sources of Ming History*, 203–207. For a discussion of *Xian bin lu*, see Yu, *Chinese Collections*, vol. 2, 652–54.

Apart from these titles, there appeared also in the latter half of the Ming dynasty a specific body of works on the "non-Chinese" (*lu*) of the northern border region. Unlike the general treatises on *si yi*, most of the texts concerning the north were written by officials who had either served in the Ministry of War or stationed in the border region. Among the more well-known of these works are Xu Lun's (1495–1566) *Illustrations and Descriptions of the Northern Borders* (*Jiu bian tu lun*; 1538), Wei Huan's (js. 1529) *Notes on the Northern Borders of the Ming Imperium* (*Huang Ming jiu bian kao*; 1541), Huo Ji's (1516–75) *Annotated Illustrations of the Northern Borders* (*Jiu bian tu shuo*; 1569), and Xiao Daheng's (1532– 1612) *Customs of the non-Chinese in the North* (*Yi su ji* or *Bei lu feng su*; pref. 1594). Although the primary aim of these works is to gather together information – such as the size of the government forces and the number of weapons – pertinent to border defense, some authors also find it important to include descriptions of the "non-Chinese" peoples in the northern region. In his *Notes on the Northern Borders*, for example, Wei Huan, who was then director of the Bureau of Operations in the Ministry of War, argues that in preparing for border defense, it is critical that officials be knowledgeable about the *lu*. For this reason, Wei Huan notes in his preface, he has included in his discussion on each of the nine northern border areas (*bian*) a section devoted to the non-Chinese active in the vicinity.[47]

With regard to the southern border zone, the desire by Ming officials to reaffirm the boundaries between "Chinese" and "non-Chinese" can also be observed through a variety of writings. Whereas some of these texts are relatively formal (and formulaic), others are more informal works by scholar-officials who, by the latter half of the Ming dynasty, were roaming through the south in an ever greater number. In addition to Tian Rucheng's *Record of Things Heard on the Torrid Frontier*, other noteworthy titles in the latter category include Guo Fei's (1529–1605) *Descriptions of the non-Chinese in South of the Range* (*Lingnan zhu yi zhi*), Chen Yongbin's (js. 1571) *Annotated Illustrations of the non-Chinese in Yunnan* (*Yunnan zhu yi tu shuo*; 1595), Cheng Zhengyi's (js. 1571) *Notes on the non-Chinese Natives in Sichuan* (*Quan Shu tu yi kao*; 1599), and Bao Ruji's (js. 1607) *Record of Things Heard in Guizhou* (*Nanzhong ji wen*; pref. 1633). Unfortunately, the texts by Guo Fei and Chen Yongbin are no longer extant. In contrast to those who wrote about the north, the authors of these texts were in

---

[47] The titles listed here are found in Huang Yuji, *Qian qing tang shu mu*, juan 8. For bibliographical information, see Franke, *Sources of Ming History*, 210–15. For Xu Lun (Hsü Lun) and Xiao Daheng (Hsiao Ta-heng), see *DMB*, 593–95, 544–46. For the need to be knowledgeable about the *lu*, see Wei Huan, *Huang Ming jiu bian kao*, preface:2b.

general concerned less about the military threats posed by the *man yi* than about the latter's distinct customs and livelihood.[48]

But this desire to reaffirm the boundaries between "Chinese" and "non-Chinese" was not reflected in texts alone. In addition to the titles discussed above, there appeared also in the latter half of the Ming dynasty a variety of illustrated works that had less to do with practical concerns such as border defense or extension of the state than with popular imaginations. In these texts, the "non-Chinese" in the border region are routinely depicted as neither entirely humans nor completely beasts; although some of such *man yi* are thought to live within the centralizing state, others are believed to reside in various kingdoms surrounding the central dominion. Among the works in this genre, the most well-known (at least among the literati) was no doubt the *Guideways through Mountains and Seas*. Compiled in as early as the first millennium before the common era, the *Guideways*, which portrays the world at and beyond the borders of the centralizing state as populated by a wide variety of hybrid creatures, was apparently so popular that it was available in several commercial editions in the sixteenth century alone. In one of the editions (1597), the *Guideways*, which had for centuries been transmitted without illustrations, is again accompanied by a set of images. Among the creatures depicted are the Rong of the north, who possess "the head of a human with three horns attached," and the Di of the south, who are noted to have "the face of a human but the body of a fish" (see Figure 5.4). Although it is difficult to say how much Ming-dynasty readers actually believed in the existence of hybrid creatures, what is clear is that even respected scholars such as Yang Shen, who is known for his preference for empirical studies, seemed to find the *Guideways* worthy of attention. Not only did Yang compose a set of commentaries for the text, which was published in 1554 under the title *Guideways through Mountains and Seas Annotated,* he also argued in a separate essay that even though some had questioned the veracity of the descriptions found in *Shan hai jing*, the text itself was extraordinary and valuable enough to deserve to be transmitted.[49]

In addition to the *Guideways*, images of hybrid creatures can also be found in the large number of late-Ming encyclopedias and almanacs

---

[48] For an extensive list of works on the "non-Chinese" of the south dated to the Ming period, see Lü Mingzhong et al., *Nan fang min zu gu shi shu lu*, 104–91; see also the titles in Huang Yuji, *Qian qing tang shu mu*, juan 7–8.

[49] For an authoritative study and translation of *Shan hai jing*, see Strassberg, *Chinese Bestiary*; for a list of Ming editions, see pp. 237–38 n. 82; for the Di and the Rong, see pp. 190, 201. For Yang Shen, see his *Shan hai jing bu zhu*; *Sheng'an quan ji*, 2.17; for a discussion, see Strassberg, *Chinese Bestiary*, 23.

Figure 5.4. The Rong (top: upper left) and the Di (bottom: lower left).
Source: Strassberg, *Chinese Bestiary,* plates LIV and LX. Courtesy of the
Regents of the University of California.

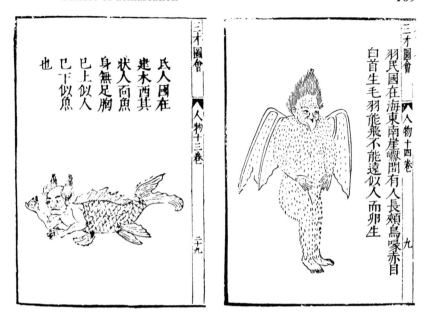

Figure 5.5. The Di (left) and the Feathered (right). *Source:* Wang Qi, *San cai tu hui,* 13:29b, 14:9b.

(*lei shu*). In his well-known *Collected Illustrations of Heaven, Earth, and People* (1609), for example, Wang Qi (js. 1565) includes in the section on "peoples and creatures" (*ren wu*) depictions of more than 175 foreign and borderland beings. While some of the peoples and creatures are from identifiable countries such as Korea and Japan, others – the Di, the Feathereds (see Figure 5.5), the One-eyeds, the Three-headeds, the Midgets, the Giants, and so on – are more difficult to place. In the accompanying text to their image, the Feathered people are described as living somewhere "southeast of the sea." Although they resemble humans, the Feathered people are born from eggs and are able to fly a short distance. Descriptions and images of similar creatures can be found also in the almanacs of the late-Ming period. For example, in his popular reference work *Authoritative Source for Myriad Uses* (*Santai wan yong zheng zong*; 1599) – which covers topics ranging from "heavenly patterns" (*tian wen*) to fortune-telling and geomancy to health and medicine – the compiler Yu Xiangdou (fl. 1596) apparently deems it worthwhile to include a long section on non-Chinese peoples and creatures. But the descriptions and depictions of the *yi* in this and other almanacs are hardly original; many of the images found are similar to those in Wang Qi's *Collected Illustrations* as well as to those in the earlier Ming work *Illustrations and Records of Foreign Regions* (*Yi yu tu zhi*). Although it is almost impossible to trace the origins of such images, it seems clear, as Richard Strassberg has argued, that there existed in the late Ming an "iconic circuit" through which images of "non-Chinese" circulated. And though we cannot be certain how Wang Qi's *Collected Illustrations* or Yu Xiangdou's *Authoritative Source* was interpreted by late-Ming readers, it seems likely that even if these texts and illustrations were read mainly for the sake of entertainment, they did serve to reinforce the readers' preconceptions of the boundaries between "Chinese" and "non-Chinese."[50]

Local knowledge

This growing desire or need among Ming officials to identify and categorize the borderland population must also be understood in the broader context of economic and social change. Even though reports on "non-Chinese" had been a standard genre in Chinese writings since at least the appearance of the *Guideways through Mountain and Sea* in the first millennium BCE, two developments seem to have encouraged their production in the second half of the Ming period. The first had to do with the rise in the popularity of travel. As Timothy Brook and others have shown, not only did more and more merchants take to the roads as the Ming economy became increasingly commercialized, a growing number of literati also found it spiritually fulfilling to roam the country and record their observations as Ming politics turned increasingly disenchanting. The second development, closely related to the first, had to do with the rise in demand by officials and by the growing reading public for geographical or local knowledge. Compared to the first half of the Ming period, not only were there in the sixteenth and seventeenth centuries more local gazetteers compiled, there was also a greater number of "geographical" works published. Although it is difficult to quantify the expansion of the publishing and printing industries – for instance, we seldom have information on how many copies of a given title were printed or how widely

---

[50] Wang Qi, *San cai tu hui*, juan 12–14. For the Feathered people, see 14:9b. For a discussion, see Goodall, *Heaven and Earth*, esp. Chap. 3. For the almanacs, see Sakai Tadao, "Mindai no nichiyō ruisho." For a catalog of Ming-period *lei shu*, see Wu Huifang, *Wan bao quan shu*, 641–58. Some of the most representative *lei shu* have been reprinted in Sakai Tadao et al., *Chūgoku nichiyō ruisho shūsei*. For *Yi yu tu zhi*, see Strassberg, *Chinese Bestiary*, 22, 70, 250 n. 227; Franke, *Sources of Ming History*, 203; Moule, "Introduction to the *Yi Yü T'u Chih*." For a discussion of the "iconic circuit," see Strassberg, *Chinese Bestiary*, 70. For a more general discussion of the visual culture in Ming China, see Clunas, *Pictures and Visuality*.

the copies of a certain title were distributed – anecdotal evidence does suggest that Ming travelers were increasingly writing not only for self-edification (though this remained important) but also for the enjoyment of the expanding literate population.[51]

The increase in mobility of the population – and the corresponding growth in demand for geographical knowledge – was clearly linked to the expansion and transformation of the Ming economy. Even in its early period, Ming society was hardly simply a collection of isolated communities. Surplus goods produced by farmers were already traded in local and regional markets, while more luxurious and specialized commodities such as embroideries, silk, paper, and porcelain were routinely sent to more distant markets to meet the demand of the rich and powerful. By the middle of the Ming, commercialization of the economy had apparently reached a new level. Not only had regional and interregional trade expanded, farmers in many areas were now producing not for their own consumption but for the market. In the lower Yangzi region where the cultivation of cotton and mulberry trees had become highly profitable, rice had to be imported to satisfy the need of the local population. By the late Ming, regional specialization had become even more evident: cotton was grown in Henan and Shandong (and later Jiangxi and Huguang) but woven into cloth in the lower Yangzi region; silk was produced in Huzhou (Zhejiang) and Baoning (Sichuan) but processed in Hangzhou, Suzhou, and Lu'an (Shanxi); sugar was exported from Fujian, whereas paper was sent from Jiangxi to Henan and the Southern Metropolitan Region; porcelain from Jingde Zhen (Jiangxi) was sought after not only by customers across China but by those abroad as well.[52]

The increased commercialization of the Ming economy also meant that merchants often needed to travel far and wide to trade. Although some sojourners became successful and soon returned home, many had to stay away for extended periods. Over time, even merchants had come to develop specializations. Those from Shanxi and Shaanxi (in the north), for example, were known to have grown wealthy through the government-instituted salt barter system, an arrangement by which selected merchants were permitted to participate in the monopolistic (and therefore highly profitable) salt trade in exchange for their deliveries of grains and animal fodder to designated border areas. Merchants from Huizhou

[51] Brook, *Confusions of Pleasure*, 173–85. For the culture of Ming (and Qing) publishing, see Chow, *Publishing, Culture, and Power*; Brokaw and Chow, *Printing and Book Culture*. For the publishing industry, see Chia, *Printing for Profit*, esp. 5–7. For the notion of the reading public, see, for example, Ko, *Teachers of the Inner Chambers*, 34 ff.

[52] Heijdra, "Socio-Economic Development," 496–513; Brook, *Confusions of Pleasure*, esp. 65–79, 112–24, 204–18.

(Southern Metropolitan Region) were also prominent in the salt trade (in part because of their proximity to the salt fields of Liang-Huai) but were most notable for their domination of the long-distance trade along the Grand Canal as well as of the distribution networks in the lower Yangzi region. Merchants from Jiangxi, by contrast, were particularly active in the interior provinces of Henan, Huguang, and Sichuan where competition was apparently less keen.[53]

The transformation of the economy did not affect merchants alone; many who took to the roads in the Ming period were in fact not tradesmen but members of the literati. Even though travel as a pastime or as a form of cultural pursuit has had a long history in the Chinese context, it was during the Ming that both the scope and scale of such travel seem to have reached a new level. As Pei-yi Wu has observed, whereas "sojourners [of earlier dynasties] went [to border regions] invariably as exiles and stayed only as long as necessary," in the Ming period, "countless travelers roamed the breadth and length of their vast country, exploring inaccessible areas for their scenic beauty and admiring the sort of wild grandeur that Europeans did not find appealing until about one century later." Reasons for this transformation were many. In terms of costs, travel, especially along popular routes, had become relatively affordable. In terms of political and cultural change, the lack of leadership and harmony at the court in the late Ming had evidently driven many would-be officials to seek other forms of fulfillment. Although some scholars would devote their energy to lecturing and forming literary associations, others opted to travel around the country. In terms of social change, the expansion of literacy and education (especially in the lower Yangzi region) and the resulted heightened competitiveness of the civil service examinations had apparently made it less appealing for some literati to follow the traditional path of success. The most famous traveler of the late Ming, Xu Hongzu, did not even take part in the examinations but instead chose to spend his life exploring the country.[54]

An example of this penchant for travel can be seen in the case of Wang Shixing, a one-time official in Guangxi whose descriptions of the so-called Yao and Zhuang we have encountered earlier. A native of Linhai (Zhejiang), Wang was born in 1547 into a poor family but was later adopted by a distant uncle Wang Zongmu (1523–91). Although Wang

---

[53] Heijdra, "Socio-Economic Development," 514–16; Brook, *Confusions of Pleasure*, 210–11.

[54] For a history of travel writing in imperial China, see Strassberg, *Inscribed Landscapes*. For the quotation, see Wu, *Confucian's Progress*, 98; for a discussion of the reasons for travel, see 93–141. For costs, see Brook, *Confusions of Pleasure*, 174.

Shixing's interest in geography might have been influenced by his adopted father, who was himself a prominent scholar-official and who had over time developed a strong interest in collecting local information, it was not until 1570, when Wang Shixing traveled as a student to Hangzhou, that the future venturer seems to have taken his first major trip outside of Linhai. Between 1573, when he passed the provincial examination, and 1577, when he succeeded (on his second attempt) at the metropolitan level, Wang Shixing undertook an extended journey to central and south-eastern Zhejiang, during which he was able to visit, perhaps for the first time, some of the more famous mountains (such as Jinhua and Xiandu) and scenic sites in his home province. Although Wang Shixing might have initially viewed this excursion as a diversion between his more serious commitments, he would soon discover his genuine passion for travel.[55]

Throughout his career, Wang Shixing would take advantage of almost every opportunity to see the country. His first assignment after he became a *jin shi* brought him to southern Henan. While there, not only did he take advantage of the opportunity to visit many of its important historical sites, he was able also to climb Mount Song, one of China's Five March-mounts (*wu yue*). Following his stay in Henan and a brief stint in another position in the capital at Beijing, Wang was forced to return home to mourn for his mother. But even in mourning, Wang Shixing's passion for travel remained unabated. While home in Zhejiang, he visited three of the most sacred Buddhist sites on the east coast – Putuo Island, Mount Ayuwang, and Mount Tiantai – as well as a range of other famous desti-nations (including Mount Jiuhua) in the Southern Metropolitan Region. At the end of his forced retirement in 1588, Wang returned to Beijing – on his way to the north he visited Mount Tai (Shandong), known then (as now) as the first among the Five Marchmounts, and Qufu, the legendary birthplace of Confucius – but was quickly offered a new assignment in Sichuan. From 1588 to 1589, Wang Shixing appears to have redoubled his efforts to travel, visiting not only the three remaining marchmounts – Hua (Shaanxi), Heng (Shanxi), and Heng (present-day Hunan) – but also many other scenic sites in the central and western parts of the country. In 1589, Wang Shixing was assigned to Guangxi as an assistant adminis-tration commissioner. And in 1591, he was transferred to Yunnan where he served for two years as the vice commissioner of the Lancang military defense circuit. It was toward the end of his stay in Yunnan that Wang

---

[55] For biographical information on Wang Shixing (Wang Shih-hsing), see Zhou Zhenhe, *Wang Shixing di li shu*, 651–59, 668–84; *DMB*, 1405–406. For Wang Zongmu (Wang Tsung-mu), see *DMB*, 1438–41. For Wang's travel to southeastern Zhejiang, see *Wu yue you cao*, in Zhou Zhenhe, *Wang Shixing di li shu*, 88–92.

finished one of his major collected writings, *Notes on Travels to the Five Marchmounts* (*Wu yue you cao*). Following his time in the southwest, Wang Shixing was given a variety of assignments in Henan and Shandong. In 1596, he was offered what would be his last post as the chief minister in the Court of State Ceremonial in the southern capital at Nanjing. Wang Shixing died two years later in 1598 at the age (*sui*) of fifty-two.[56]

Ultimately, Wang Shixing was more interested in his travel than in his official career (according to a recent biographer, Wang seems to have managed to set foot in every province and capital region in Ming China except Fujian). "The career of an official is like a play," Wang once wrote to a friend. "It can hardly be taken seriously." At a time when political candor could cost one's career (not to mention one's life), Wang appears to had no qualms about taking stands on sensitive matters. On one occasion, when he was still at his first post in Henan, Wang was said to have hosted a certain Ai Mu (jr. 1558), who was at the time on his way to exile for having criticized Zhang Juzheng (1525–82), the powerful senior grand secretary. On another occasion, Wang Shixing urged – without success – that scholars such as Gu Xiancheng (1550–1612) and Zou Yuanbiao (1551–1624), both of whom had been critical of Zhang, be brought back into government service. Toward the end of his career, Wang apparently angered the Wanli emperor by declining to serve as the grand coordinator of Henan on the grounds that he was not as qualified as another candidate. For this breach of protocol, he was given a minor post at Nanjing instead. Although Wang Shixing never followed some of his contemporaries in rejecting officialdom altogether, it is clear that political advancement was not high on his list of priorities; what seems to be important to him was travel.[57]

Not only did Ming officials and literati become more interested in travel, they also had an increased appetite for geographical knowledge. This can be seen in the publication, especially in the latter half of the Ming period, of a wide range of works under the category of *di li*. Although the majority of these publications, such as the thousands of administrative gazetteers, was compiled primarily for the consumption by officials, other "geographical" works, such as those belonging to the genre of route books, which appeared in the late sixteenth century, were evidently written for the growing number of itinerant merchants (to prevent them from venturing into dangerous areas) and other independent-minded travelers.

[56] For Wang's official career, see Zhou Zhenhe, *Wang Shixing di li shu*, 651–59. For the significance of visiting the Five Marchmounts, see Wu, "Ambivalent Pilgrim."

[57] For the extent of Wang's travel, see Foreword to Zhou Zhenhe, *Wang Shixing di li shu*, 1. For the quotation, see the letter by Wang in Zhou Zhenhe, *Wang Shixing di li shu*, 557.

A notable example of the former category of works was the *Union Gazetteer of the Great Ming* (*Da Ming yi tong zhi*; 1461), an officially sponsored compilation which gathers together a wide range of geographical information (such as maps, lists of topographical features, surveys of local customs, etc.) from all the provinces and capital regions in the country. Although it was originally an official compilation (the work includes a preface by the Tianshun emperor), the *Union Gazetteer* would become so popular that in the sixteenth century at least two commercial editions of the work were published. Although some of the works under the category of *di li* are more concerned about the history (and historical personages) of individual places, others are more interested in the unusual information of particular areas.[58]

This appetite for geographical knowledge can be observed also through indirect evidence. When Xu Hongzu was traveling in Guangxi in the late 1630s, not only did he carry with him a copy of the *Union Gazetteer* (which he frequently consulted and amended), he was also able to purchase in the provincial capital several local guidebooks, including Zhang Mingfeng's (jr. 1552) *Famous Places of Guilin* (*Gui sheng*; 1590) and *Historical Notes on Guilin* (*Gui gu*; 1590), Wei Jun's *Miscellanea of Guangxi*, and Xie Zhaozhe's *Customs of the Southern Region* (*Baiyue feng tu ji*). Whereas the two titles by Zhang Mingfeng, a native son of Guilin, comprise mostly surveys of and writings by notable visitors from the past, the works by Wei Jun and Xie Zhaozhe, both of whom had served as officials in Guangxi, are noted more for their contemporary observations. Likewise, when the early-Qing scholar Wang Sen set out to compile his anthologies, he was apparently able to collect a variety of Ming-dynasty texts concerning the geography and customs of the southern province. Among them were Tian Rucheng's *Record of Things Heard*, Zhang Qize's *Miscellanea of Wuzhou and Xunzhou* (*Wu Xun za pei*), and Cao Xuequan's (1574–1646) *Descriptions of Famous Sites of Guangxi* (*Guangxi ming sheng zhi*; 1630). Although it is difficult to gauge how widely circulated many of these texts were, that they were available to Xu Hongzu and Wang Sen, it seems, testifies to the existence of a market for such works.[59]

In part because of this growing appetite for geographical knowledge, more and more officials also seem to have found it desirable to leave

---

[58] For route books, see Brook, *Geographical Sources*, 3–9; idem, *Confusions of Pleasure*, 179–80. For the *Union Gazetteer*, see Brook, *Confusions of Pleasure*, 129. For a list of geographical works published in the Ming period, see Huang Yuji, *Qian qing tang shu mu*, juan 7–8.

[59] Xu Hongzu, *Xu Xiake you ji*, 2:346. For an incomplete list of titles on Guangxi published in the Ming, see YXCZ, preface:1–2. Neither the work by Xie Zhaozhe nor the one by Zhang Qize seems to be extant as a stand-alone text.

behind records of their travels. While some of these works are in the format of travel diaries, others are in the form of informal jottings. Consider,
for example, the case of Wang Ji, a poet from Wuxing (Zhejiang) who once
served as an assistant magistrate in Nanning prefecture. Although Wang
probably did not stay in Heng Zhou long enough (250 days to be precise) to claim much administrative accomplishment, he did leave behind
an highly informative *bi ji*, the *Hand-held Mirror for Daily Inquiries in the
Gentleman's Hall*. As Wang Ji explains in his postscript, while he was in
Guangxi, he was constantly struck by how different the customs of Heng
Zhou were from those in Zhejiang. As a result, he made it his practice
"to tirelessly inquire in detail about every matter [he] came across." And
because he had been asked time and again about his stay in Guangxi after
he had returned home, he decided that he would write down what he had
found out about Heng Zhou – from its "mountains and streams" to its
"local practices" – so that he could save the troubles of repeatedly answer-
ing the same questions. Whether such were indeed the circumstances in
which the work was produced we cannot be certain; what is clear is that
Wang's text would in time be deemed sufficiently important or popular
to be included in Shen Jiefu's (1533–1601) *Collection of Records* (*Ji lu
hui bian*; 1617), a collectanea that comprises 127 titles by some seventy
authors.[60]

Consider also the case of Wei Jun, a native of Songxi (in Fujian
province) who served in Guangxi as an education intendant (*xue zheng*)
from 1610 to 1612. Unlike Wang Ji, who was able to stay in one place for
an extended period during his time in the province, Wei Jun, as part of
his duty to conduct examinations for students, was required to travel to
different parts of Guangxi. This difference in their experiences is clearly
reflected in their writings. Whereas Wang's *Hand-held Mirror* is limited in
its focus on Heng Zhou, Wei's *Miscellanea of Guangxi* is much broader in
scope. As Wei Jun explains in the preface to his work, although people
in the past spoke of being able to learn about all-under-heaven without having to set foot outdoor, it has been his practice to inquire about
local customs and history wherever he travels. In Guangxi, because the
demand of his official duties is relatively light, Wei Jun explains, he has
been able to jot down some of what he has learned. The result is a work
of eight *juan* that covers subjects ranging from geography and climate to
historical events and contemporary affairs. Although some of the entries
in the work are based on Wei's personal observations, others are probably hearsay. Even though the works by Wang Ji and Wei Jun are quite

---

[60] Wang Ji, *Jun ji tang ri xun shou jing*, 24b–25a.

different in scope, their objectives were quite similar. In both cases, the authors believed that what they had to say about Guangxi would be of interest not only to people who might travel to the border region but also to those who might never have a chance to make it there.[61]

Not only was there in the second half of the Ming period a growing demand for and supply of information on borderland areas, there was also an increased emphasis among literati-travelers on firsthand observations. For example, Yang Shen, who was known by his contemporaries not only for his prolific scholarly outputs but also for his extensive travel in Yunnan (where he was exiled for nearly forty years), once cautioned others not to rely solely on textual records but to always try to visit notable sites in person. Similarly, in the preface to his *Further Elucidations on My Extensive Record of Travels*, a substantial work he completed around 1597, Wang Shixing laments the practice by some fellow travelers to "substitute their ears for their mouths" and to report what they did not personally observe. Unlike such travel writings, Wang Shixing assures his readers, his comments are "all based on what I have personally seen and heard; where this is not possible, I would rather leave out [the information]." His text *Further Elucidations* is divided into six chapters; the first offers an overview of the geographical features of the Ming realm, the next four provide more detail discussions on individual regions, and the last one (no longer extant) covers "the non-Chinese of the four quarters." In this work Wang Shixing is obviously interested in comparing and contrasting not only between provinces but also between different parts of a province. With regard to Guangxi, not only is Wang keen to point out where the Left and Right rivers originated (Yunnan and Guizhou, respectively) or how one part of the province is demographically distinct from another part, he is also interested in explaining why Guangxi has not had as "brilliant" a past as other provinces. The reason, Wang surmises, has to do with the fact that the rivers in Guangxi neither lead to the ocean nor come together to form a basin (instead, they form the West River, which flows into Guangdong). As a consequence, he argues, compared with other provinces such as Fujian and Sichuan, it is much more difficult for Guangxi – as well as for Guizhou which shares the same limitations – to develop major settlements and to transform itself into a prosperous region.[62]

---

[61] Apart from *Xi shi er*, Wei Jun collected some additional notes in *Qiao nan suo ji*.

[62] For Yang Shen, see Lin Qingzhang, *Ming dai kao ju xue*, 111; Feng Jiahua, *Yang Shen ping zhuan*. For Wang Shixing, see his preface to *Guang zhi yi*, 238; the quotation is adapted from Ward, *Xu Xiake*, 17. For Wang's comments on Guangxi, see *Guang zhi yi*, 5.375–83, esp. 375–76, 379, 381.

Although not all of Wang Shixing's travel writings were published during his lifetime, his influence on late-Ming and early-Qing literati was nonetheless significant. Consider again his most systematic *di li* work, *Further Elucidations on My Extensive Record of Travels*. Even though Wang did not live to witness its publication, copies of his manuscript, according to a certain Yang Tiyuan, who eventually printed the text in 1676, did find their ways into the hands of some of the bibliophiles of the time. Even when it was still in its manuscript form, Yang noted, Wang Shixing's text had already stirred much interest among the literati. To them, Yang remarked, not only did Wang's descriptions appear "learned and valid," his observations also had the quality of being "unusual" or "strange" (*qi*) without being lacking in foundations (*ben*). Among the scholars who had had the opportunity to peruse the text before its publication was none other than Gu Yanwu (1613–82), whose emphasis on empirical knowledge and preference for practical learning have been widely regarded to have helped set a new trend of scholarship in the Qing dynasty. Just how much influence Wang Shixing had on Gu it is difficult to ascertain, but as Zhou Zhenhe observes in his analysis of Wang's travel writings, in all three of Gu Yanwu's major works, including his much-admired *Strengths and Weaknesses of the Various Regions of the Realm* (*Tian xia jun guo li bing shu*; 1662), Gu has not only incorporated many of Wang Shixing's ideas but has also copied verbatim many of the passages found in Wang's texts.[63]

Boundaries of culture

This growing emphasis on firsthand observations did not occur in isolation. In various scholarly pursuits, it is evident that Ming literati had also increasingly called attention to the importance of empirical knowledge. In a preface to his monumental pharmacopoeia, *Material Medica: A General Outline* (*Ben chao gang mu*; 1596), for example, Li Shizhen (1518–93) is quoted to have said that he had spent thirty years compiling the work, that while doing so he had consulted more than eight hundred references, and that altogether he had incorporated in his survey a total of 1,892 substances. For individuals who might still doubt his thoroughness, Li made the points that "the draft text has been completely revised three times, [that] duplicate entries have been weeded, [that previously] missing materials have been added, and [that] mistaken information has been

---

[63] For Yang Tiyuan's comments, see his preface in Wang Shixing, *Guang zhi yi*, 234–35. For Wang Shixing's influence on Gu Yanwu, see Foreword to Zhou Zhenhe, *Wang Shixing di li shu*, 10–11.

corrected." What Li Shizhen did not mention was that in compiling his extraordinary work he also had had to travel widely to collect and examine specimens. Similar efforts to render a degree of order to knowledge can also be seen in the compilation of the *Exploitation of the Works of Nature* (*Tian gong kai wu*; 1637), which offers detailed descriptions of practices and processes ranging from crop production to weaving to mining. In his perface to the work, Song Yingxing, a 1615 provincial graduate from Jiangxi, would go so far as to argue that, given the benefits of the myriad things and phenomena in the realm of heaven-and-earth, a scholar who prefers to "discourse emptily on the ancient sacrificial vessels of Ju" but who does not even know "the measurements and care of cooking pots" is still "unworthy of emulation."[64]

Nor was this emphasis on empirical knowledge limited to the worlds of travel-writing and scholarship. In the world of arts, historians have shown that even though late-Ming artists and patrons continued to value painting-as-self-expression over painting-as-mirror-of-reality, a small but important group of painters had come to favor relatively realistic representations over idealized imageries. An example of such artists was Zhang Hong (1577–after 1652). In a series of so-called topographical paintings – "representations of particular places and paintings presenting stages in a journey to some particular place" – Zhang, according to James Cahill, eschews references to old masters but opts instead to supply his viewers "with detailed visual information about the place" he is painting and give them "a sense of 'what it really looks like.'" In an inscription found in his album *Ten Scenes of Yue*, which Zhang Hong painted after his return from a journey to eastern Zhejiang in 1639, Zhang notes that "about half [of the things I saw there] did not agree with what I had heard. So when I returned home I got out some silk and used it to depict what I had seen, because relying on your ears is not as good as relying on your eyes." But whereas Cahill would choose to emphasize the influence of European paintings on Zhang Hong and his small cohort, Kenneth Ganza, in his study of the genre, would locate Zhang's approach in the broader cultural context of the late Ming. Zhang Hong's paintings, in Ganza's view, no doubt express personal experiences. But unlike earlier masters whose landscape paintings were shaped as much by their inner feelings as by

---

[64] For the preface by Wang Shizhen (1526–90), see Li Shizhen, *Ben cao gang mu*, 1.17. For Li Shizhen and his work, see *DMB*, 859–65; Needham et al., *Science and Civilisation in China*, vol. 6, pt. 1, 308–21; Unschuld, *Medicine in China*, 145–63; Peterson, "Confucian Learning," 782–84. For the preface by Song Yingxing, see Pan Jixing, *Tian gong kai wu jiao zhu ji yan jiu*, 208–209; translations (with modifications) are borrowed from Sung Ying-hsing, *Chinese Technology in the Seventeenth Century*, xi–xii. For the practice of collecting in Ming China, see Elman, *On Their Own Terms*, Chap. 1.

artistic conventions, Zhang allowed his paintings to reflect the "reality of external circumstances" and "what any traveler may expect to feel when subjected to the experiences of the journey he took."[65]

Historians interested in this shift in emphasis on empirical knowledge in the late Ming have pointed to two related phenomena. One, from the perspective of intellectual history, had to do with the development of what would in time be referred to as "evidential learning" (*kao zheng xue*). Although the advent of *kao zheng xue* has most often been regarded as an eighteenth-century phenomenon, as Willard Peterson has shown, "pursuing evidence as an endeavor in learning" – a broad interpretation of the term *kao zheng* – was very much a part of the late-Ming cultural landscape. For members of the literati who for a variety of reasons were unwilling or unable to take part in the intellectual mainstream – namely, the Learning of the Way (*dao xue*) as formulated by the Song-period scholar Zhu Xi (1130–1200) – and to follow the political path that accompanied it, to engage in *ge wu* (usually translated as "investigation of things") or *kao zheng* was not only an acceptable alternative but was sometimes the preferred choice. To late-Ming scholars, what constituted "evidence" was not limited to the contents of the Four Books and the Five Classics; as Peterson argues, "data drawn from one's own perceptions of the myriad things in the realm of heaven-and-earth [*tian di wan wu*]" as well as "from earlier, not necessarily ancient, texts" could both serve as the foundation of learning. This opening of intellectual space is evidenced in the works of Li Shizhen and Xu Hongzu, and it can be observed also through the writings of Xu Guangqi (1562–1633) and Fang Yizhi (1611–71), whose interests in various fields of science would likewise be regarded by their contemporaries as outside the main current.[66]

The second development, by contrast, had to do with what Julian Ward has referred to as "the resurgence of interest in the notion of 'obsession.'" For late-Ming scholars, as Ward observes, possessing a *pi* had become something of a positive attribute. Yuan Hongdao (1568–1610), for example, once asserted that "in this world those whose words are insipid and whose appearance is detestable are all men without obsessions." An admirer of the iconoclast Li Zhi (1527–1602), whose open

---

[65] For the genre of topographical paintings, see Cahill, "Huang Shan Paintings," 253–58; quotations are taken from pp. 253, 256. For Zhang Hong, see idem, *Compelling Image*, Chap. 1; Zhang's quoted words are from p. 16. For an alternative view, see Ganza, "Artist as Traveler"; for quotations, see p. 298.

[66] Peterson, "Confucian Learning," 772–88; quotation is from p. 781. For Xu Guangqi, see Jami et al., *Statecraft and Intellectual Renewal*. For Fang Yizhi, see Peterson, *Bitter Gourd*; Luo Chi, *Fang Yizhi ping zhuan*.

rejection of norms and conventions had thoroughly scandalized the literati of his generation, Yuan was obviously not advocating for just any form of reflexive behavior but for the kind that would enable individuals to express and realize their sentiments (*qing*). To Yuan Hongdao and other late-Ming literati such as the playwright Tang Xianzu (1550–1616), the notion of *qing* (which can also be translated as feeling, emotion, passion, and love) was not antithetical to the concepts of *xing* (human nature) or *li* (coherence), two central concerns of Ming scholars; rather, it completed them. Whereas *xing* and *li* were understood as something universal, *qing* was appreciated as something particular and unique to the individuals. To many in the late Ming, to focus on one's passion – even to the extent of developing a *pi* – was thus not regarded as a flaw. In fact, to Wang Shixing and Xu Hongzu, to name two of the better-known travelers of the time, it was through their obsessions with travels and through their meticulous recordings of what they observed that they were able to express and realize their *qing* and to attain, ultimately, self-cultivation.[67]

To draw one final connection between the growing emphasis on empirical knowledge, the increased demarcation and categorization of the borderland population, and the changing cultural landscape of seventeenth-century China, let us consider, again, a passage found in a late-Ming gazetteer concerning the *man yi* in the county of Huaiyuan. According to the compiler of the text, even though there were active in Huaiyuan different types of *yi* – the six identified were Yao, Dong, Zhuang, Ling, Dàn, and Miao – many of their practices were quite similar. Not only was it customary for young men and women to gather together and sing to one another (*da ge*) during festivals in the spring and in the autumn ("The Yao have Yao songs, the Dong have Dong songs, and the Zhuang have Zhuang songs"), it was also the practice of the *yi* to take advantage of such occasions to mate. It was not until after the women had gotten pregnant and moved into their husbands' households that "restrictions on [their] lewdness became more stringent." As objectionable as these practices might appear to the compiler of the gazetteer, what to him was "most repugnant" (*zui e*) was the custom of levirate marriage, the practice of marrying one's brother's widow. To the compiler, as no doubt to his fellow literati, "this is truly a custom of the *yi di*."[68]

What is noteworthy about this passage, apart from its detailed depiction of the practices of the "non-Chinese" in Huaiyuan, is its clear affirmation

---

[67] Ward, *Xu Xiake*, 27; Peterson, "Confucian Learning," 774–76.
[68] For the passage from the gazetteer of Huaiyuan, see *YXCZ*, 18:18b–20.

of the distinction between *hua* and *yi*. As we have seen, there were among Ming observers two guiding impulses in writing about the so-called non-Chinese. On the one hand, there was an urge to draw attention to the humanity and – by extension – the potential for transformation of the *man yi*. In the 1590 edition of the *Gazetteer of Pingle Prefecture*, for example, it is reported that not only were the Yao and Zhuang in the area willing to pay taxes to the centralizing state, they were also keen on sending their children to study in government schools. On the other hand, there was also a strong inclination to emphasize the beastly nature of the "non-Chinese." In the case of the Yao, not only did Ming observers make regular references to the legend of Panhu the dog, they also frequently called attention to the Yao custom of courtship (in which young men and women were said to be free to interact and mate with one another). In the case of the Zhuang, not only were Zhuang women often described in disapproving terms similar to those for the Yao, they were also closely associated with the use of *gu* poisons. What the passage from the *Gazetteer of Huaiyuan County* illustrates then is that just as it was increasingly common for Ming officials to distinguish among the *man yi* population, it remained important also for them to reaffirm the boundary between "Chinese" and "non-Chinese."[69]

That late-Ming literati found it increasingly necessary – even as they continued to employ the rhetorics of transformation and civilization – to reaffirm the boundaries between "Chinese" and "non-Chinese" is perhaps not surprising. As Wm. Theodore de Bary, Timothy Brook, and others have noted, the commercialization and urbanization of late-Ming society, while it created more opportunities for the literati, also imposed on them an immense pressure. Not only did the educated elite have to cope with a growing body of specialized knowledge, they also had to confront the challenges posed by the rise in social mobility and what they perceived as the erosion of standards and distinctions. To defend their status as "men of culture" (*wen ren*) – especially against the competing claims by the *nouveau riches* – late-Ming literati seemed particularly eager to reaffirm the ideals of the Way as they are embodied in the Four Books and Five Classics. This affirmation of normative values assumed many forms; not only can it be found in the formal writings of late-Ming scholars, it can also be detected, as Andrew Plaks has shown, in the major literati novels of the time. The significance of the comments in the *Gazetteer of Huaiyuan County* can thus be better understood in this context.

---

[69] For Pingle, see *YXCZ*, 18:18a.

Just as there was a growing demand in the late-Ming period for detailed descriptions of the "non-Chinese" in the border region, there was also an increased need by late-Ming literati to reaffirm the boundaries between *hua* and *yi*.[70]

---

[70] de Bary, "Introduction," 8–12; Brook, *Confusions of Pleasure*, 253–60; Plaks, *Four Masterworks*, 50–51.

6   Margins in history

The history of China can no longer be innocently a history of the West or the history of the true China. It must attend to the politics of narratives – whether these be the rhetorical schemas we deploy for our own understanding or those of the historical actors who give us their world.

Prasenjit Duara, *Rescuing History from the Nation*

The practice and process of identifying and categorizing the border population in China have persisted – albeit in different contexts – through the Qing to the modern period. In late imperial times, the demarcation of the borderland population was clearly grounded on the desire of the centralizing state to extend control as well as on the imperial rhetoric of "transformation through submission" (*gui hua*). Although Qing-dynasty emperors were in general more concerned with the regions corresponding to present-day Mongolia, Xinjiang (Eastern Turkestan), and Tibet than with the border zone in the south, they did find it important to catalog the different peoples under their rule as well as to ascertain the degree of transformation or submission of individual populations. In the Republican period, by contrast, revolutionary and intellectual leaders were evidently less interested in sustaining an empire than in the creation of a modern nation-state. Although they did much to identify and categorize the "non-Han" peoples, most members of the elites were ultimately concerned with how and when the "non-Han" would be transformed through assimilation (*tong hua*) or enlightenment (*kai hua*). Finally, in post-1949 China, the central government under the rule of the Communist Party would declare the People's Republic a "unitary multi-national state" (*tong yi duo min zu guo jia*) and would in time officially recognize fifty-five "minority nationalities." Although the government would abandon the earlier rhetorics of *gui hua* and *tong hua*, it would emphasize, especially in the post-Mao era, the importance of minority peoples being transformed through modernization (*xian dai hua*).

184

But even though the contexts have changed, the continuities of the practices and processes are remarkable. From the imperial to the modern period, the demarcation of the border population has clearly been founded on the perception of cultural differences. Whether such perceived distinctions have been framed in terms of the degree of civilization (in the imperial era), the level of enlightenment (in the Republican period), or the stage of modernization (in post-1949 China), it is evident that they have all been informed by a strong sense of cultural hierarchy. Through the imperial to the modern era, the identification and categorization of the borderland population has also been closely linked to the state's concern for control. Especially in border regions where the reach of the state has been limited, it was (and is) important for the centralizing state to distinguish between peoples based on, among other considerations, their perceived ties to the central authorities. Finally, in imperial as well as in modern times, the demarcation of the border population must be viewed *not* as an afterthought but as an integral part of the creation and projection of political identities. Just as Qing-dynasty emperors wanted to be seen as overlords of a vast array of peoples, the Chinese Communist Party would also like to be perceived as presiding over a unitary state made up of a multitude of nationalities.[1]

By pursuing the story of identification and categorization into the modern period, what I seek to underscore is that what we have learned about the Ming does help explain how the modern Chinese nation-state has come into being. Although ethnic politics in contemporary China is intimately tied to the rise of modern nationalism, how Chinese political and intellectual elites have approached the task of fabricating a unitary nation-state out of a collage of distinct populations must ultimately be understood in the broader context of state-building in later imperial China. In particular, even though the political boundaries of the Ming are significantly different from that of contemporary China, how the Ming state had marked – rather than erased – the distinctions among its population has clearly shaped the ways how Chinese in modern-day China have defined themselves. To be sure, the identities of the fifty-six nationalities that officially constitute the Chinese nation-state are invented. But just as important a story, this book argues, is the essential role of the practice and process of identification and demarcation in the formation and transformation of the Chinese state.

---

[1] For a parallel discussion with a different focus, see Harrell, "Introduction: Civilizing Projects."

Multiple constituencies

During the long eighteenth century, two distinct but related impulses seem to have shaped the way the Qing state incorporated and administered its southern borderland. On the one hand, as the "Manchu" Qing – which had first emerged in the early seventeenth century as a confederation of militias ("banners") on the northeastern border of Ming China – doubled the size of the territory and population under its rule, it was imperative that it develop an effective system of control. The issue of control was important because of the unprecedented territorial and demographic expansion, but it was critical also because Qing emperors were still deemed by many of their subjects as alien conquerors, both unfit and unprepared to preside over as immense and cultured a realm as the central dominion. On the other hand, as Qing rulers gained more confidence in their roles, they also began to see themselves as emperors of a universal empire that comprised not only the domain of the Ming but also, in time, the territories corresponding to present-day Mongolia (Inner and Outer), Xinjiang (Eastern Turkestan), and Tibet. Not only did Qing emperors think of themselves as rulers of the Han (a label now used increasingly frequently in the official records), they also viewed themselves as overlords of peoples (or what Pamela Crossley would call "constituencies") from a variety of regions. What fueled this sense of universalism was more than territorial ambition. For eighteenth-century Qing emperors, their success in bringing order to an immense and diverse empire was a compelling testimony not only to the military prowess of the Qing state but also to their personal authority and power.[2]

In the border region in the south, concerns for control by Qing rulers had in turn led to two competing approaches. The first was to be assertive. Although Qing emperors had originally adopted the Ming practice of recognizing native chieftains, in time they would come to support the conversion of native domains into regular administrative units. Enthusiasm for this process of *gai tu gui liu* was most evident in the case of the Yongzheng emperor (r. 1723–35), who, perhaps more so than any other ruler of the "high" Qing, was concerned about centralizing power and eliminating what one scholar has referred to as "all mediating influences that came between ruler and minister and ruler and subject." Even though Qing emperors were no doubt keen on enhancing their control of

---

[2] For the nature of early- to mid-Qing rulership, see, for example, Kuhn, *Soulstealers*; Rawski, *Last Emperors*; Crossley, *Translucent Mirror*; Elliott, *Manchu Way*; Spence, *Treason by the Book*; Perdue, *China Marches West*. See also the chapters by Jerry Dennerline, Jonathan Spence, Madeleine Zelin, and Alexander Woodside in Peterson, *Cambridge History of China*.

the south and the southwest in part because of the abundance of mineral and other resources in the region, they nevertheless sought to justify their actions by projecting themselves as benevolent rulers who wanted nothing more than to protect the natives from exploitation by chieftains. In addition to converting native domains into regular administrative units, Qing emperors and their representatives were also interested in "civilizing" the native population through education. This can be seen in as early as the Shunzhi reign (1644–61), when favorable quotas were established for the *miao yao* (understood here as a general reference for the "non-Chinese" peoples in the south) candidates in the civil service examination system, and this can be observed in the official drive, at least until the second half of the eighteenth century, to establish in border areas so-called charity schools (*yi xue*). But such efforts had their limits. In Guangxi, for example, although a large number of native domains were converted into regular units, powerful chieftain families, notably the Cens of Tianzhou, would continue to defy the Qing attempts to assert control.[3]

By contrast, the second approach to control of the southern region was more circumspect. Although it was the rhetoric of Qing rulers to "civilize" the *miao yao*, it would become clear to them that such transformations would come only at a high cost. Not only did chieftains rebel when pressed to give up power, native peoples whose land was the target of encroachment by newly arrived settlers also fought back. The result was a variety of warfare. To maintain order, Qing emperors apparently found it necessary to defend rather than demolish the boundaries between natives and settlers. This can be seen in the policy of quarantine imposed on Taiwan (to limit migration from the mainland) when the island was first brought under Qing control at the turn of the eighteenth century. This can be observed also in the promulgation in western Hunan in the early eighteenth century of a set of so-called *miao* substatutes (*miao li*), whose purposes were to reduce local conflicts and to prevent what might be seen as exploitation of non-Han natives by Han settlers. Even efforts to educate the *miao yao*, as manifested in the establishment of schools mentioned earlier, would in time be viewed by the Qianlong emperor (r. 1736–95) as largely futile. Thus, even though it was in the interest of Qing rulers to extend control to areas once held

---

[3] For the quotation, see Zelin, "The Yung-cheng Reign," 193. For the project of *gai tu gui liu*, see Herman, "Empire in the Southwest." For a survey of "Han" and "non-Han" relations in early to mid-Qing, see Rowe, "Social Stability and Social Change," 502–11. For the notion of "civilization" as interepreted by Qing-dynasty officials, see Rowe, *Saving the World*, Chap. 12. For the complex project of state making in the Qing period, see Crossley et al., *Empire at the Margins*.

by native chieftains, to maintain order, it was often to the emperors' benefit to reinforce the boundaries between Han and non-Han.[4]

At the same time, Qing emperors, more consciously so than their Ming counterparts, liked to think of themselves as rulers of a universal empire. This is reflected, for instance, in the imperial sponsorship of the compilation of the *Illustrations of the Tributaries of the Qing Imperium* (*Huang Qing zhi gong tu*), a collection of illustrations and descriptions of "peoples" who had purportedly maintained tributary relations with the Qing. Originally commissioned by the Qianlong emperor, the *Illustrations* was eventually completed, probably in stages and by different hands, in 1805. As early as 1751, the emperor was reported to have instructed his Grand Council to provide sample submissions for senior provincial officials so that they could in turn prepare and submit to the Council illustrations of not only the "Miao, Yao, Li, and Zhuang" under their jurisdiction but also that of the "multitude of outer *yi* and *fan*" active along the borders. Of the 301 entries that comprise the so-called Xie Sui edition of the *Illustrations*, about one quarter are devoted to peoples from foreign lands (including Korea, Russia, and France), while the remaining three quarters are set aside for the "non-Han" peoples in the border regions of Qing China. As in the cases of all entries, each of the thirty-three illustrations associated with the "peoples" of Guangxi features a man and a woman invariably dressed in what was thought to be their typical attire. The Yao, Zhuang, and Miao (among other groups) so included are always identified in the *Illustrations* with a specific administrative area ("the Yao people of Xiuren county," "the Lang people of Cenxi county," etc.) and are often depicted carrying tools that are meant to suggest their modes of livelihood (see Figure 6.1). The commentary that accompanies each entry (in both Chinese and Manchu in the "Xie Sui" edition) includes many stock descriptions, but its also incorporates historical and seemingly firsthand observations that are not found in earlier records. The *Illustrations*, with its professed focus on the Qing tributary relations, was no doubt compiled to display in one practical format the "splendors of the realm" (as suggested in the 1751 edict). Through the practice of inclusion and exclusion, the work is clearly also, in the words of Pamela Crossley, "a document of objectification and alienation." But even as Qing-dynasty emperors thought of themselves as rulers of universal appeal, the issue of control was never far away from their mind. For Qing rulers, As Laura Hostetler argues, "it was important to have a record of the

---

[4] For Taiwan, see Shepherd, *Statecraft and Political Economy on the Taiwan Frontier*. For *miao li*, see the essay by Donald Sutton in Crossley et al., *Empire at the Margins*. For the closing of schools, see Rowe, "Social Stability and Social Change," 507.

修仁縣頂板猺婦

修仁縣頂板猺人

岑溪縣狼婦

岑溪縣狼人

Figure 6.1. The Yao of Xiuren (top) and the Lang of Cenxi (bottom).
Source: Huang Qing zhi gong tu, 4:36, 54.

provenance of each group, of what point it came under central authority, and in which precise jurisdiction."[5]

This desire of Qing rulers and officials to identify and categorize the peoples under their rule can also be observed in the creation and compilation of the so-called *miao* albums (*miao man tu* or *bai miao tu*). As in the *Illustrations*, in these *miao* albums (some of which are actually in the form of scrolls) one could find images and descriptions of a variety of "non-Han" peoples who were thought to populate the border regions of Qing China. But in contrast to the *Illustrations*, such albums are at once more narrow in scope and more in-depth in content. With each *miao man tu* usually devoted to a single province (mostly Guizhou or Yunnan) or an even smaller administrative area, the authors of the albums were often able to portray in graphic detail what was thought to be the everyday life of various "non-Han" groups. And while the commentaries in the *Illustrations* tend to focus on the origins and history of individual "peoples," those found in the *miao* albums are generally more concerned with the customs and practices of the "non-Han" groups in question. Although some of the pictures and commentaries in the *miao man tu* are clearly copied from earlier gazetteers, in general, the pictorial representations and textual descriptions in such albums do appear to reflect firsthand observations. And although very little is known about the origins and authorship of these *miao* albums (we do know that the Kangxi emperor [r. 1662–1722] had requested drawings of similar nature to be submitted to him), the appearance of such *miao man tu* in the eighteenth century does seem to reflect not only the efforts by Qing borderland officials to identify and catalog the "non-Han" peoples under their jurisdiction but also the desire of Qing observers to distinguish between peoples of different levels of "transformation" or "civilization."[6]

This penchant of mid-Qing officials to identify and categorize the border population can also be observed through local gazetteers. In the 1733 edition of the *General Gazetteer of Guangxi*, for example, at least eighteen categories of *man* are identified (see Table 6.1). In addition to familiar categories such as "Yao," "Zhuang," "Lao," "Lang," and "Ling," the compilers also recognize several that are not found in earlier gazetteers, among which are "Sha," "Kang," "Nong," "Ya," "Li," and "Làng." While

[5] For an introduction to the *Illustrations*, see Chuang Chi-fa, *Xie Sui "Zhi gong tu,"* 1–37; Hostetler, *Qing Colonial Enterprise*, 41–49, 205–206. For the edict of 1751, see Chuang Chi-fa, *Xie Sui "Zhi gong tu,"* 11. For quotations, see Crossley, *Translucent Mirror*, 335; Hostetler, *Qing Colonial Enterprise*, 206.

[6] For an introduction to the *miao* albums, see Hostetler, *Qing Colonial Enterprise*, 159–79, 206–207. For a discussion of such albums in the context of Qing-dynasty Taiwan, see Teng, *Taiwan's Imagined Geography*. Samples of such *miao man tu* can also be found in Song Guangyu et al., *Hua nan bian jiang min zu tu lu*.

Table 6.1. *Categories of "non-Chinese" in Guangxi, 1493–1801*

		1493	1531	1599	1733	1801
Lao	獠	•	•	•	•	•
Yao	猺	•	•	•	•	•
Zhuang	獞	•	•	•	•	•
Ling	狑	•		•	•	•
Man of Guangyuan	廣源蠻		•	•		
Man of Xiyuan	西原蠻		•	•		
Banyizhongnü	斑衣種女			•		
Daliang	大良			•		
Yin	狁			•		
Dan	蜑			•	•	•
Dong	狪			•	•	•
Shanzi	山子			•	•	•
Bing	狉				•	•
Ge	犵				•	•
Kang	犺				•	•
Lang	狼				•	•
Làng	浪				•	•
Li	狸				•	•
Miao	苗				•	•
Nong	獩				•	•
Sha	狖				•	•
Ya	犽				•	•
Yang	𦍙				•	•
Ba	巴					•
Dàn	狚					•
Guo	猓					•
Lai	狭					•
Ma	馬					•
Zhong	狆					•

Sources:
1493: *GXTZ* (1531), "Guangxi jiu zhi xu," 3–4.
1531: *GXTZ* (1531), 53:1–2.
1599: *GXTZ* (1599), 33:1–4a.
1733: *GXTZ* (1733), juan 92–93.
1801: Xie Qikun et at., *Guangxi tong zhi*, juan 278–79.

the so-called Sha people are noted for their preferences for living near water and for relocating periodically, people identified as Làng are said to have come from Guangdong, Hunan, and what is now Vietnam. Just as significant, in the gazetteer the compilers apparently also finds it useful to include county-level descriptions of the distribution of individual *man* groups. Although it is difficult to gauge the reliability of such descriptions, they are by far the most detailed that had been compiled for the province. This pattern of increased demarcation can be seen also in the 1801 edition of the *General Gazetteer of Guangxi*. There, in addition to the *man* categories that had been identified, the compilers also recognize "Ma" "Lai," "Ba," "Guo," and "Zhong" as distinct "peoples." Although the identification of such groups was most likely not based on firsthand observations (the compilers of the gazetteer in question were unusually diligent in citing their sources), it does illustrate the propensity of Qing officials to identify and categorize the population under their rule.[7]

Imagining the nation

The need to account for the unity and diversity of the people of China evidently took on an added degree of urgency in the Republican period. On the one hand, as revolutionary leaders and intellectual elites of this era struggled to construct a modern nation-state (*guo jia*) out of the wreckage of the Qing empire, it became apparent to them that they had to insist that people who lived in this new *guo jia* belonged to a common *zhong zu* or *min zu*. (Although the terms *zhong zu* and *min zu* have often been translated as "race" and "nation," respectively, I have in general left them untranslated as a reminder that their meanings were – and are – far from stable.) Of the revolutionary leaders who lectured on the subject, the most passionate, if not necessarily the most original, was Sun Yat-sen (1866–1925). In his "Principle of the Nation," which was first delivered as a series of lectures in early 1924 and which would in time form part of his *Three Principles of the People* (*San min zhu yi*), Sun argues that unlike other *guo jia* in the world, China has since the Qin and Han dynasties been made up of a single *min zu*. In his view, the human species can be categorized first into races (*ren zhong*), of which there are five (White, Black, Red, Yellow, and Brown), and then within each race into a variety of *min zu*. For Sun Yat-sen, a *min zu* is constituted by natural (rather than coercive) forces; members of a *min zu* share a common ancestry, a common mode of living, a common language, a common religion, and a common set of customs. Although there are in China "several million Mongols, more than a million Manchus, several million Tibetans, and a million some Muslim Turks," Sun contends in a much-quoted passage, "as far as the majority is concerned, the four hundred million Chinese people [*Zhongguo ren*] can all be regarded as Han people, with shared blood ties, a common spoken and written language, a common religion, and common habits – all in all, [members of] a single *min zu*."[8]

---

[7] *GXTZ* (1733), juan 92–93; Xie Qikun et al., *Guangxi tong zhi*, juan 278–79.
[8] For the usage of the terms *zu*, *zhong zu*, and *min zu*, see Crossley, "Thinking about Ethnicity," 12, 19–20; Dikötter, *Discourse of Race in Modern China*, 28–29, 70–711, 108–10, esp. n. 41. For Sun Yat-sen's impassioned though not always logical arguments, see his

By contrast, it was apparent to the political and intellectual elites of the Republican period that there lived in this new and fragile *guo jia* called China people who were clearly distinct – whether territorially, physically, culturally, socially, or economically – from the majority. To secure support from these groups (especially the peoples of Mongolia, Xinjiang, and Tibet, who had threatened to seek independence), leaders of the early Republic including Sun Yat-sen and Yuan Shikai (1859–1916) had chosen to speak of China as a republic of five *min zu* (i.e., Han, Manchus, Mongols, Hui [Muslims], and Tibetans). To underscore its commitment to "the peaceful coexistence of the five *zu*" (*wu zu gong he*), the early Republican government even featured on its national flag a design of five stripes of equal width. In 1924, the Nationalist Party, then led by Sun and obviously influenced by the Soviet Union, even went so far as to declare in its manifesto of its First National Congress its support of "the right of self-determination of all the *min zu* within China." In time, however, both Sun Yat-sen and his successor, Chiang Kai-shek (1888–1975), would distance themselves from this position. In *China's Destiny*, first published in Chinese in 1943 and translated into English in 1947, Chiang Kai-shek would again insist on China's inherent unity: "The fact that it [China] comprises five stocks is due not to diversity in race or blood but to dissimilarity in creed and geographical environment. In a word, the distinction between the five stocks is territorial as well religious, but not ethnological."[9]

The desire among intellectuals in the Republican period to account for the unity and diversity of the people of China can be readily observed through their writings. Among the more representative of such works are Li Chi's *Formation of the Chinese People* (1928), Zhang Qiyun's *Study of the Chinese Nation* (*Zhongguo min zu zhi*; 1928), and four versions of *History of the Chinese Nation* (*Zhongguo min zu shi*) by, respectively, Wang Tongling (1928), Lü Simian (1934), Song Wenbing (1935), and Lin Huixiang (1936). Although these writings differ in their approaches, at their core they invariably affirm the essential unity or inevitable unification of the Chinese people. For example, in his *Formation of the Chinese People*, Li Chi (1896–1979), who had studied at Harvard, is ultimately interested in the question of what makes up the population of modern-day China. Combining techniques from physical anthropology with textual historical research, Li Chi concludes that Chinese people, not unlike

"Min zu zhu yi," esp. 184–89; quotations are from p. 188. See also Fitzgerald, *Awakening the Nation*.

[9] For the early policies of the Republican government, see Mackerras, *China's Minorities*, 54–56, 59–60. For the declaration of the Nationalist Party, see Sun Yat-sen, "Zhongguo Guo min dang di yi ci quan guo dai biao da hui xuan yan," 119. For Chiang Kai-shek's claims, see his *China's Destiny*, 13.

an organic chemical compound, are made up of a variety of elements. As the "silk-wearing, rice-eating, and city-building Descendants of the Yellow Emperor" expanded outward, Li argues, they absorbed or incorporated, among others, the "horse-riding, kumiss-drinking, flesh-eating Hsiung-nus," the "yak-driving Ch'iangs," the "pig-rearing Tungus," the "cattle-stealing Mongols," the "tattooing Shan-speaking group," the "cremating Tibeto-Burman-speaking group," and the "Kanlan-dwelling Mon-Khmer-speaking group." Li's choice of metaphor might be unintentional but was certainly not arbitrary; the people of China might be a diverse and changing lot, but as with any chemical compound, Li Chi seems to suggest, the particular configuration of their constituents is what allows them to appear as an independent and identifiable unit.[10]

Other historians and anthropologists of the period would come up with different organizing schemes. In his *History of the Chinese Nation*, for example, Lin Huixiang (1901–58), an anthropologist who was for years head of the History and Sociology department at Xiamen University, is particularly interested in the distinctions and links between what he refers to as the *min zu* in history (*li shi shang zhi min zu*) and the *min zu* of modern times (*xian dai zhi min zu*). It is because of their lack of attention to such distinctions and links, he argues, that earlier scholars (such as Li Chi, Wang Tongling, Lü Simian, and Song Wenbing) have come up with a variety of often incommensurable schemes to explain the composition of the people of China. According to Lin, what he seeks to achieve in his study is to document the origins and transformations of the *min zu* of the past and to show how such *min zu* are linked to those of the modern period. In his scheme (see Figure 6.2), the people of early China are divided into fourteen *xi* ("lineages") and two *zhong* ("white" and "black"), whereas the people of the modern period are grouped into eight *zu*. Although each of the modern *min zu* could trace its origins to at least one *xi* in the past (as indicated by the solid lines in the diagram), Lin Huixiang argues, it is evident from the textual records that all have incorporated elements from a variety of *xi* and *zhong* (as indicated by the dotted lines). This phenomenon, according to Lin, is particularly evident in the case of the Han (bottom, 1), which could trace its origins not only directly to the Huaxia (top, 1), the Dongyi (2), the Jingwu (3), and the Baiyue (4) but also indirectly to all other *xi* and *zhong* from the past. To Lin, just as the Huaxia *xi* had in the past succeeded in absorbing or incorporating other *xi* and *zhong*,

---

[10] Li, *Formation of the Chinese People*, esp. 273–76. On Li Chi, see Dikötter, *Discourse of Race in Modern China*, 132–34.

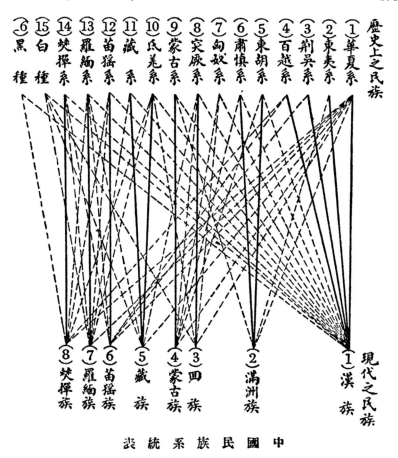

Figure 6.2. Genealogy of the Chinese Nation. *Source:* Lin Huixiang, *Zhongguo min zu shi*, 9.

the Han of modern times would also come to assimilate (*tong hua*) other *min zu*.[11]

With regard to Guangxi, the desire by Repulican-period officials and intellectuals to account for the unity and diversity of its population can also be observed through various publications. Consider first the local gazetteers from this period. Although the quality of these compilations varies, their structure and content do differ significantly from those of earlier gazetteers. This was especially the case for gazetteers

[11] Lin Huixiang, *Zhongguo min zu shi*, esp. 1:1–17, 22–24, 39–40. For a biographical sketch of Lin, see Guldin, *Saga of Anthropology*, 36–39.

completed in or after 1934 when a more concerted effort was launched by the government of Guangxi to collect local data. Of the many changes found in the gazetteers of this period, the most noteworthy is probably the widespread use of the terms *she hui* and *min zu*. As Michael Tsin, among others, has pointed out, for the political and intellectual elites of the Republican period, the greatest challenge was to transform "a heap of sand" that was the people of China (as they were often compared with) into a cohesive "society" or *she hui* that was committed to placing collective gains above individual benefits. The introduction of a separate section on *she hui* in many of the gazetteers compiled during this period was thus not arbitrary. As the compilers of the 1936 edition of the *Gazetteer of Rong County* explained, a "society" was different from a "grouping" (*ren qun*) in that people of a society shared "common relationships, common behaviors, and common [modes of] living." By asserting that the various *min zu* of Rong county (Han, Miao-Yao, Dong-Zhuang, etc.) were in fact members of the same *she hui*, the compilers were clearly making a case for unity over diversity.[12]

But not all *min zu* were deemed equal. Although "non-Han" peoples were often presented in this period as just other rightful *min zu* alongside the "Han," references to the former were frequently couched in culturalist or evolutionary terms. Not only were the beliefs and practices of the "non-Han" often deemed "backward" (*luo hou*), it was also commonly assumed that through intervention or evolution such *min zu* would eventually be assimilated into the "Han." In the 1937 edition of the *Gazetteer of Yongning County*, for instance, even though the compilers acknowledge the presence in the area of four distinct *min zu*, they are quick to remind the reader that people of Hui, Tu, and Zhuang – except in the areas of "religion, language, and attire" – "are now all assimilated into the Han" (*xian jie tong hua yu Han*). Whereas Zhuang women used to blacken their teeth, tattoo their faces, walk around on bare feet, and dress in blouses that expose their chests and shoulders, by the early Republican period, according to the compilers, almost all of the original Zhuang customs have vanished. In ten years' time, the compilers predict, with the disappearance of the remaining Zhuang markers (*hui zhang*), the label (*hui hao*) of the Zhuang race (*zhong*) would also become extinct. The authors of the gazetteer observe also that many of the children of mixed Han and Zhuang parentage have turned out to be bright and handsome. To the

---

[12] For a discussion of *she hui* as a modernist category, see Tsin, *Nation, Governance, and Modernity*, esp. 5–9, 29–31. For Rong county, see Huang Zhixun and Long Tairen, *Rong xian zhi*, 55 (reprint pagination). For Guangxi in the Republican period, see Lary, *Region and Nation*; Levich, *Kwangsi Way*.

compilers, this only proves that human races can indeed be improved (*xin hu ren zhong zhi gai liang*). This conviction on the inevitability of human evolution is best summed up by the authors as thus: "That barbaric people [*ye man ren*] would eventually be overcome by enlightened ones [*wen ming ren*] is the law of natural evolution."[13]

Efforts to understand the relationships between "Han" and "non-Han" can also be found in an array of field reports published in the Republican period. Although ethnology (*min zu xue*) had been established as an academic discipline in China by the late 1920s, some of the most detailed studies of the "non-Han" *min zu* in Guangxi in the 1930s and 1940s were conducted by officials and researchers who had never been trained in the discipline. Take for example the *Notes on the non-Han of Guangxi* by Liu Xifan first published in 1934. A native son of Guangxi, Liu Xifan, who would in time be appointed headmaster of a provincial-level institute dedicated to training "non-Han" teachers, was particularly concerned with the difficulties and urgency of transforming the *man*. Liu's argument in his study is two-fold. First, at least in Guangxi, Liu Xifan argues, the Han and *man* (of the latter he identifies Miao, Yao, Dong, and Zhuang as the most numerous) are in fact members of the same *zu*. This Liu seeks to prove by pointing out that both Han and non-Han share similar family names and that both have much in common in their languages and social customs. Second, Liu Xifan contends, given the level of disdain and ignorance the Han have developed toward the non-Han, it has become unnecessarily difficult for the latter to be assimilated into the Han. To conclude his study, Liu offers a list of what he considers the characteristics (*te dian*), strengths (*you dian*), and weaknesses (*ruo dian*) of the non-Han as well as a series of recommendations he believes would facilitate their "enlightenment" (*kai hua*). In a separate report on the progress of "special education" (*te zhong jiao yu*) in Guangxi, Liu Xifan would in time reiterate his argument that to educate and assimilate China's "special" *min zu*, the government must commit its resources to conduct field investigations. Only with a firm knowledge of the various *min zu*, Liu contends, could the government be able to formulate proper policies to assist their transformations.[14]

Consider also the works by Xu Songshi (1900–99). In his well-known study, *History of the People of the Yue River Region* (1939), Xu, a native

---

[13] Mo Bingkui et al., *Yongning xian zhi*, 5.1611–15; quotations are from pp. 1611, 1615.

[14] For the establishment of ethnology as an academic discipline, see Guldin, *Saga of Anthropology*, esp. 30–34; Wang Jianmin, *Zhongguo min zu xue shi*, Vol. 1, esp. Chap. 4. For Liu Xifan's observations, see his *Ling biao ji man*, esp. Chaps. 28–30; *Guangxi te zhong jiao yu*, esp. 67–75.

son of Guangxi and a Christian minister by calling, sets out to show that the so-called Miao, Yao, Zhuang, and so on, in south China are not members of distinct *zhong zu* or *min zu* but are instead members of *bu zu* ("tribes") of an inclusive Han *zu*. Xu argues that the label "Han" should be applied to not only the heirs of the Yellow Emperor but also the descendants of various *bu zu* active in the Yellow, Yangzi, and Yue river regions in the ancient period. Noting the resemblance between ancient Chinese and the Miao, Yao, and Zhuang languages and citing the frequent usage of Zhuang words in the creation of place-names in south China, Xu Songshi contends that the various *man* in the southern provinces were in fact the earliest settlers in the region and should in some sense be regarded as "the purest Han people" (*zui chun cui de Han ren*). To Xu, the distinctions between Han and *man* are not genetic but historical; it is people from the central plains, he maintains, who have persistently sought to distinguish between those who are closely associated with the cultural center and those who are not. "It is only after the culture of the central plains had become the orthodox culture of China," Xu Songshi argues, "that there emerged the boundary between *hua* and *man*." Unlike Liu Xifan, Xu was not primarily interested in assimilating the *man* (as a Christian minister, he was no doubt more concerned with their religious conversion). What informs Xu's works, however, is his conviction that there is a nation or *min zu* that constitutes the state that is China and that this Chinese nation (*Zhonghua min zu*) is both unitary in its core and diverse in its composition.[15]

Making of minorities

In contrast to the Republican period, China since 1949 has witnessed a more concerted effort by the state to recognize its "minority nationalities." Whether its objective was to gain support from the "non-Han" *min zu* or to demonstrate its commitment to the Marxist–Leninist–Stalinist ideology, in as early as the 1930s, the Chinese Communist Party was on record as supporting the theory of equality and the right to self-governance of China's minority *min zu*. In the 1931 "Constitution of the Chinese Soviet Republic," for example, it is stated that "the Soviet Government of China recognizes the right of self-determination of the minority nationalities in China, to the extent that every weak and small *min zu* has the right to separate from China and to establish for itself an independent state." This position was later subtly modified by Mao

---

[15] Xu Songshi, *Yuejiang liu yu ren min shi*; for quotations, see his preface to the original edition and p. 40.

Zedong (1883–1976), who declared in a speech in 1938 that minority
min zu should be allowed the right to administer their own affairs "while
at the same time joining the [people of] Han *zu* in establishing a unified
state." This principle of "limited autonomy" would later be codified in
the "Common Guidelines" (*Gong tong gang ling*), a political blueprint
drafted on the eve of the founding of the People's Republic, in which it
is declared that all *min zu* in China are equal, that "autonomous administrative areas" (*zi zhi qu*) would be established in minority territories,
and that all *min zu* are free to develop their languages and scripts, preserve and reform their customs, and observe their religious faiths. Most
of these clauses would in time be incorporated into the Constitution of
the People's Republic of 1954, in which China is formally proclaimed a
"unitary multi-national state."[16]

To implement "self-rule" among the so-called minority nationalities,
the central government decided in 1952 to issue a set of further guidelines.
Autonomous administrative areas, according to the expanded "Guidelines," would be set up in areas where a substantial portion of the population was constituted by one or more minority *min zu*. The government of a *zi zhi qu* would be headed by members of the minority group
or groups in question but efforts would be made to include members
of other *min zu*. The governments of such autonomous administrative
areas would be allowed to promulgate their own regulations so long as
such regulations were approved by the local authorities of higher level.
Although the total number of *zi zhi qu* would fluctuate, by 1984, when
the Law of Autonomy for Minority Nationality Regions (which codifies
the "Guidelines" of 1952), was finally passed, there were according to
official data 119 autonomous administrative areas, of which 5 were at the
region (*qu*) level, 31 at the prefecture level, and 83 at the county level. In
the case of Guangxi, although the establishment of a provincial-level *zi
zhi qu* had not been high on the official agenda, by 1958, the establishment of the Guangxi Zhuang Autonomous Region would be seen by the
central government as a key step in integrating the "Zhuang" and other
minority nationalities into the state.[17]

---

[16] For the early policies of the Chinese Communist Party, see Dreyer, *China's Forty Millions*,
Chaps. 4–5; Mackerras, *China's Minorities*, 72–78, 139–50. Excerpts from the "Constitution of the Chinese Soviet Republic," the 1938 speech by Mao, and the "Common
Guidelines" are found in Zhongguo she hui ke xue yuan min zu yan jiu suo min zu wen
ti li lun yan jiu shi, *Dang de min zu zheng ce*, 16–17, 50, 113–15.

[17] For the establishment of autonomous administrative areas, especially with regard to the
Guangxi Zhuang Autonomous Region, see Kaup, *Creating the Zhuang*, 78–93. For the
"Guidelines," see Ren min chu ban she, *Min zu zheng ce wen xian hui bian*, 67–72. For
the 1984 figures, see in Zhongguo da bai ke quan shu chu ban she bian ji bu, *Zhongguo
da bai ke quan shu: min zu*, 538.

To enforce its overall control of the autonomous administrative areas, the central government has from very early on implemented programs to recruit and train minority cadres. As early as November 1950, the government approved the setting up of the Central Institute of Nationalities at Beijing (which was opened in 1951 and renamed in 1993 as the Central University of Nationalities) and three regional institutes in northwest, southwest, and south-central China. These institutes of nationalities were expected to offer training in political studies and minority languages to both "Han" and "non-Han" cadres as well as to conduct research on subjects (including language, history, culture, society, and economy) related to minority nationalities. In addition, the government also approved in principle in 1950 the establishment of provincial-level cadre schools as well as the setting up at various administrative levels primary, secondary, and higher-education institutions for minority students. In Guangxi, an institute of nationalities was established in Nanning in as early as 1952. In time, numerous minority cadre schools would also be set up in various parts of the autonomous region.[18]

The implementation of these policies, however, relied to a great extent on a practical *min zu* classification scheme. As early as the summer of 1950, teams of cadres and scholars were dispatched by the central government to minority areas to explain to the people there the policies of the government and to investigate the conditions of the *shao shu min zu*. As a result of this apparent openness of the new government, more than four hundred "nationalities" are reported in the National Census of 1953. To sort out the claims and to reduce the number of officially recognized *min zu*, the Nationalities Affairs Committee, which had been set up in 1949 to formulate and implement policies concerning minority nationalities, initiated in that same year the project of "nationality identification" (*min zu shi bie*). With the help of newly reorganized academic and research institutes, the Commission sent out teams of investigators – many of whom were prominent ethnologists, linguists, and historians – to conduct fieldwork among the various *min zu*. Although many of these researchers were conscious of the criteria stated by Stalin in 1913 that "a nation is a historically constituted, stable community of people, formed on the basis of a common language, territory, economic life, and psychological make-up manifested in a common culture," they were aware that they must adjust the four criteria to suit the situations in China. As a result of the works of *min zu shi bie*, fifty-three minority nationalities are reported in the Second National Census of 1964 (by the time of the Third National Census in

---

[18] Dreyer, *China's Forty Millions*, 108–14. For Guangxi, see Kaup, *Creating the Zhuang*, 132–33. For the guidelines in setting up the institutes of nationalities, see Ren min chu ban she, *Min zu zheng ce wen xian hui bian*, 12–15.

1982, the number of *shao shu min zu* would stand at fifty-five). In the case of Guangxi, although the project of "nationality identification" was complicated by the fact that some people who seemed to fit the criteria of being members of a particular *min zu* either did not want to be perceived as a minority or did not want to be assigned a particular nationality label, by 1964, eleven "non-Han" *min zu* – Zhuang, Yao, Miao, Dong, Mulao, Maonan, Hui, Jing, Yi, Shui, and Gelao (most would now be identified by modified Chinese characters) – would be officially recognized.[19]

The official classification of *min zu* was accompanied also by the creation of a more formal body of knowledge. As we have seen, the carrying out of state-sponsored field research in minority areas had already begun in the summer of 1950, but it was in the summer of 1956 that the Nationalities Affairs Committee of the National People's Congress formally endorsed the implementation of a large-scale "investigation of the societies and histories of minority nationalities" (*shao shu min zu she hui li shi diao cha*). The guiding principle for the project, as explained in the Committee's directive, was to "first investigate the productivity level, system of ownership, and class conditions of each minority nationality society and then to collect as much as possible materials concerning the historical development and special customs and habits [of each *min zu*]." Researchers from various disciplines were divided into eight teams (to which eight more would be added in 1958), with each team responsible for a province or a region. In the case of Guangxi, several dozen researchers were reported to have participated in the investigation. Special attention was apparently given to the Zhuang, the Yao, the Mulao, and the Maonan. Together, the investigators of Guangxi are said to have produced more than twenty-six million characters' worth of research materials, a significant portion of which was eventually re-edited and published in the 1980s as part of the "Five-part Series on Nationalities Issues" (*Min zu wen ti wu zhong cong shu*) under the general editorship of the Nationalities Affairs Commission of the State Council.[20]

---

[19] For the early investigation teams and a history of the project of "nationality identification," see Wang Jianmin et al., *Zhongguo min zu xue shi*, vol. 2, 50–56, 106–29. Stalin's quotation is found in Mackerras, *China's Minorities*, 141. For Guangxi, see Kaup, *Creating the Zhuang*, 88–91. For brief descriptions of the minority nationalities in Guangxi, see Guangxi bai ke quan shu bian zuan wei yuan hui, *Guangxi bai ke quan shu*, 52–59.

[20] For a history of the investigation project, see Wang Jianmin et al., *Zhongguo min zu xue shi*, Vol. 2, Chaps. 6–7; the directive is quoted in pp. 159–60. For the implementation of the project in Guangxi, see Guangxi bai ke quan shu bian zuan wei yuan hui, *Guangxi bai ke quan shu*, 650–51; Guangxi Zhuangzu Zizhiqu di fang zhi bian zuan wei yuan hui, *Guangxi tong zhi: min su zhi*, 408. For a discussion of the officially-sponsored five-part series, see Wang Jianmin et al., *Zhongguo min zu xue shi*, vol. 2, 340–42. For an innovative study that makes use of the rich materials collected in the investigation reports, see Took, *A Native Chieftaincy in Southwest China*.

For the "Han" majority and more generally the Chinese state, the identification and objectification of the "non-Han" have contributed to at least two levels of discourse. On one level, as Dru Gladney, among others, has argued, the continual representation of the "minority nationalities" across a wide range of popular media as exotic and even erotic actually tells us less about the *shao shu min zu* themselves than about the construction of the majority identity in contemporary China. In contrast to the "non-Han," who are still often portrayed in Chinese popular print and visual media as leading a "traditional," "colorful," and "carefree" lifestyle, the "Han," despite their internal diversity, are regularly presented as a homogeneous group who can be counted on to lead the way to China's modernity. On another level, the objectification of "non-Han" groups in contemporary China has also served to reinforce the notion of a "unitary multi-national state." In his widely cited essay, "The Pattern of Diversity in Unity of the Chinese Nation," which was first delivered as a lecture in Hong Kong in 1988 and which would in time spawn a high-profile conference sponsored by the Nationalities Affairs Commission, for example, Fei Xiaotong maintains that the fifty-six *min zu* in China have had in fact a long history of interactions. Since at least the Neolithic period, Fei argues, the various *min zu* have had to engage in a complicated process of "give and take" (*wo zhong you ni, ni zhong you wo*). But even though each of the fifty-six "nationalities" has contributed to the making of *Zhonghua min zu*, it is the Han people, Fei contends, who have been the centripetal force in this process.[21]

But "Han" people and state representatives have not been alone in imagining *min zu* identities. Members of individual minority groups, as recent ethnographies have testified, have also actively engaged in self-representation. Consider for instance the case of the Miao, China's fifth largest *shao shu min zu*. Although state agents and the "Han" population at large have been instrumental in refashioning "Miao" as a legitimate and unitary category of nationalities, as Louisa Schein argues, people who have come to identify themselves as Miao have also found it beneficial (and, in some cases, even imperative) to embrace their perceived Miaoness. In the arena of culture, this can be seen, especially during the Mao era, in the regular performances in state-sponsored celebrations and functions of "traditional" *min zu* songs and dances by recognized expert minority performers, and this readiness on the part of the so-called Miao people to incorporate their *min zu* identity can be observed

---

[21] For "Han" representations of "non-Han," see, for example, Gladney, *Dislocating China*; Blum, *Portraits of "Primitives."* For the idea of "diversity in unity," see Fei Xiaotong, "Zhonghua min zu duo yuan yi ti ge ju."

also, particularly in the post-Mao period, in the race among minority entrepreneurs to market their "Miaoness" as ultimate symbols of authenticity. Nor, as Schein has shown, is this urge by the "Miao" to embrace their identity invariably a result of economic considerations. Whereas for some minority members the double jeopardy of the Cultural Revolution (1966–76) and the economic reforms since the early 1980s have generated a feeling of nostalgia and a desire to recover the essence of Miaoness, for others members the yearning to be seen as modern has led to their distinction between Miao people who remain "backward" and those who, as in their cases, have made significant progress.[22]

Consider also the case of the Yao. As Ralph Litzinger explains, minority elites – intellectuals, scholars, officials, cadres, and so on – have long occupied a strategic position in the representation of *min zu* identities. Not only have they participated in debates concerning minority classification, they have also taken an active part in the formulation of the official histories of individual *min zu*. In the case of the Yao, for example, minority scholars have been particularly interested in documenting not only the long and continuous history of the so-called Yao people but also how the resourceful and resilient *min zu* had been able to stand against the oppressive "feudal" order. But as Litzinger has shown, "Yao" elites in the post-Mao period have had to engage in a complex balancing act. Whereas during the Mao era their overriding concern had been to project an image of a *min zu* committed to participating in the socialist revolution, in the reform period, when "tradition" and "culture" have again come to be seen as valuable assets, they have found themselves having not only to uphold the ideals of progress and development but also to recover and to showcase, both literally and metaphorically, what are deemed to be the traditional beliefs and practices of the Yao people.[23]

Such projects of self-representation, perhaps not surprising, have been transformed in recent years by the information revolution. As more and more people in China gained access to the Internet, they have also created a range of online communities. Among such cyberspace networks, the most intriguing (for our purpose) are the ones founded by members of various minority *min zu*. Although it is impossible to determine precisely the size or composition of such imagined communities, their appearance does illustrate how the use of technology has supplemented other more conventional means of asserting one's identities. And although in many cases members of such online communities seem content and ready to celebrate their official *min zu* identities, in other cases they appear

[22] Schein, *Minority Rules*.
[23] Litzinger, *Other Chinas*.

more ambivalent. Consider for instance the community associated with Web site Rauz.net. Although the Chinese name of the site is *Zhuang zu zai xian* ("Zhuang nationality online"), visitors would quickly learn that the objective of the site is "to facilitate the transmission and development of the culture of the Rau people." According to the site, "Rau" (a label not officially recognized) is a general designation not only for the Zhuang and Buyi nationalities found mostly in south China but also for the Tay (Chinese: Dai) and Nung (Nong) minorities in Vietnam. Visitors to Rauz.net could find not only descriptions of the history, culture, and current state of affairs of the reputed Rau (Chinese: Lao) collective but also an online forum through which they could interact with one another. Although we know very little about this particular site except that it was founded in 2001 and that its members are most likely relatively young, educated, and affluent, it is clear that its organizers have to walk a fine line: although it is their desire to promote a collective, cross-national Rau identity (an endeavor that might be looked on with suspicion by the Chinese government), they are quick to remind visitors to their site that they are opposed to "any conspiracy or action that uses any *min zu* issue as an excuse to break up the motherland."[24]

Boundaries of history

To understand China's past is to recognize how the boundaries of "China" and "Chinese" have transformed over time. Although it is common wisdom that the physical and political boundaries of China have changed over time, scholars are far from agreed on how "Chineseness" itself has transformed. Whereas some would point to the centrality of the literary tradition or the apparent uniformity of cultural practices as evidence that the essence of being Chinese has remained relatively constant, others would argue that to be Chinese is little more than to pledge allegiance to the polity of China or to maintain an affinity with the ideals of a perceived Chinese civilization. It is not my aim in this book to resolve this debate; instead, my purpose is to insist that we must approach the ideas of "China" and "Chineseness" historically and locate their transformations within the broader context of political, socio-economic, and cultural change.

In particular, this study argues that to recognize how the boundaries of "China" and "Chinese" have transformed, it is important that we pay particular attention to the subjects at the margins. The "margins" I

---

[24] The disclaimer can be found in http://www.rauz.net/about.htm.

speak of are of course not limited to geographical ones. Although men with minimal literacy and women in general – to mention two of the marginalized groups in imperial China – have for the most part been left silent in the historical records, it is inconceivable now for one to write a general history of China without having taken into consideration the roles such groups played in society. And although we must continue to take seriously the dominant discourses of the educated and the powerful, it is equally important that we expose the gaps and limitations inherent in any master narrative of China and trace how such discourses have changed over time.

But although there are different types of margins, it is at the geographical ones, this study maintains, that historians are best positioned to take note of the changing boundaries of "China" and "Chinese." As we have seen, it was at the borderlands that travelers from the central plains were especially conscious of the challenges posed by the diversity of climates and landscapes, and it was in the border regions that the centralizing state was particularly aware of the limits of its administrative and military reach. And as we have noted also, it was in the border zones that agents and representatives of the state were especially keen on distinguishing between people who were deemed subjects of the state and those who were not, and it was in the border areas that the political and cultural elites of China were particularly interested in differentiating the "non-Chinese" from the "Chinese." In brief, what this study has shown is that while observers in the later imperial period might disagree on how they perceived the limits of "China" and "Chinese," as the centralizing state extended its reach in the border regions, its representatives and agents did find it important to create and perpetuate an increasingly complex set of parameters to mark out China's political and cultural boundaries.

By focusing on the practice and process of demarcation and categorization, the story of expansion told here thus clearly departs from the conventional frontier narratives of confrontation and assimilation. Although territorial and cultural expansion have been integral to almost all borderland experiences, the desire of people in power to demarcate and to differentiate was evidently just as important a driving force behind frontier processes as their urge to integrate and to assimilate. My goal here is not to dismiss the significance of warfare and the undertaking of cultural integration in borderland history; rather, my objective is to challenge historians and others to reexamine some of their most cherished assumptions (especially their confidence in the continual utility of the conceptual binary of "Han" and "non-Han") and encourage them to view the history of China not through the lens of self-evidenced peoples or cultures but first and foremost as a history of boundary formation and transformation.

By framing the history of China's expansion in terms of boundary formation, this study also compels us to reexamine certain conventional wisdoms concerning the making of the Chinese nation-state. If the official narrative – that China, despite its diversity, has long been a unitary state – has been supplanted in recent scholarship by one that emphasizes the *pursuit* for national unity, what the findings of this book remind us then are two important though often neglected elements of this revised narrative. First, although political and intellectual elites in the past century have sought to underline the essential unity of China, they have done so, as I have argued, as much by imagining the cohesion of its people as by marking the presumed differences between the "Han" majority and the "non-Han" minorities. Second, although historians have traced the early-twentieth-century practice of officially recognizing the Han, the Manchus, the Mongols, the Hui, and the Tibetans as the five major *min zu* of China to the conception of the empire by Qing-dynasty emperors (notably Qianlong), to fully understand how the "ethnic landscape" of modern China – both in terms of the categorization of minority nationalities and in terms of specific *min zu* policies – has evolved, this study argues, we must search for its roots not only in Qing times but also earlier in the imperial period.[25]

But even though I have sought in this book to draw attention to the margins, I have not attempted to write a history of the "non-Chinese" (or "non-Han") as it is commonly understood. In fact, I have come to doubt whether such an enterprise – with the underlying assumption that identities such as "Yao" and "Zhuang" are self-evident – is possible or even desirable. (For that matter, I question also the validity of historical writings that take for granted the identity of "Chinese.") To be sure, people who were identified as Yao or Zhuang have long appeared in the historical records. But although some of the "non-Chinese" did leave behind textual records (and hence possess something of a historical voice), it is far from evident that most would find it intrinsically meaningful to represent themselves as members of particular "non-Chinese" collectives. Identities, as we have come to understand, are multi-layered and situational. Rather than take as its point of departure the primordial nature of identities, a more satisfactory account of the history of the Yao or the Zhuang

---

[25] For two collections of stimulating studies concerning the pursuit for unity in modern China, see Unger, *Chinese Nationalism*; Fogel and Zarrow, *Imagining the People*. For the Qing practice of identifying its five major constituencies, see, for example, Elliott, *Manchu Way*, 359–60.

(or any other "non-Chinese" people) would have to place as its focus the very construction, contestation, and transformation of such identities. This book has gone some way in tracing such developments, especially from the perspectives of the representatives and agents of the centralizing state; a more thorough account, however, will have to wait for a more systematic exploration of the records the so-called non-Chinese have left behind.

Nor are the challenges of writing a conventional history of the "non-Chinese" ("non-Han" in the modern context) limited to the lack of documentary evidence. In his 1995 essay "The History of the History of the Yi," Stevan Harrell observes that although the "Yi" (who number nearly eight million, according to the census of 2000) are made up of peoples who are linguistically and culturally diverse, since the late nineteenth century, Western diplomats and missionaries, "Han" Chinese scholars, as well as Communist party cadres and minority intellectuals have all sought to project onto the category a coherent, linear "Yi history." Whereas Western visitors to southwest China in the late nineteenth and early twentieth centuries tended to frame the history of the Yi (also known as Lolo) in racialist terms, Harrell reports, intellectual elites in the Republican period were more interested in tracing the lineage of the Yi through Chinese historical records and in marking the level of "civilization" of individual Yi groups. And whereas in post-1949 China cadres and scholars of an earlier generation were most concerned about configuring the history of the Yi to fit the Marxist scheme of developments, since the 1980s (and this is observed by Harrell and his co-author in a more recent essay), some self-identifying Yi scholars have begun to subvert the orthodox version of Yi history by placing the Yi at the very center of Chinese civilization. The case of the Yi is instructive not only because it shows how in different contexts different interested parties would trace the history of the Yi to different origins; it is instructive also because it shows how in order to write a history of the Yi (or a history of the Yao, or a history of the Zhuang), we must treat the construction of identities not as an afterthought to be dispensed with in a footnote but as the very center of historical inquiry.[26]

In conclusion, what I am suggesting is that just as the construction of the boundaries of "Chinese" (or "Han") has depended on the creation of the boundaries of "non-Chinese" (or "non-Han"), the converse is also true. Just as the construction of the Yi identity has since the early twentieth century been closely tied to the making of the modern Chinese

---

[26] Harrell, "History of the Yi"; Harrell and Li, "History of the Yi, Part II."

nation-state, the appearance in the records of various "non-Chinese" categories in the southern border zone in the imperial period should also be viewed as a result of the expansion of the centralizing state. Although historians committed to recovering the agency of the marginalized and the dominated should continue to read between the lines and against the grain, decode what James Scott calls public and hidden transcripts, and track what Gyan Prakash refers to as "the failures, silences, displacements, and transformations" produced by the functioning of colonialism, in the case of China, a history of the "non-Chinese" would make very little sense if considered independently from the context of the expansion of the state. Rather than consider the discourses of the dominant and the dominated, the colonizing and the colonized, and the majority and the minority, as inevitably oppositional, this book argues, it would be more productive, to think of them as inherently interdependent.[27]

---

[27] For strategies in recovering the history of the "subaltern," see Hershatter, "The Subaltern Talks Back"; Scott, *Arts of Resistance*; Prakash, "Introduction: After Colonialism."

Works cited

ABBREVIATIONS

BBCSJC   *Bai bu cong shu ji cheng* 百部叢書集成. Taipei: Yi wen yin shu guan, 1965–70.

SKQS   *Ying yin Wen yuan ge Si ku quan shu* 影印文淵閣四庫全書. Taipei: Taiwan shang wu yin shu guan, 1983–86.

SKQSCM   *Si ku quan shu cun mu cong shu* 四庫全書存目叢書 Jinan: Qi Lu shu she chu ban she, 1995–97.

XXSKQS   *Xu xiu Si ku quan shu* 續修四庫全書 [Shanghai]: Shanghai gu ji chu ban she, 1995–2002.

CHINESE AND JAPANESE MATERIALS

Bai Yaotian 白耀天. "'Lang' kao" 「狼」考 [Notes on "Lang"]. *Guangxi min zu yan jiu* 广西民族研究 1988.4: 65–76.

Bao Ruji 包汝楫 (js. 1607). *Nan zhong ji wen* 南中紀聞 [Record of things heard in Guizhou] (pref. 1633). 1 juan. BBCSJC ed.

Cai Ying'en 蔡迎恩 and Gan Dongyang 甘東陽, eds. *Taiping fu zhi* 太平府志 [Gazetteer of Taiping prefecture] (1577). 3 juan. Reprint, Beijing: Shu mu wen xian chu ban she, [1990].

Cao Shuji 曹樹基. *Zhongguo ren kou shi* 中国人口史 [Demographic history of China]. Vol. 4, *Ming shi qi* [The Ming period]. Shanghai: Fu dan da xue chu ban she, 2000.

———. *Zhongguo yi min shi* 中国移民史 [History of migration in China]. Vol. 5, *Ming shi qi* 明时期 [The Ming period]. Fuzhou: Fujian ren min chu ban she, 1997.

Cao Xuequan 曹學佺 (1574–1646). *Guangxi ming sheng zhi* 廣西名勝志 [Descriptions of famous sites in Guangxi] (1630). 10 juan. XXSKQS ed.

Chen Lian 陳璉 (1370–1454). *Qinxuan ji* 琴軒集 [Collected writings of Chen Lian] (pref. 1615). 10 juan. Ju de tang kan ben ed.

Chen Liankai 陈连开. "Zhongguo, Hua–Yi, Fan–Han, Zhonghua, Zhonghua min zu" 中国·华夷·蕃汉·中华·中华民族. In Fei Xiaotong, *Zhonghua min zu duo yuan yi ti ge ju*, 211–53.

Chen Xiangyin 陈相因 and Qin Yongjiang 秦邕江, eds. *Guangxi fang zhi yi shu kao lu* 广西方志佚书考录 [Notes on the lost gazetteers of Guangxi]. Nanning: Guangxi ren min chu ban she, 1990.

Cheng Zhengyi 程正誼 (js. 1571). *Quan Shu tu yi kao* 全蜀土夷考 [Notes on the non-Chinese natives in Sichuan] (1599). 4 juan. Copy in Sonkeikaku.

Chuang Chi-fa [Zhuang Jifa] 莊吉發, ed. *Xie Sui "Zhi gong tu" Man wen tu shuo jiao zhu* 謝遂《職貢圖》滿文圖說校注 [Annotated Manchu-language edition of the Xie Sui edition of the *Illustrations of the Tributaries*]. Taipei: Guo li gu gong bo wu yuan, 1989.

Dang Dingwen 党丁文, ed. *Guangxi li dai ming ren ming sheng lu* 广西历代名人名胜录 [A catalog of famous historical personages and famous historical sites of Guangxi]. Guilin: Guangxi min zu chu ban she, 1991.

Fan Chengda 范成大 (1126–93). *Fan Chengda bi ji liu zhong* 范成大筆記六種 [Six informal jottings by Fan Chengda]. Beijing: Zhonghua shu ju, 2002.

———. *Gui hai yu heng zhi* 桂海虞衡志 [Descriptions of forests and marshes of the Gui region] (1175). [3] juan. In *Fan Chengda bi ji liu zhong*, 71–177.

Fan Honggui 范宏贵. "Tan tan Ling ren de cun zai yu xiao shi" 谈谈伶人的存在与消失 [On the appearance and disappearance of the Ling people]. *Guangxi min zu yan jiu* 1988.1: 44–48.

Fan Ye 范曄 (398–445) et al., eds. *Hou Han shu* 後漢書 [History of the Latter Han] (fifth century). 120 juan. Beijing: Zhonghua shu ju, 1965.

Fan Yuchun 范玉春. "Ming dai Guangxi de jun shi yi min" 明代广西的军事移民 [Military migration to Guangxi during the Ming dynasty]. *Zhongguo bian jiang shi di yan jiu* 中国边疆史地研究 8.2 (1998): 34–43.

Fang Yu 方瑜 (js. 1544), ed. *Nanning fu zhi* 南寧府志 [Gazetteer of Nanning prefecture] (1564). 11 juan. Reprint, Beijing: Shu mu wen xian chu ban she, [1990].

Fei Xiaotong 费孝通. "Zhonghua min zu duo yuan yi ti ge ju" 中华民族多元一体格局 [The pattern of diversity in unity of the Chinese nation]. In *Zhonghua min zu duo yuan yi ti ge ju*, 3–38.

———, ed. *Zhonghua min zu duo yuan yi ti ge ju* 中华民族多元一体格局 [The pattern of diversity in unity of the Chinese nation]. Rev. ed. Beijing: Zhong yang min zu da xue chu ban she, 1999.

Feng Jiahua 丰家骅. *Yang Shen ping zhuan* 杨慎评传 [Critical biography of Yang Shen]. Nanjing: Nanjing da xue chu ban she, 1998.

Gao Xiongzheng 高熊徵, ed. *Siming fu zhi* 思明府志 [Gazetteer of Siming prefecture] (1690). 6 juan. Naikaku Hishi copy.

Gao Yanhong 高言弘 and Yao Shun'an 姚舜安. *Ming dai Guangxi nong min qi yi shi* 明代广西农民起义史 [History of peasant uprisings in Guangxi during the Ming]. Nanning: Guangxi ren min chu ban she, 1984.

Gong Yin 龚荫. *Zhongguo tu si zhi du* 中国土司制度 [The institution of native chieftaincy of China]. Kunming: Yunnan min zu chu ban she, 1992.

Gu Yanwu 顧炎武 (1613–82). *Tian xia jun guo li bing shu* 天下郡國利病書 [Strengths and weaknesses of the administrative regions of the realm] (1662). 34 ce. Si bu cong kan san bian ed.

Guangxi bai ke quan shu bian zuan wei yuan hui 广西百科全书编纂委员会, ed. *Guangxi bai ke quan shu* 广西百科全书 [Encyclopedia of Guangxi]. Beijing: Zhongguo da bai ke quan shu chu ban she, 1994.

Guangxi min zu yan jiu suo 广西民族研究所, ed. *Guangxi shao shu min zu di qu shi ke bei wen ji* 广西少数民族地区石刻碑文集 [Collection of stone inscriptions from the minority nationality areas in Guangxi]. Nanning: Guangxi ren min chu ban she, 1982.

————, ed. *"Ming shi lu" Guangxi shi liao zhai lu* 〈明实录〉广西史料摘录 [Extracts of source materials on Guangxi from the *Veritable Records of the Ming*]. Nanning: Guangxi ren min chu ban she, 1990.

Guangxi tong zhi guan 广西通志馆, ed. *Guangxi fang zhi ti yao* 广西方志提要 [Introduction to the local gazetteers of Guangxi]. Nanning: Guangxi ren min chu ban she, 1988.

Guangxi Zhuangzu Zizhiqu bian ji zu 广西壮族自治区编辑组, ed. *Guangxi Zhuang zu she hui li shi diao cha* 广西壮族社会历史调查 [Investigations on the society and history of the Zhuang nationality in Guangxi]. 7 vols. Nanning: Guangxi min zu chu ban she, 1984–87.

Guangxi Zhuangzu Zizhiqu di fang zhi bian zuan wei yuan hui 广西壮族自治区地方志编纂委员会, ed. *Guangxi tong zhi: min su zhi* 广西通志 · 民俗志 [General gazetteer of Guangxi: popular customs]. Nanning: Guangxi ren min chu ban she, 1992.

————, ed. *Guangxi tong zhi: ren kou zhi* 广西通志 · 人口志 [General gazetteer of Guangxi: population]. Nanning: Guangxi ren min chu ban she, 1993.

————, ed. *Guangxi tong zhi: zi ran di li zhi* 广西通志 · 自然地理志 [General gazetteer of Guangxi: physical geography]. Nanning: Guangxi ren min chu ban she, 1994.

Gui yuan shu lin bian ji wei yuan hui 桂苑书林编辑委员会, ed. *Yue xi shi zai jiao zhu* 粤西诗载校注 [*Anthology of Poetry of Guangxi*, collated and annotated]. Nanning: Guangxi ren min chu ban she, 1988.

Guilin Zhang shi jia cheng 桂林张氏家乘 [Genealogy of the Zhang lineage of Guilin]. 15 juan. N.p., 1921. Copy in the East Asian Library at Columbia University.

Guo Yingpin 郭應聘 (1500–86). *Xi nan ji shi* 西南紀事 [Records of events in the southwest] (1580s). 6 juan. Reprint, Beijing: Shu mu wen xian chu ban she, [1988].

He Linxia 何林夏. "*Cangwu zong du jun men zhi* yan jiu" 蒼梧總督軍門志研究 [On *Cangwu zong du jun men zhi*]. In Ying Jia et al., *Cangwu zong du jun men zhi*, 486–522.

Hu Renzhao 胡人朝, Wu Enyang 吴恩扬, and Zhang Wei 张瑋, eds. *Zhongguo xi nan di qu li dai shi ke hui bian* 中国西南地区历代石刻汇编 [Collection of historical stone inscriptions from southwest China]. 20 vols. Tianjin: Tianjin gu ji chu ban she, 1998.

Huang Kaihua 黃開華. "Ming dai tu si zhi du she shi yu xi nan kai fa" 明代土司制度設施与西南發展 [Implementation of the institution of native chieftaincy and the development of the southwest during the Ming]. In *Ming dai tu si zhi du* 明代土司制度, ed. Bao Zunpeng 包遵彭, 27–217. Taipei: Xue sheng shu ju, 1972.

Huang Shuguang 黄书光 et al. *Yao zu wen xue shi* 瑶族文学史 [Literary history of the Yao nationality]. Nanning: Guangxi ren min chu ban she, 1988.

Huang Tirong 黄体荣. *Guangxi li shi di li* 广西历史地理 [Historical geography of Guangxi]. Nanning: Guangxi min zu chu ban she, 1985.

Huang Yu 黄鈺, ed. *Ping huang juan die ji bian* 评皇卷牒集编. [Collection of "certificates from Emperor Ping"]. Nanning: Guangxi ren min chu ban she, 1990.

Huang Yu 黃瑜 (1426–97). *Shuang huai sui chao* 雙槐歲鈔 [Periodic jottings from the Pavilion of Double Locust Trees] (pref. 1495). 10 juan. Beijing: Zhonghua shu ju, 1999.

Huang Yuji 黃虞稷 (1626–91), ed. *Qian qing tang shu mu* 千頃堂書目 [Catalog of the Thousand-Acre Hall] (late seventeenth century). 32 juan. Reprint, Shanghai: Shanghai gu ji chu ban she, 1990.

Huang Zhixun 黃志勛 and Long Tairen 龍泰任, eds. *Rong xian zhi* 融縣志 [Gazetteer of Rong county] (1936). Reprint, Taipei: Cheng wen chu ban she, 1975.

Huang Zuo 黃佐 (1490–1566) et al., eds. *Guangxi tong zhi* 廣西通志 [General gazetteer of Guangxi] (1531). 60 juan. Reprint, Beijing: Shu mu wen xian chu ban she, [1988].

Huo Ji 霍冀 (1516–75). *Jiu bian tu shuo* 九邊圖說 [Annotated illustrations of the northern borders] (1569). Xuan lan tang cong shu ed.

Jiang Mian 蔣冕 (1463–1533). *Xiang gao ji* 湘皋集 [Collected writings from the banks of the Xiang River] (1554). 33 juan. SKQSCM ed.

Jin Hong 金鉷 (1678–1740) et al., eds. *Guangxi tong zhi* 廣西通志 [General gazetteer of Guangxi] (1733). 128 juan. SKQS ed.

Kuang Lu 鄺露 (1604–50). *Chi ya* 赤雅 [Explanations of matters concerning the south] (1635). 3 juan. BBCSJC ed.

Lee Cheuk Yin [Li Zuoran] 李焯然. "Qiu Jun *Da xue yan yi bu* dui Ming dai bian fang de jian tao" 丘濬《大學衍義補》對明代邊防的檢討 [Evaluations of the Ming border defense in Qiu Jun's *Da xue yan yi bu*]. In *Yamane Yukio kyōju taikyū kinen Mindaishi ronsō* 山根幸夫教授退休記念明代史論叢, ed. Mindaishi kenkyūkai Mindaishi ronsō henshū iinkai 明代史研究会明代史論叢編集委員会, vol. 1, 627–44. Tokyo: Kyūko shoin, 1990.

Li Guoxiang 李国祥, ed. *Ming shi lu lei zuan: Guangxi shi liao juan* 明实录类纂 · 广西史料卷 [Topical compilations from the *Veritable Records of the Ming*: historical materials on Guangxi]. Guilin: Guangxi shi fan da xue chu ban she, 1990.

Li Jifu 李吉甫 (758–814). *Yuanhe jun xian tu zhi* 元和郡縣圖志 [Illustrated descriptions of the administrative regions in the Yuanhe period (806–20)] (814). 40 juan. BBCSJC ed.

Li Jinyou 李晋有 et al., eds. *Zhongguo shao shu min zu gu ji lun* 中国少数民族古籍论 [Essays on the early textual records of the minority nationalities of China]. Multiple vols. Chengdu: Ba Shu shu she, 1997–.

Li Shizhen 李時珍 (1518–93). *Ben cao gang mu* 本草綱目 [Material medica: a general outline] (1603). 52 juan. [Beijing]: Ren min wei sheng chu ban she, 1975.

Li Shunan 李樹枏 et al., eds. *Zhaoping xian zhi* 昭平縣志 [Gazetteer of Zhaoping county] (1934). 8 vols. Reprint, Taipei: Cheng wen chu ban she, 1967.

Li Xian 李賢 (1408–66) et al., eds. *Da Ming yi tong zhi* 大明一統志 [Union gazetteer of the Great Ming] (1461). 90 juan. Reprint, Taipei: Wen hai chu ban she, 1965.

Li Zengbo 李曾伯 (thirteenth century). *Ke zhai za gao* 可齋雜藁 [Collected writings of Li Zengbo]. 34 juan. SKQS ed.

Lin Huixiang 林惠祥. *Zhongguo min zu shi* 中國民族史 [History of the Chinese nation]. 2 vols. [Shanghai]: Shang wu yin shu guan, 1936.

Lin Qingzhang 林慶彰. *Ming dai kao ju xue yan jiu* 明代考據學研究 [Evidential learning in the Ming period]. Rev. ed. Taipei: Xue sheng shu ju, 1986.

Liu Xifan 劉錫蕃 [Liu Jie 劉介]. *Guangxi te zhong jiao yu* 廣西特種教育 [Special education in Guangxi]. Guilin: Guangxi Sheng zheng fu bian yi wei yuan hui, 1940.

———. *Ling biao ji man* 嶺表紀蠻 [Notes on the non-Han of Guangxi] (1934). Shanghai: Shang wu yin shu guan, 1935.

Lü Mingzhong 呂名中 et al., eds. *Nan fang min zu gu shi shu lu* 南方民族古史书录 [Annotated bibliography of early textual sources on the nationalities in the south]. Chengdu: Sichuan min zu chu ban she, 1989.

Lü Simian 呂思勉. *Zhongguo min zu shi* 中國民族史 [History of the Chinese nation] (1934). Shanghai: Zhongguo da bai ke quan shu chu ban she, 1987.

Luo Chi 罗炽. *Fang Yizhi ping zhuan* 方以智评传 [Critical biography of Fang Yizhi]. [Nanjing]: Nanjing da xue chu ban she, 1998.

Luo Xianglin 羅香林. "Lang bing Lang tian kao" 狼兵狼田考 [On Lang soldiers and Lang land]. In *Baiyue yuan liu yu wen hua* 百越源流與文化, rev. ed., 281–93. Taipei: Guo li bian yi guan Zhonghua cong shu bian shen wei yuan hui, 1978.

Luo Yuejiong 羅曰褧 (jr. 1585). *Xian bin lu* 咸賓錄 [Record of tribute guests] (pref. 1591). 8 juan. Beijing: Zhonghua shu ju, 1983.

Ma Duanlin 馬端臨 (ca. 1254–ca. 1323). *Wen xian tong kao* 文獻通考 [Comprehensive study of important documents] (1324). 348 juan. Shang wu yin shu guan wan you wen ku shi tong ben (1935–37) ed. Reprint, Beijing: Zhonghua shu ju, 1986.

Mao Kun 茅坤 (1512–1601). *Mao Lumen xian sheng wen ji* 茅鹿門先生文集 [Collected writings of Master Mao Kun] (pref. 1588). 36 juan. XXSKQS ed.

Mao Ruizheng 茅瑞徵 (js. 1601). *Huang Ming xiang xu lu* 皇明象胥錄 [Record of the interpreters of the Ming imperium] (pref. 1629). 8 juan. In Guo li Beiping tu shu guan shan ben cong shu di yi ji. Reprint, Taipei: Hua wen shu ju, [1968].

Ming shi lu 明實錄 [Veritable records of the Ming] (1418 to mid–seventeenth century). 133 vols. Reprint, Taipei: Zhong yang yan jiu yuan li shi yu yan yan jiu suo, 1961–66.

Mo Bingkui 莫炳奎 et al., eds. *Yongning xian zhi* 邕寧縣志 [Gazetteer of Yongning county] (1937). 5 vols. Reprint, Taipei: Cheng wen chu ban she, 1975.

Mo Junqing 莫俊卿 and Lei Guangzheng 雷广正. "Lang ren Lang min Lang bing yan jiu" 俍人俍民俍兵研究 [On Lang people, Lang subjects, and Lang soldiers]. In *Ling wai Zhuang zu hui kao* 岭外壮族汇考, ed. Xie Qihuang 谢启晃, Guo Zaizhong 郭在忠, Mo Junqing 莫俊卿, et al., 144–52. Nanning: Guangxi min zu chu ban she, 1989.

Okada Koji 岡田宏二. *Chūgoku Kanan minzoku shakaishi kenkyū* 中国華南民族社会史研究 [Studies on the social history of the ethnic groups in south China]. Tokyo: Kyūko shoin, 1993.

Ouyang Roxiu 欧阳若修 et al. *Zhuang zu wen xue shi* 壮族文学史 [Literary history of the Zhuang nationality]. 3 vols. Nanning: Guangxi ren min chu ban she, 1986.

Pan Jixing 潘吉星. *Tian gong kai wu jiao zhu ji yan jiu* 天工开物校注及研究 [*Exploitation of the works of nature*, collated, annotated, and examined]. Chengdu: Ba Shu shu she, 1989.

Qi Yi 齐易, ed. *Guangxi hang yun shi* 广西航运史 [History of water transportation in Guangxi]. Beijing: Ren min jiao tong chu ban she, 1991.

Qin Cailuan 覃采鸾 and Huang Mingbiao 黄明标, eds. *Washi fu ren lun ji* 瓦氏夫人论集 [Studies on Madame Washi]. Nanning: Guangxi ren min chu ban she, 1992.

Qin [Tan] Guiqing 覃桂清. *Guangxi Xincheng tu si shi hua* 广西忻城土司史话 [Historical notes on the native domain of Xincheng in Guangxi]. Liuzhou: Guangxi min zu chu ban she, 1990.

Qin [Tan] Yanhuan 覃延欢 and Liao Guoyi 廖國一, eds. *Guangxi shi gao* 广西史稿 [History of Guangxi]. Guilin: Guangxi shi fan da xue chu ban she, 1998.

Qiu Jun 丘濬 (1421–95). *Da xue yan yi bu* 大學衍義補 [Supplement to the *Extended Meaning of the Great Learning*] (1487). 164 juan. In *Qiu Wenzhuang gong cong shu* 丘文莊公叢書. Reprint, Taipei: Qiu Wenzhuang gong cong shu ji yin wei yuan hui, 1972.

———. *Qiongtai shi wen hui gao* 瓊臺詩文會稾 [Collected writings of Qiu Jun] (1621). 24 juan. In *Qiu Wenzhuang gong cong shu*. Reprint, Taipei: Qiu Wenzhuang gong cong shu ji yin wei yuan hui, 1972.

Qu Dajun 屈大均 (1630–96). *Guangdong xin yu* 廣東新語 [News from Guangdong] (1700). 28 juan. Beijing: Zhonghua shu ju, 1985.

Qu Jiusi 瞿九思 (1546–1617). *Wanli wu gong lu* 萬曆武功錄 [Record of military accomplishments of the Wanli period] (pref. 1612). 14 juan. Reprint, Taipei: Yi wen yin shu guan, 1980.

Ren min chu ban she 人民出版社, ed. *Min zu zheng ce wen xian hui bian* 民族政策文獻彙編 [Collected documents on nationality policies] (1953). Enlarged ed. Beijing: Ren min chu ban she, 1958.

Sakai Tadao 酒井忠夫. "Mindai no nichiyō ruisho to shomin kyōiku" 明代日用類書庶民教育 [Household almanacs and popular education in the Ming period]. In *Kinsei Chūgoku kyōiku shi kenkyū* 近世中国教育史研究, ed. Hayashi Tomoharu 林友春, 25–154. Tokyo: Kokudosha, 1958.

Sakai Tadao, Sakade Yoshinobu 坂出祥伸, and Ogawa Yōichi 小川陽一, eds. *Chūgoku nichiyō ruisho shūsei* 中國日用類書集成 [The Chinese household almanacs series]. Multiple titles. Tokyo: Kyūko shoin, 1999–.

Satō Fumitoshi 佐藤文俊. *Mindai ōfu no kenkyū* 明代王府の研究 [Studies on the princely estates of the Ming]. Tokyo: Kenbun shuppan, 1999.

She Yize 佘貽澤. *Zhongguo tu si zhi du* 中國土司制度 [The institution of native chieftaincy of China]. Shanghai: Zheng zhong shu ju, 1947.

Shen Defu 沈德符 (1578–1642). *Wanli ye huo bian* 萬曆野獲編 [Random gleanings from the Wanli period] (1619). 30+4 juan. Beijing: Zhonghua shu ju, 1959.

Shen Jiefu 沈節甫 (1533–1601), ed. *Ji lu hui bian* 紀錄彙編 [Collection of records] (1617). 224 juan. Beijing: Quan guo tu shu guan suo wei fu zhi zhong xin, 1994.

Shen Shixing 申時行 (1535–1614) et al., eds. *Ming hui dian* 明會典 [Collected statutes of the Ming] (1587). 228 juan. Beijing: Zhonghua shu ju, 1989.

Shi Wei 石卫 and Luo Chang'ai 罗昌爱. "Guangxi Yongning Xian shou zai 16 yi; 40 wan gan qun fen qi sheng chan zi jiu" 广西邕宁县受灾16亿·40万干群奋起生产自救 [Damage to Yongning county, Guangxi, reached 1.6 billion yuan; 400,000 cadres and citizens made a rigorous start to produce to help themselves]. *Ren min wang di fang lian bao wang* 人民网地方联报网, 19 July 2001. http://www.unn.com.cn/GB/channel21/939/2260/200107/19/82862.html (accessed 31 March 2004).

Song Guangyu 宋光宇 et al., eds. *Hua nan bian jiang min zu tu lu* 華南邊疆民族圖錄 [Illustrated records of the borderland ethnic groups in southern China]. Taipei: Guo li zhong yang tu shu guan, 1991.

Song Wenbing 宋文炳. *Zhongguo min zu shi* 中國民族史 [History of the Chinese nation]. Shanghai: Zhonghua shu ju, 1935.

Su Jianling 苏建灵. "Lun Ming dai Guangxi dong bu de tu si" 论明代广西东部的土司 [On the native domains in eastern Guangxi during the Ming]. In *Ming Qing shi qi Zhuang zu li shi yan jiu*, 120–76.

———. "Ming dai Guangxi de wei suo" 明代广西的卫所 [Guards and battalions in Guangxi during the Ming]. In *Ming Qing shi qi Zhuang zu li shi yan jiu*, 191–206.

———. "Ming Qing shi qi Zhuang Han min zu rong he wen ti yan jiu" 明清时期壮汉融合问题研究 [A study of the integration of the Zhuang and Han nationalities in the Ming and Qing periods]. In *Ming Qing shi qi Zhuang zu li shi yan jiu*, 1–116.

———. *Ming Qing shi qi Zhuangzu li shi yan jiu* 明清时期壮族历史研究 [Studies on the history of the Zhuang nationality in the Ming and Qing periods]. [Nanning]: Guangxi min zu chu ban she, 1993.

Su Jun 蘇濬 (1541–99), ed. *Guangxi tong zhi* 廣西通志 [General gazetteer of Guangxi] (1599). 42 juan. Reprint, Taipei: Xue sheng shu ju, n.d. With additional materials to 1622.

Su Tongbing 蘇同炳. *Ming dai yi di zhi du* 明代驛遞制度 [The courier system of the Ming dynasty]. Taipei: Zhonghua cong shu bian shen wei yuan hui, 1969.

Sun Yat-sen 孫逸仙 [Sun Wen 孫文] (1866–1925). "Min zu zhu yi" 民族主義 [Principle of the nation]. In *Sun Zhongshan quan ji* 孫中山全集, ed. Guangdong sheng she hui ke xue yuan li shi yan jiu shi 广东省社会科学院历史研究室 et al., vol. 9, 183–254. Beijing: Zhonghua shu ju, 1986.

———. "Zhongguo guo min dang di yi ci quan guo dai biao da hui xuan yan" 中國國民黨第一次全國代表大會宣言 [Manifesto of the first national representative meeting of the Chinese Nationalist Party]. In *Sun Zhongshan quan ji*, vol. 9, 114–25.

Tan Qixiang 谭其骧, ed. *Zhongguo li shi di tu ji* 中國歷史地圖集 [Historical atlas of China]. 8 vols. Shanghai: Di tu chu ban she, 1982.

Tang Shunzhi 唐順之 (1507–60). *Guang you zhan gong lu* 廣右戰功錄 [Record of military accomplishments in Guangxi] (1559). 1 juan. BBCSJC ed.

Taniguchi Fusao 谷口房男. *Kanan minzokushi kenkyū* 華南民族史研究 [Studies on the history of ethnic groups in south China]. Tokyo: Ryokuin shobō, 1997.

———. "Kōsei doshi seido no isshuku" 広西土司制度の一齣 [A case study of the institution of native chieftaincy in Guangxi]. In *Kanan minzokushi kenkyū*, 249–80.

———. "Mindai Kōsei no dojunkenshi ni tsuite" 明代広西の土巡検司について [On the native police offices in Guangxi during the Ming]. In *Kanan minzokushi kenkyū*, 231–48.

———. "Ō Shujin to shōsū minzoku" 王守仁と少数民族 [Wang Yangming and minority nationalities]. In *Kanan minzokushi kenkyū*, 211–30.

Taniguchi Fusao [Gukou Fangnan] 谷口房男 and Bai Yaotian 白耀天, eds. *Zhuang zu tu guan zu pu ji cheng* 壮族土官族谱集成 [Collected genealogies of Zhuang native chieftains]. Nanning: Guangxi min zu chu ban she, 1998.

Taniguchi Fusao 谷口房男 and Kobayashi Takao 小林隆夫, eds. *Mindai seinan minzoku shiryō: Min jitsuroku shō* 明代西南民族資料: 明実録抄 [Sources on the ethnic groups in the southwest during the Ming: extracts from the *Veritable Records of the Ming*]. Tokyo: Tōyō Daigaku Ajia Afurika Bunka Kenkyūjo, 1983–.

Tian Rucheng 田汝成 (js. 1526). *Yan jiao ji wen* 炎徼紀聞 [Record of things heard on the torrid frontier] (1558). 4 juan. Jia ye tang cong shu ed.

Tsukada Shigeyuki 塚田誠之. *Chiwan-zoku bunkashi kenkyū: Mindai ikō chūshin to shite* 壮族文化史研究: 明代以降を中心として [Studies on the cultural history of the Zhuang nationality: centering on the Ming period and after]. Tokyo: Daiichi Shobō, 2000.

———. *Chiwan-zoku shakaishi kenkyū: Min Shin jidai o chūshin to shite* 壮族社会史研究: 明清時代を中心として [Studies on the social history of the Zhuang nationality: centering on the Ming and Qing periods]. Suita: Kokuritsu Minzokugaku Hakubutsukan, 2000.

———. "Min Shin jidai ni okeru Chiwan-zoku tōchi taisei" 明清時代における壮族統治体制 [Structure of control among the Zhuang in the Ming and Qing periods]. In *Chiwan-zoku shakaishi kenkyū*, 157–85.

Tu guan di bu 土官底簿 [Record of native chieftains] (early sixteenth century). 2 juan. SKQS ed.

Wang Chongwu 王崇武. *Ming ben ji jiao zhu* 明本紀校注 [*Basic Annals of the Ming*, collated and annotated]. Shanghai: Shang wu yin shu guan, 1948.

Wang Ji 王濟 (d. 1540). *Jun ji tang ri xun shou jing* 君子堂日詢手鏡 [Hand-held mirror for daily inquiries in the Gentleman's Hall] (pref. 1522). 1 juan. Ji lu hui bian ed.

Wang Jianmin 王建民. *Zhongguo min zu xue shi* 中國民族學史 [History of ethnology in China]. Vol. 1, 1903–1949. Kunming: Yunnan jiao yu chu ban she, 1997.

Wang Jianmin et al. *Zhongguo min zu xue shi* [History of ethnology in China]. Vol. 2, 1950–1997. Kunming: Yunnan jiao yu chu ban she, 1998.

Wang Mingke 王明珂. *Huaxia bian yuan: li shi ji yi yu zu qun ren tong* 華夏邊緣: 歷史記憶與族群認同 [Chinese borders: historical memory and ethnic identification]. Taipei: Yun chen, 1997.

Wang Qi 王圻 (js. 1565), ed. *San cai tu hui* 三才圖會 [Collected illustrations of heaven, earth, and people] (1609). 106 juan. Reprint, Shanghai: Shanghai gu ji chu ban she, 1988. Supplemented by Wang Siyi.

Wang Sen 汪森 (1653–1726), ed. *Yue xi cong zai* 粤西叢載 [Anthology of miscellanies of Guangxi] (ca. 1704). 30 juan. SKQS ed.

———, ed. *Yue xi wen zai* 粤西文載 [Anthology of belles-lettres of Guangxi] (ca. 1704). 75 juan. SKQS ed.

Wang Shixing 王士性 (1547–98). *Guang you zhi* 廣遊志 [Record of extensive travels] (pref. 1593). 2 juan. In Zhou Zhenhe, *Wang Shixing di li shu san zhong*, 210–29.

———. *Guang zhi yi* 廣志繹 [Further elucidations on my extensive record of travels] (pref. 1597). 5 juan. In Zhou Zhenhe, *Wang Shixing di li shu san zhong*, 230–402.

Wang Shouren 王守仁 (1472–1529). *Yangming quan shu* 陽明全書 [Complete works of Wang Shouren] (1572). 38 juan. Si bu bei yao ed.

Wang Tongling 王桐齡 (b.1878). *Zhongguo min zu shi* 中國民族史 [History of the Chinese nation] (1928). Reprint, Taipei: Hua shi chu ban she, 1977.

Wang Wanfu 王萬福. *Ming Qiu Wenzhuang gong Jun nian pu* 明丘文莊公濬年譜 [Chronological biography of Qiu Jun]. Taipei: Shang wu yin shu guan, 1985.

Wang Yuquan 王毓銓. *Ming dai de jun tun* 明代的軍屯 [Military colonies in the Ming period]. Beijing: Zhonghua shu ju, 1965.

Wei Dongchao 韦东超. "Ming dai Guangxi tu si di qu de bian hu yu fu yi kao lüe" 明代广西土司地区的编户与赋役考略 [A study of household registration, taxation, and corvée in the native domains of Guangxi during the Ming]. *Zhongnan min zu xue yuan xue bao* 中南民族学院学报 1996.3: 76–79.

Wei Huan 魏煥 (js. 1529). *Huang Ming jiu bian kao* 皇明九邊考 [Notes on the northern borders of the Ming imperium] (1541). 10 juan. In Guo li Beiping tu shu guan shan ben cong shu di yi ji. Reprint, Taipei: Hua wen shu ju, [1968].

Wei Jun 魏濬 (js. 1604). *Qiao nan suo ji* 嶠南瑣記 [Miscellaneous notes on Guangxi] (pref. 1612). 2 juan. BBCSJC ed.

———. *Xi shi er* 西事珥 [Miscellanea of Guangxi] (pref. 1612). 8 juan. National Library of Beiping microfilm copy.

Wei Zheng 魏微 (580–643) et al., eds. *Sui shu* 隋書 [History of the Sui] (636). 85 juan. Beijing: Zhonghua shu ju, 1973.

Wu Huifang 吳蕙芳. *Wan bao quan shu: Ming Qing shi qi de min jian sheng huo shi lu* 萬寶全書: 明清時期的民間生活實錄 [Complete book of ten thousand treasures: records of everyday life in the Ming and Qing periods]. Taipei: Guo li zheng zhi da xue li shi xue xi, 2000.

Wu Wenhua 吳文華 (1521–98). *Yue xi shu gao* 粵西疏稿 [Memorials concerning Guangxi] (pref. 1587). 3 juan. SKQSCM ed.

Wu Xiaofeng 吳小风. "Ming dai Guangxi cheng shi xu shi jian she yan jiu" 明代广西城市圩市建设研究 [A study of the development of cities and market towns in Guangxi during the Ming]. *Guangxi min zu yan jiu* 2004.2: 91–99.

———. "Ming dai Guangxi jiao tong jian she shu lüe" 明代广西交通建设述略 [A survey of the development of transportation in Guangxi during the Ming]. *Zhongguo bian jian shi di yan jiu* 13.4 (2003): 52–61.

Wu Yongzhang 吳永章. *Zhongguo tu si zhi du yuan yuan yu fa zhan shi* 中国土司制度渊源与发展史 [The origin and development of the institution of native chieftaincy of China]. Chengdu: Sichuan min zu chu ban she, 1988.

———, ed. *Zhongnan min zu guan xi shi* 中南民族关系史 [History of ethnic relations in south central China]. Beijing: Min zu chu ban she, 1992.

Xiao Daheng 蕭大亨 (1532–1612). *Yi su ji* 夷俗記 [Customs of the non-Chinese in the north] (pref. 1594). 1 juan. BBCSJC ed.

Xiao Tengfeng 蕭騰鳳 (js. 1568). *Liang Yue yi gao* 兩粵議稿 [Memorials concerning Guangdong and Guangxi] (ca. 1568). 5 juan. Naikaku Hishi copy.

Xie Jin 解縉 (1369–1415) et al., eds. *Yongle da dian* 永樂大典 [The Yongle encyclopedia] (1408). Reprint, Beijing: Zhonghua shu ju, 1986.

Xie Junhui 謝君惠 et al., eds. *Wuzhou fu zhi* 梧州府志 [Gazetteer of Wuzhou prefecture] (1631). 20 juan. Naikaku Hishi copy.

Xie Qikun 謝啟昆 (1737–1802) et al., eds. *Guangxi tong zhi* 廣西通志 [General gazetteer of Guangxi] (1801). 279+1 juan. Reprint, Taipei: Wen hai chu ban she, 1966. With additional information to 1865.

Xu Hongzu 徐弘祖 (1586–1641). *Xu Xiake you ji* 徐霞客遊記 [Travel diaries of Xu Hongzu] (ca. 1641). 10 juan. Shanghai: Shanghai gu ji chu ban she, 1995 [1987].

Xu Jieshun 徐杰舜. *Han min zu fa zhan shi* 汉民族发展史 [History of development of the Han nationality]. Chengdu: Sichuan min zu chu ban she, 1992.

Xu Lun 許論 (1495–1566). *Jiu bian tu lun* 九邊圖論 [Illustrations and descriptions of the northern borders] (1538). 1 juan. BBCSJC ed.

Xu Song 徐松 (1781–1848) et al., eds. *Song hui yao ji gao* 宋會要輯稿 [Essential documents of the Song] (1936). 200 ce. Reprint, Beijing: Zhonghua shu ju, 1957.

Xu Songshi 徐松石. *Yuejiang liu yu ren min shi* 粵江流域人民史 [History of the people of the Yue River region] (1963). Rev. ed. Reprinted in *Xu Songshi min zu xue yan jiu zhu zuo wu zhong* 徐松石民族學研究著作五種. Guangzhou: Guangdong ren min chu ban she, 1993.

Yan Congjian 嚴從簡 (js. 1559). *Shu yu zhou zi lu* 殊域周咨錄 [Exhaustive inquiries on the strange lands] (pref. 1574). 24 juan. Beijing: Zhonghua shu ju, 1993.

Yang Fang 楊芳 (js. 1577) et al., eds. *Dian Yue yao zuan* 殿粵要纂 [Essential information for governing Guangxi] (1602). 4 juan. Reprint, Beijing: Shu mu wen xian chu ban she, [1988].

Yang Shen 楊慎 (1488–1559). *Shan hai jing bu zhu* 山海經補注 [*Guideways through Mountains and Seas*, annotated] (1554). 1 juan. BBCSJC ed.

———. *Sheng'an quan ji* 升菴全集 [Complete works of Yang Shen] (1582). 81 juan. Guo xue ji ben cong shu ed.

Yao Silian 姚思廉 (557–637), ed. *Liang shu* 梁書 [History of the Liang] (636). 56 juan. Beijing: Zhonghua shu ju, 1973.

Yao Mo 姚鏌 (1465–1538). *Dongquan wen ji* 東泉文集 [Collected writings of Yao Mo] (1547). 8 juan. National Central Library (Taipei) microfilm. Pagination is slightly different in the SKQSCM ed.

Ye Sheng 葉盛 (1420–74). *Ye Wenzhuang gong liang Guang zou cao* 葉文莊公兩廣奏草 [Memorials concerning Guangdong and Guangxi by Ye Sheng] (pref. 1551). 16 juan. In *Ye Wenzhuang gong zou yi* 葉文莊公奏議 (1631). XXSKQS ed.

Ye Xianggao 葉向高 (1559–1627). *Si yi kao* 四夷考 [Notes on the non-Chinese of the four quarters] (1606). 8 juan. BBCSJC ed.

Yin Geng 尹畊 (js. 1532). *Teng xia ji lüe* 藤峽紀略 [Record of the Rattan Gorge] (ca. 1540). 1 juan. In *Ming chen ning rang yao bian* 名臣寧攘要編 (Wanli period), ed. Xiang Dezhen 項德楨 (js. 1586). Naikaku Hishi copy.

Ying Jia 應檟 (1494–1554), Ling Yunyi 凌雲翼 (js. 1547), and Liu Yaohui 劉堯誨 (1522–1585), eds. *Cangwu zong du jun men zhi* 蒼梧總督軍門志 [Record of the office of the supreme commander at Cangwu] (1581). 34 juan. Reprint, Beijing: Quan guo tu shu guan wen xian shu wei fu zhi zhong xin, 1991. First compiled in 1552.

Yu Beishan 于北山. *Fan Chengda nian pu* 范成大年譜 [Chronological biography of Fan Chengda]. Shanghai: Shanghai gui ji chu ban she, 1987.

Yu Dayou 俞大猷 (1503–79). *Zheng qi tang ji* 正氣堂集 [Collected writings from the Hall of Uprightness] (1578). 17 juan. Naikaku Hishi copy. Pagination is slightly different in the edition in the Si ku wei shou shu ji kan 四庫未收書集刊 series.

Yu Ji 虞集 (1272–1348). *Daoyuan xue gu lu* 道園學古錄 [Records of learning from the ancients] (1456). 50 *juan*. Si bu cong kan ed.

Yu Xiangdou 余象斗 (fl. 1596), ed. *Santai wan yong zheng zong* 三台萬用正宗 [Authoritative source for myriad uses] (1599). 43 juan. Reprinted in Sakai Tadao et al., *Chūgoku nichiyō ruisho shūsei*.

Zhang Ji 張吉 (1451–1518). *Gucheng ji* 古城集 [Collected writings of Zhang Ji] (1691). 6 juan + *bu yi*. SKQS ed.

Zhang Mingfeng 張鳴鳳 (jr. 1552). *Gui sheng-Gui gu jiao dian* 桂勝 · 桂故校點 [*Famous Places of Guilin* and *Historical Notes on Guilin,* annotated and punctuated] (1590). 16 + 8 juan. Nanning: Guangxi ren min chu ban she, 1988.

Zhang Ning 張寧 (js. 1454). *Fangzhou za yan* 方洲雜言 [Miscellaneous words of Zhang Ning] (late fifteenth century). 1 juan. BBCSJC ed.

Zhang Qiyun 張其昀. *Zhongguo min zu zhi* 中國民族志 [Study of the Chinese nation] (1928). Reprint, Taipei: Shang wu yin shu guan, 1969.

Zhang Shengzhen 张声震, ed. *Zhuang zu tong shi* 壯族通史 [General history of the Zhuang]. 3 vols. Beijing: Min zu chu ban she, 1997.

Zhang Tingyu 張廷玉 (1672–1755) et al., eds. *Ming shi* 明史 [History of the Ming] (1739). 332 juan. Beijing: Zhonghua shu ju, 1974.

Zhang Xuan 張瑄 (1417–94). *Nan zheng lu* 南征錄 [Record of the military campaign in the south] (pref. 1464). 1 juan. SKQSCM ed.

Zhang Yigui 張益桂 and Xu Shiru 徐碩如. *Ming dai Guangxi nong min qi yi shi gao* 明代广西农民起义史稿 [History of peasant risings in Guangxi during the Ming]. Nanning: Guangxi ren min chu ban she, 1988.

Zhang Zimo 张子模, ed. *Ming dai fan feng ji Jingjiang wang shi liao cui bian* 明代藩封及靖江王史料萃编 [Collection of historical materials on enfeoffment and the Prince of Jingjiang of the Ming dynasty]. Guilin: Guangxi shi fan da xue chu ban she, 1994.

Zheng Xiao 鄭曉 (1499–1566). *Huang Ming si yi kao* 皇明四夷考 [Notes on the non-Chinese of the four quarters of the Ming imperium] (pref. 1564). 2 juan. Taipei: Hua wen shu ju, [1968].

Zhong Wendian 钟文典, ed. *Guangxi tong shi* 广西通史 [General history of Guangxi]. 3 vols. Nanning: Guangxi ren min chu ban she, 1999.

Zhongguo da bai ke quan shu chu ban she bian ji bu 中国大百科全书出版社编辑部, ed. *Zhongguo da bai ke quan shu: min zu* 中国大百科全书: 民族 [Encyclopedia Sinica: nationalities]. Beijing and Shanghai: Zhongguo da bai ke quan shu chu ban she, 1986.

Zhongguo guo jia tong ji ju ren kou tong ji si 中国国家统计局人口统计司, ed. *Zhongguo ren kou tong ji nian jian* 中国人口统计年鉴 [China population statistics yearbook]. Beijing: Zhongguo zhan wang chu ban she, 1988–.

Zhongguo she hui ke xue yuan min zu yan jiu suo min zu wen ti li lun yan jiu shi 中国社会科学院民族研究所民族问题理论研究室, ed. *Dang de min zu zheng ce wen xian zi liao xuan bian, 1922.7–1949.10* 党的民族政策文献资料选编 [Selected documents on the nationality policies of the Party, 1922.7–1949.10]. Beijing: Zhongguo she hui ke xue yuan min zu yan jiu suo min zu wen ti li lun yan jiu shi, 1981.

Zhou Hongwei 周宏伟. *Qing dai liang Guang nong ye di li* 清代两广农业地理 [Agricultural geography of Guangdong and Guangxi in Qing dynasty]. Changsha: Hunan jiao yu chu ban she, 1998.

Zhou Qufei 周去非 (js. 1163). *Ling wai dai da jiao zhu* 嶺外代答校注 [*Answers about Areas Beyond the Southern Range,* collated and annotated] (1178). 10 juan. Beijing: Zhonghua shu ju, 1999.

Zhou Zhenhe 周振鹤, ed. *Wang Shixing di li shu san zhong* 王士性地理書三種. [Three treatises on geography by Wang Shixing]. Shanghai: Shanghai gu ji chu ban she, 1993.

Zhu Baojiong 朱保烱 and Xie Peilin 謝沛霖, eds. *Ming Qing jin shi ti ming bei lu suo yin* 明清進士題名碑錄索引 [Index to the names of Ming- and Qing-period metropolitan degree holders listed in the official steles]. 3 vols. Shanghai: Shanghai gu ji chu ban she, 1980.

WESTERN LANGUAGE MATERIALS

Anderson, Benedict. *Imagined Communities: Reflections on the Origin and Spread of Nationalism.* Rev. ed. London and New York: Verso, 1991.

Appleby, Joyce, Lynn Hunt, and Margaret Jacob. *Telling the Truth about History.* New York: Norton, 1994.

Barth, Fredrik, ed. *Ethnic Groups and Boundaries: The Social Organization of Culture Difference.* Boston: Little, Brown, 1969.

Blum, Susan D. *Portraits of "Primitives": Ordering Human Kinds in the Chinese Nation.* Lanham, Md.: Rowman & Littlefield, 2001.

Breisach, Ernst. *Historiography: Ancient, Medieval & Modern.* 2nd ed. Chicago: University of Chicago Press, 1994.

Brokaw, Cynthia, and Kai-wing Chow, eds. *Printing and Book Culture in Late Imperial China.* Berkeley and Los Angeles: University of California Press, 2005.

Brook, Timothy. *The Chinese State in Ming Society.* London and New York: RoutledgeCurzon, 2005.

_____. "Communications and Commerce." In Twitchett and Mote, *Cambridge History of China,* vol. 8, 579–707.

_____. *The Confusions of Pleasure: Commerce and Culture in Ming China.* Berkeley and Los Angeles: University of California Press, 1998.

_____. "The Gazetteer Cartography of Ye Chunji." In *Chinese State in Ming Society,* 43–59.

_____. *Geographical Sources of Ming-Qing History.* 2nd ed. Ann Arbor: Center for Chinese Studies, University of Michigan, 2002.

_____. "The Spatial Organization of Subcounty Administration." In *Chinese State in Ming Society,* 19–42.

Brown, Melissa J. *Is Taiwan Chinese? The Impact of Culture, Power, and Migration on Changing Identities.* Berkeley and Los Angeles: University of California Press, 2004.

Burguière, André, and Raymond Grew, eds. *The Construction of Minorities: Cases for Comparison Across Time and Around the World.* Ann Arbor: University of Michigan Press, 2001.

Cahill, James. *The Compelling Image: Nature and Style in Seventeenth-Century Chinese Painting.* Cambridge, Mass.: Harvard University Press, 1982.

_____. "Huang Shan Paintings as Pilgrimage Pictures." In *Pilgrims and Sacred Sites in China,* ed. Susan Naquin and Chün-fang Yü, 246–92. Berkeley and Los Angeles: University of California Press, 1992.

Chan, Hok-lam. "The Chien-wen, Yung-lo, Hung-hsi, and Hsüan-te Reigns, 1399–1435." In Mote and Twitchett, *Cambridge History of China,* vol. 7, 182–304.

Chia, Lucille. *Printing for Profit: The Commercial Publishers of Jianyang, Fujian (11th–17th Centuries).* Cambridge, Mass.: Harvard University Asia Center, 2002.

Chiang-Kai-shek. *China's Destiny.* Translated by Wang Chung-hui. New York: Macmillan, 1947.

Chow, Kai-wing. *Publishing, Culture, and Power in Early Modern China.* Stanford: Stanford University Press, 2004.

Chu, Hung-lam. "Ch'iu Chün (1421–1495) and the *Ta-Hüeh Yen-I Pu: Statecraft Thought in Fifteenth-Century China.*" Ph.D. dissertation. Princeton University, 1983.

Clunas, Craig. *Fruitful Sites: Garden Culture in Ming Dynasty China.* Durham: Duke University Press, 1996.

———. *Pictures and Visuality in Early Modern China.* Princeton: Princeton University Press, 1997.

Crossley, Pamela Kyle. "Thinking about Ethnicity in Early Modern China." *Late Imperial China* 11.1 (1990): 1–35.

———. *A Translucent Mirror: History and Identity in Qing Imperial Ideology.* Berkeley and Los Angeles: University of California Press, 1999.

Crossley, Pamela Kyle, Helen F. Siu, and Donald S. Sutton, eds. *Empire at the Margins: Culture, Ethnicity, and Frontier in Early Modern China.* Berkeley and Los Angeles: University of California Press, 2005.

Cushman, Richard D. "Rebel Haunts and Lotus Huts: Problems in the Ethno-history of the Yao." Ph.D. dissertation. Cornell University, 1970.

Daniels, Christine, and Michael V. Kennedy, eds. *Negotiated Empires: Centers and Peripheries in the Americas, 1500–1820.* New York and London: Routledge, 2002.

de Bary, Wm Theodore. "Introduction." In *Self and Society in Ming Thought,* 1–24. New York: Columbia University Press, 1970.

de Heer, Philip. *The Caretaker Emperor: Aspects of the Imperial Institution in Fifteenth-Century China as Reflected in the Political History of the Reign of Chu Ch'i-yü.* Leiden: E.J. Brill, 1985.

Di Cosmo, Nicola. *Ancient China and Its Enemies: The Rise of Nomadic Power in East Asian history.* Cambridge: Cambridge University Press, 2002.

Diamond, Norma. "The Miao and the Poison: Interactions on China's Southwest Frontier." *Ethnology* 21.1 (1988): 1–25.

Dikötter, Frank. *The Discourse of Race in Modern China.* Stanford: Stanford University Press, 1992.

Dirks, Nicholas B., ed. *Colonialism and Culture.* Ann Arbor: University of Michigan Press, 1992.

Dreyer, June Teufel. *China's Forty Millions: Minority Nationalities and National Integration in the People's Republic of China.* Cambridge, Mass.: Harvard University Press, 1976.

Duara, Prasenjit. *Rescuing History from the Nation: Questioning Narratives of Modern China.* Chicago: University of Chicago Press, 1995.

Eberhard, Wolfram. "Kultur und Siedlung der Randvölker China." *T'oung Pao,* Supplement to Vol. 36 (1942).

Elliott, Mark C. *The Manchu Way: The Eight Banners and Ethnic Identity in Late Imperial China.* Stanford: Stanford University Press, 2001.

Elman, Benjamin A. *On Their Own Terms: Science in China, 1550–1900.* Cambridge, Mass.: Harvard University Press, 2005.

Faure, David. "The Lineage as a Cultural Invention: The Case of the Pearl River Delta." *Modern China* 15.1 (1989): 4–36.

Fitzgerald, John. *Awakening China: Politics, Culture, and Class in the Nationalist Revolution.* Stanford: Stanford University Press, 1996.

Fogel, Joshua A., and Peter Zarrow G., eds. *Imagining the People: Chinese Intellectuals and the Concept of Citizenship, 1890–1920.* Armonk, N.Y.: M.E. Sharpe, 1997.

Franke, Wolfgang. *An Introduction to the Sources of Ming History.* Kuala Lumpur and Singapore: University of Malaya Press, 1968.

_____. "Historical Writing During the Ming." In Mote and Twitchett, *Cambridge History of China*, vol. 7, 726–82.

Fried, Morton H. "Tribe to State or State to Tribe in Ancient China?" In *The Origins of Chinese Civilization*, ed. David N. Keightley, 467–94. Berkeley and Los Angeles: University of California Press, 1983.

Ganza, Kenneth Stanley. "The Artist as Traveler: The Origin and Development of Travel as a Theme in Chinese Landscape Painting of the Fourteenth to Seventeenth Centuries." Ph.D. dissertation. Indiana University, 1990.

Giersch, C. Pat. "'A Motley Throng:' Social Change on Southwest China's Early Modern Frontier, 1700–1880." *Journal of Asian Studies* 60.1 (2001): 67–94.

Gladney, Dru C. *Dislocating China: Reflections on Muslims, Minorities, and Other Subaltern Subjects.* Chicago: University of Chicago Press, 2004.

_____. "Introduction: Making and Marking Majorities." In *Making Majorities*, 1–9.

_____, ed. *Making Majorities: Constituting the Nation in Japan, Korea, China, Malaysia, Fiji, Turkey, and the United States.* Stanford: Stanford University Press, 1998.

Goodall, John A., ed. *Heaven and Earth: Album Leaves from a Ming Encyclopedia: San-ts'ai t'u-hui, 1610.* Boulder, Colo.: Shambhala Publications, 1979.

Goodrich, L. Carrington, and Chaoying Fang, eds. *Dictionary of Ming Biography, 1368–1644.* 2 vols. New York: Columbia University Press, 1976.

Guldin, Gregory Eliyu. *The Saga of Anthropology in China: From Malinowski to Moscow to Mao.* Armonk, N.Y.: M.E. Sharpe, 1994.

Hargett, James M. *On the Road in Twelfth Century China: The Travel Diaries of Fan Chengda (1126–1193).* Stuttgart: Franz Steiner Verlag Wiesbaden, 1989.

Harrell, Stevan, ed. *Cultural Encounters on China's Ethnic Frontiers.* Seattle and London: University of Washington Press, 1995.

_____. "The History of the History of the Yi." In *Cultural Encounters on China's Ethnic Frontiers*, 63–91.

_____. "Introduction: Civilizing Projects and the Reaction to Them." In *Cultural Encounters on China's Ethnic Frontiers*, 3–36.

Harrell, Stevan, and Yongxiang Li. "The History of the History of the Yi, Part II." *Modern China* 29.3 (2003): 362–96.

Hazelton, Keith. *A Synchronic Chinese–Western Daily Calendar, 1341–1661 A.D.* Minneapolis: Department of History, University of Minnesota, 1984; second printing, 1985.

Heijdra, Martin. "The Socio-Economic Development of Rural China during the Ming." In Twitchett and Mote, *Cambridge History of China*, vol. 8, 417–578.

Herman, John E. "Empire in the Southwest: Early Qing Reforms to the Native Chieftain System." *Journal of Asian Studies* 56.1 (1997): 47–74.

Hershatter, Gail. "The Subaltern Talks Back: Reflections on Subaltern Theory and Chinese History." *positions* 1.1 (1993): 103–30.

Ho, Ping-ti. "In Defense of Sinicization: Rebuttal of Evelyn Rawski's 'Reenvisioning the Qing.'" *Journal of Asian Studies* 57.1 (1998): 123–55.

———. *The Ladder of Success in Imperial China: Aspects of Social Mobility, 1368–1911.* New York: Columbia University Press, 1962.

Hostetler, Laura. *Qing Colonial Enterprise: Ethnography and Cartography in Early Modern China.* Chicago: University of Chicago Press, 2001.

Hucker, Charles O. *A Dictionary of Official Titles in Imperial China.* Stanford: Stanford University Press, 1985.

——— "Ming Government." In Twitchett and Mote, *Cambridge History of China*, vol. 8, 9–105.

Hutchinson, John, and Anthony D. Smith. *Ethnicity.* Oxford and New York: Oxford University Press, 1996.

Jami, Catherine, Peter M. Engelfriet, and Gregory Blue. *Statecraft and Intellectual Renewal in Late Ming China: The Cross-Cultural Synthesis of Xu Guangqi, 1562–1633.* Leiden: E.J. Brill, 2001.

Johnston, Alastair I. *Cultural Realism: Strategic Culture and Grand Strategy in Chinese History.* Princeton: Princeton University Press, 1995.

Karpat, Kemal H., and Robert W. Zens, eds. *Ottoman Borderlands: Issues, Personalities, and Political Changes.* Madison: Center of Turkish Studies, University of Wisconsin, 2003.

Kaup, Katherine Palmer. *Creating the Zhuang: Ethnic Politics in China.* Boulder, Colo.: L. Rienner, 2000.

Ko, Dorothy. *Teachers of the Inner Chambers: Women and Culture in Seventeenth-Century China.* Stanford: Stanford University Press, 1994.

Kuhn, Philip A. *Soulstealers: The Chinese Sorcery Scare of 1768.* Cambridge, Mass.: Harvard University Press, 1990.

Langlois, John D., Jr. "The Hung-wu Reign, 1368–1398." In Mote and Twitchett, *Cambridge History of China*, vol. 7, 107–81.

Lary, Diana. *Region and Nation: The Kwangsi Clique in Chinese Politics, 1925–1937.* Cambridge: Cambridge University Press, 1974.

Lattimore, Owen. *Inner Asian Frontiers of China.* New York: American Geographical Society, 1940.

Lee, James Z. "The Political Economy of a Frontier: Southwest China, 1250–1850." Book manuscript.

Levich, Eugene William. *The Kwangsi Way in Kuomintang China, 1931–1939.* Armonk, N.Y.: M.E. Sharpe, 1993.

Li, Chi. *The Formation of the Chinese People: An Anthropological Inquiry* (1928). Reprint, New York: Russell and Russell, 1967.

Litzinger, Ralph A. *Other Chinas: The Yao and the Politics of National Belonging.* Durham and London: Duke University Press, 2000.

Mackerras, Colin. *China's Minorities: Integration and Modernization in the Twentieth Century.* Hong Kong: Oxford University Press, 1994.

March, Andrew L. "An Appreciation of Chinese Geomancy." *Journal of Asian Studies* 27.2 (1968): 253–67.

Marks, Robert B. *Tigers, Rice, Silk, and Silt: Environment and Economy in Late Imperial South China*. Cambridge: Cambridge University Press, 1998.

Mote, Frederick W. "The Ch'eng-hua and Hung-chih Reigns, 1465–1505." In Mote and Twitchett, *Cambridge History of China*, vol. 7, 343–402.

———. *Imperial China, 900–1800*. Cambridge, Mass.: Harvard University Press, 1999.

———. "Introduction." In Mote and Twitchett, *Cambridge History of China*, vol. 7, 1–10.

Mote, Frederick W., and Denis Twitchett, eds. *The Cambridge History of China*. Vol. 7, *The Ming Dynasty, 1368–1644, Part 1*. Cambridge: Cambridge University Press, 1988.

Moule, A. C. "An Introduction to the *Yi Yü T'u Chih* or 'Pictures and Descriptions of Strange Nations' in the Wade Collection at Cambridge." *T'oung Pao* 27.2–3 (1930): 179–88.

Needham, Joseph, Gwei-Djen Lu, and Hsing-Tsung Huang. *Science and Civilisation in China*. Vol. 6: Biology and Biological Technology, Pt. 1: Botany. Cambridge: Cambridge University Press, 1986.

Perdue, Peter C. *China Marches West: The Qing Conquest of Central Eurasia*. Cambridge, Mass.: The Belknap Press of Harvard University Press, 2005.

Peterson, Willard J. *Bitter Gourd: Fang I-Chih and the Impetus for Intellectual Change*. New Haven: Yale University Press, 1979.

———. "Confucian Learning in Late Ming Thought." In Twitchett and Mote, *Cambridge History of China*, vol. 8, 708–88.

———, ed. *The Cambridge History of China*. Vol. 9, Part 1: *The Ch'ing Empire to 1800*. Cambridge: Cambridge University Press, 2002.

Plaks, Andrew H. *The Four Masterworks of the Ming Novel*. Princeton: Princeton University Press, 1987.

Prakash, Gyan. "Introduction: After Colonialism." In *After Colonialism: Imperial Histories and Postcolonial Displacements*, 3–17. Princeton: Princeton University Press, 1995.

Rawski, Evelyn S. *The Last Emperors: A Social History of Qing Imperial Institutions*. Berkeley and Los Angeles: University of California Press, 1998.

———. "Reenvisioning the Qing: The Significance of the Qing Period in Chinese History." *Journal of Asian Studies* 55.4 (1996): 829–50.

Robinson, David M. *Bandits, Eunuchs, and the Son of Heaven: Rebellion and the Economy of Violence in Mid-Ming China*. Honolulu: University of Hawai'i Press, 2001.

———. "Images of Subject Mongols Under the Ming Dynasty." *Late Imperial China* 25.1 (2004): 59–123.

Rossabi, Morris. "The Ming and Inner Asia." In Twitchett and Mote, *Cambridge History of China*, vol. 8, 221–71.

Rowe, William T. *Saving the World: Chen Hongmou and Elite Consciousness in Eighteenth-Century China*. Stanford: Stanford University Press, 2001.

———. "Social Stability and Social Change." In Peterson, *Cambridge History of China*, vol. 9, pt. 1, 473–562.

Said, Edward W. *Orientalism.* New York: Pantheon Books, 1978.

Schafer, Edward H. *The Vermilion Bird: T'ang Images of the South.* Berkeley and Los Angeles: University of California Press, 1967.

Schein, Louisa. *Minority Rules: The Miao and the Feminine in China's Cultural Politics.* Durham and London: Duke University Press, 2000.

Scott, James C. *Domination and the Arts of Resistance: Hidden Transcripts.* New Haven: Yale University Press, 1990.

————. *Seeing Like a State: How Certain Schemes to Improve the Human Condition Have Failed.* New Haven: Yale University Press, 1998.

Shepherd, John R. *Statecraft and Political Economy on the Taiwan Frontier, 1600–1800.* Stanford: Stanford University Press, 1993.

Shin, Leo K. "The Last Campaigns of Wang Yangming." *T'oung Pao* (forthcoming).

————. "Ming China and Its Border with Annam." In *The Chinese State at the Borders,* ed. Diana Lary. Vancouver: University of British Columbia Press, forthcoming.

Skinner, G. William. "Presidential Address: The Structure of Chinese History." *Journal of Asian Studies* 44.2 (1985): 271–92.

Smith, Paul J., and Richard von Glahn, eds. *The Song-Yuan-Ming Transition in Chinese History.* Cambridge, Mass.: Harvard University Asia Center, 2003.

Spence, Jonathan D. *Treason by the Book.* New York: Viking, 2001.

Strassberg, Richard E., ed. and trans. *A Chinese Bestiary: Strange Creatures from the Guideways through Mountains and Seas.* Berkeley and Los Angeles: University of California Press, 2002.

————. *Inscribed Landscapes: Travel Writing from Imperial China.* Berkeley and Los Angeles: University of California Press, 1994.

Struve, Lynn A., ed. *The Qing Formation in World-Historical Time.* Cambridge, Mass.: Harvard University Asia Center, 2004.

Sunderland, Willard. *Taming the Wild Field: Colonization and Empire on the Russian Steppe.* Ithaca, N.Y.: Cornell University Press, 2004.

Sung Ying-hsing [Song Yingxing]. *Chinese Technology in the Seventeenth Century.* Translated by E-tu Zen Sun and Shiou-chuan Sun. University Park: Pennsylvania State University, 1966.

Teng, Emma. *Taiwan's Imagined Geography: Chinese Colonial Travel Writing and Pictures, 1683–1895.* Cambridge, Mass.: Harvard University Asia Center, 2004.

Took, Jennifer. *A Native Chieftaincy in Southwest China: Franchising a Tai Chieftaincy under the Tusi System of Late Imperial China.* Leiden: E.J. Brill, 2005.

Tsai, Shih-shan Henry. *Perpetual Happiness: The Ming Emperor Yongle.* Seattle and London: University of Washington Press, 2001.

Tsin, Michael. *Nation, Governance, and Modernity in China: Canton, 1900–1927.* Stanford: Stanford University Press, 1999.

Twitchett, Denis, and Herbert Franke, eds. *The Cambridge History of China.* Vol. 6, *Alien Regimes and Border States, 910–1368.* Cambridge: Cambridge University Press, 1995.

Twitchett, Denis, and Tilemann Grimm. "The Cheng-t'ung, Ching-t'ai, and T'ien-shun Reigns, 1436–1464." In Mote and Twitchett, *Cambridge History of China,* vol. 7, 305–342.

Twitchett, Denis, and Frederick W. Mote, eds. *The Cambridge History of China.* Vol. 8, *The Ming Dynasty, 1368–1644, Part 2.* Cambridge: Cambridge University Press, 1998.

Unger, Jonathan, ed. *Chinese Nationalism.* Armonk, N.Y.: M.E. Sharpe, 1996.

Unschuld, Paul U. *Medicine in China: A History of Pharmaceutics.* Berkeley and Los Angeles: University of California Press, 1986.

von Glahn, Richard. *The Country of Streams and Grottoes: Expansion, Settlement, and the Civilizing of the Sichuan Frontier in Song times.* Cambridge, Mass.: Council on East Asian Studies, Harvard University, 1987.

Wade, Geoff, trans. *Southeast Asia in the Ming Shi-lu: An Open Access Resource.* Singapore: Asia Research Institute and the Singapore E-Press. http://epress.nus.edu.sg/msl/.

Waldron, Arthur. *The Great Wall of China: From History to Myth.* Cambridge: Cambridge University Press, 1990.

Wang Gungwu. "The Chinese Urge to Civilize: Reflections on Change." In *The Chineseness of China,* 145–64. Hong Kong: Oxford University Press, 1991.

———. "Ming Foreign Relations: Southeast Asia." In Twitchett and Mote, *Cambridge History of China,* vol. 8, 301–32.

Ward, Julian. *Xu Xiake (1587–1641): The Art of Travel Writing.* Richmond: Curzon, 2001.

White, Richard. *The Middle Ground: Indians, Empires, and Republics in the Great Lakes Region, 1650–1815.* Cambridge and New York: Cambridge University Press, 1991.

Whittaker, C. R. *Rome and Its Frontiers: The Dynamics of Empire.* London and New York: Routledge, 2004.

Wiens, Herold J. *China's March Toward the Tropics.* Hamden, Conn.: Shoe String Press, 1954. Reissued in 1967 as *Han Chinese Expansion in South China.*

Wu, Pei-yi. "An Ambivalent Pilgrim to T'ai-shan in the Seventeenth Century." In *Pilgrims and Sacred Sites in China,* ed. Susan Naquin and Chün-fang Yü, 65–88. Berkeley and Los Angeles: University of California Press, 1992.

———. *The Confucian's Progress: Autobiographical Writings in Traditional China.* Princeton: Princeton University Press, 1990.

Yu, Ping-kuen, ed. *Chinese Collections in the Library of Congress: Excerpts from the Annual Report(s) of the Librarian of Congress, 1898–1971.* 3 vols. Washington, D.C.: Center for Chinese Research Materials Association of Research Libraries, 1974.

Zelin, Madeleine. "The Yung-cheng Reign." In Peterson, *Cambridge History of China,* vol. 9, pt. 1, 183–229.

Glossary-Index

CPSIA information can be obtained at www.ICGtesting.com
Printed in the USA
BVOW071442071211

277743BV00002B/4/P